Gestalt Approaches in Counseling

William R. Passons

Chief of Service
Consultation and Education
Northeast Community Center for
Mental Health/Mental Retardation
Philadelphia, Pennsylvania

HOLT, RINEHART AND WINSTON
New York   Chicago   San Francisco   Atlanta
Dallas   Montreal   Toronto   London   Sydney

This book is dedicated to
Betty Ann Passons
Jolie Ann Passons
Corey Richard Passons

Library of Congress Cataloging in Publication Data

Passons, William R.
  Gestalt approaches in counseling.

  Includes bibliographies.
  1. Counseling. 2. Gestalt therapy. I. Title.
BF637.C6P28   616.8'914   74–22223

ISBN 0–03–089421–2

Preface

During the past several years Gestalt therapy has emerged as a major force in the field of mental health. Evidence for this is readily noted in the increase in publications prepared in response to the requests for more knowledge on the theory and practice of Gestalt therapy. At national conventions of various professional organizations, such as the American Psychological Association and the American Personnel and Guidance Association, practitioners at all levels of training and competence endeavor to attend workshops in Gestalt therapy. The appeal of Gestalt therapy, thus, has a broad base.

This book is not designed for those who wish to become Gestalt therapists. Other texts that delve more deeply into theory are. For prospective Gestalt therapists, as opposed to counselors, require much more extensive training, including participation in their own therapy and supervised experience as a therapist.

In this book I am attempting to reach another population which consists of such counselors—those who will not be Gestalt therapists but who wish to employ some Gestalt approaches in their work. In my experience, teaching in counselor education and doing school consultation, I have encountered numerous individuals who have asked me for readings in Gestalt that would be useful to them. In most instances they have found the readings stimulating, provocative, and difficult to translate into their daily counseling work.

Being convinced that Gestalt therapy is a rich resource from which certain approaches could be gleaned for use by these persons, I prepared a paper

v

entitled "Gestalt Therapy Interventions for Group Counselors." The response to the paper by my graduate students and practicing counselors suggested two things to me. First, I had been correct in my hunch that there are Gestalt approaches which can be gainfully used by practicing counselors in school settings. Second, I had formulated an approach for presenting these approaches which rendered them understandable and usable. As requests came for more of these materials I began preparing them, and the book evolved.

Gestalt Approaches in Counseling has three purposes. First, an attempt is made to present a brief overview of the theoretical dimensions of Gestalt therapy. Such attention to theory is necessary for understanding the source of the interventions and interrelatedness between the two.

The second purpose is to engage the readers in some self-awareness work of their own. Many of the concepts discussed and written "about" in the book will stay at the "about" level until linked to the individual reader's experience. Thus, self-exercises are interspersed throughout the book so that readers can experience in themselves some of the same kinds of awareness elicited in counselees by a specific approach.

The third purpose is to offer a number of Gestalt approaches for use by practicing counselors and counselor trainees. The approaches are not presented as "this is what you should do" strategies. Rather, they are conveyed with the attitude of "here are some approaches you might try." Suggesting experiments for possible use in particular situations is something Gestalt therapists are accustomed to doing, so I feel more comfortable with this approach.

There are numerous individuals to whom I wish to extend thanks and appreciation for assisting in the preparation of the book. First and foremost, there is my wife Betty, whose love, patience, and sacrifices are recorded on each page of the book just as clearly as her skillful editing. Then there is my daughter, Jolie, who during the preparation of the manuscript provided well-needed and delightful diversions by climbing up in my lap to do her "writing." My son Cory is not yet aware that his birth coincided beautifully with the completion of the manuscript.

I am particularly grateful to Peter J. Kuriloff for the interest, support, and encouragement which was so evident in his feedback and reactions to the manuscript. Others who offered significant suggestions on content and format are Thomas Cutolo, Robert Harman, Fran Keller, Tom Niland, Clyde Parker, and Eric Shelley.

I extend special appreciation to Marilyn B. Rosanes-Berrett and Helen Fusaro for many rich experiences in Gestalt therapy.

I also wish to extend thanks to Glen Dey, Art Dole, Ace Griffiths, and

Lee Olsen for their significant contribution to my personal and professional development.

Finally, thanks are due to Helen Gintvain for the fine job she did in typing the manuscript.

Philadelphia, Pa.   W. R. P.
January 1975

Contents

Practical Dimensions
of a Theory of Counseling

Practicing counselors often eschew theories of counseling as having little or no relevance to the everyday demands confronting them. Comments such as the following reflect this attitude: "I'm on the firing line and I haven't got the time for theorizing"; "Those professors would be less concerned with theory if they came out of their ivory towers into the real world"; "Theories look nice in books, but I find little practical value in them." Individuals who make such statements assume for all practical purposes that their behavior does not emanate from a theoretical base.

One of the notions just mentioned is true; the other is not. It cannot be denied that many counselors experience themselves as not behaving in accordance with a theory of counseling. That they *are* devoid of theoretical guidelines in their work, however, is subject to doubt. The latter position reflects the highly probable condition that the counselor has implicit theoretical notions of which he may not be aware. Careful observation and discussion of certain counselor behaviors often reveal the values and assumptions behind them.

On this point Stefflre (1965) has written: "The real question then is not whether we shall operate from theory since we have no choice in this matter, but rather what theories shall we use and how shall we use theories" (p. 3). Implicit in this statement is the assumption—one with which the writer is in complete agreement—that it is desirable for the counselor to be aware of his theoretical point of view.

Uses and Misuses of a
Personal Theory of Counseling

A theory, like any other scientific tool, has little intrinsic value. This is not to say that certain qualities such as comprehensiveness, simplicity, predictive power, and the generation of meaningful research cannot be used to evaluate theories. But this is assessing the adequacy of a theory according to scientific criteria and is thus still a step removed from reality.

The real worth of a theory is its usefulness. If a counselor finds no practical assistance from his theory, then the theory clearly has no value. Many counselors, however, are unaware of the benefits of using their theory constructively because these benefits often seem vague and nebulous. Thus, it is important for the counselor to understand how he can use this important tool.

Constructive Uses
of a Theory of Counseling

A counselor can employ his theory as a framework that offers suggestions about the meaning of a counselee's behavior. The theory can help him to differentiate the relevant from the irrelevant elements of the behavior he observes. From his theory the counselor can derive hypotheses about the meaning of one student's shyness and the overt hostility of another. A counselor can also use a theory constructively to interrelate apparently disjointed bits of behavior and thus enhance his understanding of a counselee. The contiguity of specific behaviors such as losing a boyfriend and failing a math test can often be best understood with the aid of a theoretical base providing a link between the two.

From his theory and the understanding he derives from its use, the counselor is better equipped to assess how the counselee can change his behavior patterns and the directions these changes may take. This will assist the counselor in working with the counselee in establishing goals or purposes for counseling.

In a similar vein the counselor can use his theory to predict how he may be able to influence the counselee. With some perspective on the dynamics of the person and the proposed directions of the counseling, the counselor can be more attuned to the potential impact of his person and his interventions. The counselor's use of questions, self-disclosure, clarification, feedback, silence, confrontation, and other process variables, while not consciously planned, can be roughly assessed for appropriateness against the hypothesis about the counselee derived from his theory.

Just as the theory can be used in conceptualizing the objectives of counseling, so can it also suggest the achievement of those objectives. Such formulations can help the counselor to recognize positive outcomes which might otherwise go unnoticed. For example, the behavior of a severely restricted counselee, who one day quite unexpectedly throws an eraser at his teacher, may be placed in a context in which the developmental value of this "disruptive" event can be understood. Furthermore, viewing the counselee, his own counseling behavior, and the outcomes of counseling in a systematic fashion affords the counselor a perspective for comprehending the total counseling process and reviewing it for future reference.

The counselor may find some value in his theory for situations other than direct contact with counselees. He may, for example, find that some of the hypotheses which are useful to him in understanding counselees may be of value in assisting teachers to understand the behavior of students. Furthermore, he may find that some of his counseling behaviors can be modified and adapted for use in the classroom or the broader guidance program. Finally, it may be that the counselor can translate some of his observations and theoretical notions into action-research programs within the school. The counselor's creativity and imagination are the only limits to generating useful implications from his theory.

Through the systematic and constructive use of his theory the counselor may reap some benefits for himself as a person as well as a functioning professional. Equipped with a set of flexible guidelines for observing and behaving, the counselor is less likely to feel that each new situation may hit him with a sense of impotence. He can use his theory as a framework to explore "What would I do if . . ." questions pertaining to experiences he has not yet had. As he continues to integrate the experiences he does have into his theoretical framework, the richness of this backlog becomes more apparent in formulating strategies and alternatives for new situations. Thus, the theory can afford the counselor a means to better understand himself in process. In so doing he may experience an increase in his sense of confidence along with a decrease in anxiety over anticipating the ambiguous and unexpected events which are part and parcel of his job. This type of awareness can be used by both counselors and counselees to enhance self-corrective growth and development.

Misuses of a Theory of Counseling

Now that a case has been built for how the counselor can constructively use his theory of counseling, it seems equally advantageous to mention some of the ways he can misuse it. In this way it can be more clearly seen how the "user" of the theory carries the responsibility for the ultimate worth of the theory. Theories do not act; counselors do, and they can easily misuse the same tool which can yield the benefits mentioned in the previous section.

One of the chief misuses of a theory of counseling occurs when the counselor does not recognize the limitations of his theory—when he assumes that his theory is fact rather than a tool for understanding and inquiry. When the counselor accepts notions from his theory as dicta rather than guidelines to be investigated, then the theory is being pushed beyond its limits. As the theory becomes "truth," the counselor will then often assume the burden of proving it. In this process the filtering function by which the theory helps sort out meaningful observations can become so restricted that the counselor becomes myopic. An unconstructive result can be that the counselor becomes a slave of his theory rather than a user of it. The theory then becomes a Procrustean bed into which the servant must force the world around him, regardless of whether it fits.

A second common way that counselors can misuse a theory is in what has been called "sacrificing a person to the theory." A counselee comes in upset about a problem. The counselor uses his theory to understand the dynamics of the counselee and to formulate (for himself) the directions that counseling "ought" to take. The counselor may then proceed accordingly. If the counselee does not respond in the ways the counselor predicted, the counselor may go on dogmatically as though the counselee will eventually come around. There are undoubtedly numerous counselees who go misunderstood and unhelped due to this process.

Another misuse of theory occurs when the user views his theory as "the way" and begins to proselytize others into the fold. Each counselor's theory is a personal statement. There may be many counselors who share some theoretical territories, but the overlaps between them are rarely complete. Thus, the counselor is misusing his theory when he tries to impose it on other counselors. Messages such as "This is the way—how can you not see it?" are of little value to the sender or the receiver.

Formulating a Personal
Theory of Counseling

Formulating a personal theory of counseling is much easier said than done. There are three key ingredients in approaching the task. These are the counselor as a person, the existent theories, and the synthesizing processes used by the counselors to formulate a personal theory.

The Counselor as a Person

Currently, it is recognized that the person of the counselor is the essential instrument in his work. Stripped of all professional accouterments and rhetoric, who the counselor is remains the primary factor in his functioning. His values, beliefs, needs, and other personal characteristics permeate everything he does in his many functions as a counselor.

These components and the total person they comprise, then, are the bedrock upon which the professional counselor stands. In discussing the counselor's "personal" theory Lister (1964) stated:

> Each beginning counselor has already spent years formulating hypotheses about himself and others and the nature of the world in which he lives. In the broadest sense, the counselor's personal theory refers to the hypotheses he has come to view as reliable guides to satisfying human relations. Although many such hypotheses are largely implicit and inarticulate, they nevertheless constitute patterns for counseling behavior or personality theory. For example, the student whose experience has led him to believe that his effectiveness in human relations requires that he prevent others from getting the upper hand is apt to maintain tight control of topics covered in the counseling interview. . . . If a student believes that people are basically trustworthy and capable of responsible behavior, he will probably have a higher threshold for the perception of "clear and imminent danger" than the student who has found others untrustworthy and irresponsible. (p. 209)

Congruence between the counselor as a person and his theory of counseling is inevitable if the counselor formulates his own theory. Attempts to impose onto himself a theory which does not fit him results in a mismatch which has deleterious results. The counselor cannot feel familiar or together with such an imposition, whether it comes from himself or counselor educators, and will experience a state of dissonance.

Thus, an important first step in formulating his theory is for the counselor to attain a high level of awareness of his philosophical beliefs, values, needs, and so on. Without this awareness the base of his theory is shaky. Too often counselors will determine those personal positions which are "desirable" and impute them to themselves. The problems engendered by this approach are legion as the counselor ambles assuredly down a rosy path in the wrong direction!

A counselor, like a counselee, may try to deny a feeling or belief he holds in deference to the way he thinks counselors ought to be. A more constructive approach is to become aware of who he is rather than who he should be. In this way the counselor becomes aware of himself and how he can use himself to help counselees. Through the process of enhancing this awareness the counselor may realize for himself some changes he desires and work on them. This growth may contribute to his effectiveness as a counselor if the changes are brought about for him as a person and not with the objective of making himself closer to a model counselor. As the counselor becomes more aware of himself, he increases his ability to consider theories of counseling in themselves, and in terms of their appropriateness for him. On this subject Shoben (1962) has stated:

> In the psychological realm, then, it is hardly surprising that the touchstones by which we often evaluate a theory are our own experience, our previously developed ideas about the ways in which men do and should behave, and our particular complex of values associated with ourselves and our fellows as interacting and sentient organisms.

Shoben (1962) has also related this process to the proliferation of theories of counseling and the variations in adherents to them. If there were a theory that was "right" for every counselor, there would not be so many of them.

Problems in Formulating
a Personal Theory

The paths that a counselor follows in formulating his personal theory of counseling are diverse. There are several pitfalls on these paths which merit mention.

Sometimes counselors frustrate themselves with the question, "Who am I to think I can formulate a theory of counseling, even if it is a personal one?" The important point to remember here is that the "major" theorists have formulated formal theories from their "personal" points of view. Carl Rogers has stated that his theory was significantly related to the kind of relationship and assistance he seeks when he needs it. Persons who have seen Albert Ellis in action can see how his theory seems to fit his personality. Fritz Perls, in formulating Gestalt therapy, started with a Freudian base and later rejected much of it on the basis of his observations and changes in himself over the years. If people such as these allow room for their own personalities, cannot the counselor afford himself the same privilege?

A second common error in formulating a personal theory of counseling is adopting an existent theory wholesale, and swallowing it without proper chewing or digestion. The counselor may become excited with a theory and see himself so much in agreement with it that he then considers himself a "labeled" counselor. Sometimes this actually works, but only for the rare few. Usually there is a period of infatuation, a honeymoon so to speak, which may be of some duration. As the counselor gains experience he begins to feel changes in himself that don't fit with the theory. Hopefully he will make changes in the latter rather than the former. For individuals who can and do make these modifications the "wholesale" mistake is often averted. Too often, however, the theory is grasped without a sufficient awareness of self, and clutched even more tightly when dissonances are experienced.

Another often noticed problem is formulating a personal theory of counseling to amalgamate an assortment of techniques and interventions and referring to them as a theory. Counselors frequently see in films or demonstrations counseling interventions which they believe they can use effectively. Such a process can be profitable if the counselor weaves the new approaches into the overall fabric of his theory, which hopefully has room for a few new angles. However, if the process *is* his theory, the most likely result is a nonstable collection of unrelated techniques which are applied in a hit-or-miss fashion devoid of any of the constructive uses of a theory.

A fourth problem in the formulation process occurs when an examined theory is totally rejected because it cannot be carried out to the letter. I have had several students who saw films of Fritz Perls doing rather deep and intense dream work with patients. After further study the students wanted to work some Gestalt interventions into their counseling but hesitated because they did not feel competent enough to go all the way into the dream work they had seen. The aversion to trying the dream work was quite appropriate as it was far beyond their expertise. Deciding they could not use any Gestalt approaches, however, was a non sequitur. After having worked through this all-or-nothing conflict on the issue, they were then able to use effectively some of the approaches which fit them personally and which were in accordance with their level of competence.

A dynamic similar to this sometimes occurs when the counselor sees an approach he likes but is turned off by labels, including the term "therapy"—Behavioral therapy, Gestalt therapy, Rational-Emotive therapy, and so forth. One often hears, "We don't do 'therapy' in the schools, so these don't apply to us." This is another version of an all-or-nothing situation. A school counselor does not have to have a couch and practice free-association psychoanalysis in order to operate from a Freudian framework! This orientation, however, can be reflected in the nature of the questions he asks, topics he pursues, interpretations of behavior he makes, and hypotheses he draws up about the dynamics of his counselee.

Sometimes the formulation process is halted, usually when the counselor considers his theory complete. "Well, now that I've built it, let's get on with putting it into practice." While to a certain degree this attitude is desirable, especially when the counselor experiences his theory as useful, the feeling of being "finished" with the formulation can lead to difficulties. Input contrary to the tenets of the theory may be dismissed as exceptions rather than taken as occasions to re-examine some of the basic assumptions of the theory. When the user of the theory becomes closed and rigid in his formulations he is stifling one of the most crucial processes for keeping the theory viable. That is the continual process of allowing the theory to grow and develop, much like a person. This is not to say that the theory is rewritten each day and modified to fit all possible cases. Under these circumstances the theory would soon collapse of its own weight. But neither should the theory be considered a sacrosanct and inviolable code.

A related reformulation difficulty takes place when the counselor himself changes but tries to continue with the same theory. Many new counselors emerge from their training program with some theoretical formulations that fit them at the time. However, as their experience accrues they begin to sense changes in their values, beliefs, and those counseling interventions which they find effective. If at this point they continue to assess their behavior in terms of the theory they learned, they may experience a sense of dissonance. What they learned in training thus becomes a monkey on their back, impeding professional development. The counselor who professes one theory but practices another could benefit himself by examining the relationship between himself and his personal theory of counseling.

Suggestions for Formulation

The problems in formulating a personal theory of counseling are by no means unavoidable. Adopting some of the suggestions presented below can help the counselor to circumvent them:

1. *Sharpening* awareness of his own feelings, values, beliefs, expectancies, thought processes, and other personal characteristics relevant to his personal theory of counseling;
2. *Seeking* information about various theories of counseling and new developments that occur in counseling theory;
3. *Studying* existing theories;
4. *Setting* a theoretical framework which addresses itself to the components of a theory of counseling as discussed in Chapter 2;

5. *Screening* out theoretical formulations which are incongruent with this personality;
6. *Selecting* diminsions of theories and techniques which fit him as a person;
7. *Synthesizing* what he selects with his own beliefs and thoughts about others and how he can be helpful to them;
8. *Subjecting* his evolving theory to practical applications in various counseling situations;
9. *Shifting* his theory according to his experience with it and in accordance with changes that come about in himself;
10. *Stabilizing* the theory as time and experience accrue, while keeping in mind that the theory can be solidified to the point that it becomes an albatross.

With reference to these processes Shoben (1962) wrote:

> In general, these systematized ideas may be regarded to a significant degree as a part of the counselor as a person. The utility of this cognitive personality trait represented by his theoretical allegiance is largely a function of the extent to which he "knows himself"—that is, he knows the pitfalls as well as the advantages that his theory entails—and the extent to which he is able to use his theoretical tools flexibly and discriminately. The counselor who achieves this kind of honesty in dealing with his cognitive self is likely to enjoy a sense of personal growth that is denied to others. (p. 621)

My wish is that the reader will use this text as a source of input in formulating and reformulating his personal theory of counseling according to processes such as those just mentioned.

Summary

The basic assumption of this chapter is that all counselors operate according to a theory. Further, many counselors are unaware of their own theoretical formulations and could enhance their functioning by making explicit some of their implicit theorizing.

Counselors can use their theory constructively and likewise can misuse it. Effective uses include understanding the counselee's behavior, assessing possible changes and goals, making predictions, judging the impact of selected interventions, and evaluating outcomes. The counselor can also derive implications from his theory for use in classrooms and other school programs. Finally, feelings of competence can result from effectively using a theory. Ways that a counselor can misuse his theory include not recognizing its limitations, sacrificing counselees to the theory, and imposing his theory on colleagues.

The counselor's personal theory of counseling is significantly related to his values, beliefs, needs, feelings, and other personality characteristics. Thus, a first step in formulating a personal theory of counseling is for the counselor to know himself. Counselors often encounter problems in formulating their personal theory of counseling. These problems include not allowing their personal self to be expressed in the theory, adopting an existent theory totally, referring to an assortment of techniques as a theory, rejecting a formal theory because it cannot be practical to the letter, making the theory too rigid, and not changing the theory in accordance with personal changes that occur. Ten suggestions to avoid some of these problems center around the following words: sharpening, seeking, studying, setting, screening, selecting, synthesizing, subjecting, shifting, and stabilizing.

REFERENCES

Lister, J. L., The counselor's personal theory. *Counselor Education and Supervision*, 1964, **3**, 207–213.

Shoben, E. J., Jr., The counselor's theory as a personality trait. *American Personnel and Guidance Journal*, 1962, **40**, 617–621.

Stefflre, B. (ed.), *Theories of Counseling.* New York: McGraw-Hill Book Company, 1965.

2

Theoretical Components
of Gestalt Therapy

Theories of counseling have, for the most part, been derived from theories of psychotherapy. For example, Client-centered therapy is referred to as Client-centered counseling, Behavioral therapy as Behavioral counseling, and so on. While counselors may not practice therapies in their pure sense, they do operate according to the basic theories of the therapies. Considerable counseling literature has been devoted to pointing out the implications of therapies for practicing counselors.

The main purpose of this text is to introduce practicing counselors to some of the implications of Gestalt therapy for their work. It is the writer's impression that there are many approaches used in Gestalt therapy that can be effectively used by counselors of various theoretical persuasions. An understanding of the theoretical rationale underlying these approaches may help the reader to decide how they can be relevant in counseling situations. The degree to which the theory behind a Gestalt approach is consistent with the theoretical notions of the counselor will be positively related to the likelihood that they will match and fit into his style.

Historical Development
of Gestalt Therapy

Gestalt therapy was developed by the late Frederick (Fritz) Perls. Actually, it is more appropriate to say that Perls was developing Gestalt therapy because he did not consider it a finished product at the time of his death. Perls's thinking was as evolutionary as it was revolutionary. Just as he believed that a person never finishes developing, so did he view his own theoretical formulation processes. He was not one to "finish" his theory and then go on from there assuming the truth of it. Rather, he appropriately used the theory to understand what he saw and was able to remain detached enough to change some of his ideas when the consistency of persons' behavior refuted them.

Perls began his psychiatric career as a Freudian analyst and later became a training analyst. Because of this background there are many important analytical influences present in the theory of Gestalt therapy. Likewise there are numerous differences and criticisms leveled at psychoanalysis by Gestalt therapists. *Ego, Hunger and Aggression* (Perls, 1947) and *Gestalt Therapy* (Perls, Hefferline, and Goodman, 1951) are excellent primary resources for the reader to pursue comparisons and contrasts between Gestalt therapy and psychoanalysis.

In the 1920s Perls became interested in Gestalt psychology as it was being developed by Max Wertheimer, Wolfgang Köhler, and Kurt Koffka. These theorists were conceptualizing a system of psychology that was in direct opposition to the analytical, stimulus-response, associative behaviorism which was also popular at the time. Their contribution was a theory of behavior based on the concept that psychological phenomena are organized and synthesized wholes rather than constellations of specific, molecular parts.

The namesake of this system of psychology was Gestalt. While Gestalt does not translate precisely from German to English, the flavor of the concept can be grasped. English and English (1958) have defined a Gestalt as

> a form, a configuration or a totality that has, as a unified whole, properties which cannot be derived by summation from the parts and their relationships. . . . It may refer to physical structures, to physiological and psychological functions, or to symbolic units. (p. 225)

While Gestalt psychology focused primarily on describing perceptual and learning processes. Perls noted several propositions within the theory which had powerful implications for psychotherapy. A few of these deserve mention.

1. *A person tends to seek closure.* A Gestalt which is incomplete or unfinished demands attention until it is unified and stabilized. A series of dots is seen as a line. A total conversation is disrupted when someone asks, "Who starred in that film?" and no one can remember. Finally someone recalls the name and the immediate Gestalt is closed and the conversation flows again.
2. *A person will complete Gestalts in accordance with his current need.* Flash

a circular object in front of a group of playful children and they will report it as a ball. Hungry children may perceive an apple or a hamburger. Sexually deprived men may "see" a woman's breast. This process is referred to as projection.

3. *A person's behavior is a whole which is greater than the sum of its specific components.* Reading, for example, is comprised of a number of specific behaviors. The act of reading, however, is an experience which in totality transcends those behaviors. Listening to a piece of music is a process which involves something more than hearing specific notes, just as a melody is more than the constellation of notes.

4. *A person's behavior can be meaningfully understood only in context.* Seeing a man wiggle his hips can have no meaning and even be amusing. Then, when the hips are found to be those of Jack Nicklaus starting a Gestalt of hitting a golf ball 250 yards, the meaning of the behavior becomes evident. The cowering of a child when approached by a teacher carrying a ruler is understood in light of beatings by parents with sticks. The scars carved on the bodies of some primitive tribes are seen as adornment only in that environment. In sum, a person is an integral part of his environment and cannot be understood out of its immediate and broader context.

5. *A person experiences the world in accordance to the principles of figure and ground.* When regarding a painting, the colors and shapes are attended to as figure. At the moment the frame and wall are ground. If attention is shifted to admiring the frame, it becomes figure and the painting itself is ground. If a stranger rudely bumps the viewer with a sharp elbow it is likely that the pain and the stranger will emerge as figures, the painting receding into the ground.

Perls ingeniously assimilated ideas from other theorists. Influenced by Wilhelm Reich, Perls came to appreciate how psychological defenses were inextricably entwined in muscular position or "body armor." Experiencing feelings by acting them out was consistent with Moreno's psychodrama, yet Perls attempted to improve upon this method by having persons project upon an empty chair to remove the confounding effects of the role-player's personality. Perls expanded on Rogers's idea of feedback as a therapeutic agent by including body posture, voice tone, eye movements, feelings, and gestures. Also, throughout Gestalt therapy there is evidence of the existential and humanistic view of man from Eastern religion and thought.

Theoretical Components
of Gestalt Therapy

An adequate theory of therapy or counseling must be comprehensive in scope, including certain philosophical tenets. There will be a set of assumptions about the nature of man which will pervade the theory and offer a sense of consistency. The theory will be inextricably linked with a theory of personality. This dimension of the theory focuses on *who* the counselee is and suggests hypotheses about the nature and dynamics of his behavior. Finally, the theory will offer some formulations with regard to the operational processes of counseling. The remainder of this chapter will present a brief overview of Gestalt therapy in terms of components of a comprehensive theory.

The discussion that follows is not intended as a definitive theoretical statement on Gestalt therapy. Aspects of the theory which deal with pathological individuals are not considered here because they are outside the realm of counseling in schools. Included are some highlights of the theory and practice of Gestalt therapy which are offered as a perspective for understanding the approaches presented in the text. The counselor's grasp of the rationale underlying these approaches will increase his ability to judge the appropriateness of their use and provide stimulus to invent additional approaches according to the tenets of the Gestalt theory. Resources are available for the reader who desires a more extensive treatment of the theory and practice of Gestalt therapy (Fagan and Shepherd, 1971; Perls, 1947, 1969, 1973; Perls, Hefferline, and Goodman, 1951; Polster and Polster, 1973; Pursglove, 1968).

Assumptions about Man

Several pivotal assumptions about the nature of man form the base of Gestalt therapy:

1. Man is a whole who is (rather than has) a body, emotions, thoughts, sensations, and perceptions, all of which function interrelatedly.
2. Man is part of his environment and cannot be understood outside of it.
3. Man is proactive rather than reactive. He determines his own responses to external and proprioceptive stimuli.
4. Man is capable of being aware of his sensations, thoughts, emotions, and perceptions.
5. Man, through self-awareness, is capable of choice and is thus responsible for covert and overt behavior.
6. Man possesses the wherewithal and resources to live effectively and to restore himself through his own assets.
7. Man can experience himself only in the present. The past and the future can be experienced only in the now through remembering and anticipating.
8. Man is neither intrinsically good nor bad.

The reader will note that these assumptions are shared by other theories which are currently referred to as "humanistic" approaches. At the philosophical level these parallels are evident. However, as each of the components is discussed the differences and specifics of the theory of Gestalt therapy will emerge and its uniqueness will become evident.

Motivation

According to Perls (1969), "Every individual, every plant, every animal has only one inborn goal—to actualize itself as it is." All behavior, then, derives its purpose from the individual's quest to become himself. As such, achieving this actualizing or becoming process is the person's primary need. It can be assumed that at any moment a person's behavior, regardless of how it may appear to any observer, is his current chosen means toward actualization.

As a part of this actualization need there are other biological and social needs. Basic biological needs include air, food, water, shelter, expression of self, sex, and aggression. Social needs are learned from environmental contacts, including coping with other persons, maintaining one's identity, and dealing with environmental restrictions.

The question then becomes, "To which need does a person respond in a given now?" The explanation of this dynamic is best understood through the figure and ground relationship. Needs move in and out of the figure and ground fields. At a given moment a particular need may emerge and direct the person's behavior. The need moves from ground to figure. After this need is met it recedes into ground, and the most pressing need in the "new" now emerges from the ground as figure.

This situation plays a prominent part in the process of motivation. For example, the reader may be responding to a need which is being met by learning about Gestalt therapy. A long-lost friend walks into the room. Learning about Gestalt therapy recedes into ground, and being with the friend, a need which a moment before may have been in the outer recesses of ground, becomes the dominant need in the figure field. The reader will resume reading when the balance between the needs is readjusted by spending time with the friend.

There is no universal hierarchy of needs. Each person has an individual formula that dictates which needs will dominate a given situation. This means that there could be a person who would finish reading and then greet his friend! The point is that it is difficult to predict the relative value of a person's needs. Again this can be situational. Reading done for pleasure and reading done for an important exam could result in different behaviors upon the entrance of the friend.

In situations where needs are in competition, one will dominate as the movement of needs from figure to ground and back is fluid and flexible. There are grey areas. At any moment, however, one of the needs will have a greater emergent (hence emergency—"I must do this now") quality to it.

Development

A basic tenet of both Gestalt psychology and Gestalt therapy is that a person cannot be considered as separate from his environmental field. This field includes physical and social objects as well as forces with which the person is in contact. Virtually all of a person's behavior is in some way related to this person-environment complex.

From the moment of conception a person is in contact and is interacting with his environment. This interaction between himself and his environment is the basis through which his needs are met. The environmental-person contacts are holistic relations which take the form of Gestalts. Poorly defined, unclear Gestalts result in contacts that are not to the person's benefit. On the other hand, the formulation of clear person-environment (figure-ground) Gestalts which take the form of creative adjustments allow the person to meet his needs in his environment. The process of formulating these creative adjustments is growth.

The self has a dual role in growth processes. In terms of function, the main role of the self is formulating the creative adjustment contacts within the environment. Thus, the self is active, dynamic, and changing according to emergent needs and environmental presses. At the same time, the self *is* the system of creative adjustments that are present at any given moment. The self, then, is defined by both the processes and contents of the person's behavior in his environment.

At any time the person may identify with his self or try to alienate himself from it. When he identifies with his self he frees it so that creative and self-regulatory behaviors can take place. This allows for situations to be finished, problems to be solved, and environmental contacts to be focused on those things which have interest and excitement for him. Conversely, when the person tries to alienate himself from his self he is interfering with the processes of his self, thus reducing the potentials for creative adjustments. The person's contacts become fuzzy and he is unable to cope or live effectively. This network of identifications and alienations is the ego (Perls, Hefferline, and Goodman, 1951).

The definition of maturity also relies heavily upon the place of the environment in personal development. A keystone of development is "transcendence from environmental- to self-support." Immaturity is characterized by dependency and helplessness, with heavy reliance on manipulating the environment for support and meeting needs. Maturity is approached as the person demonstrates that he can and will assume responsibility for his behavior and looks to himself for the support he needs. Ideally, the person will achieve a level of self-support that will afford him a sense of autonomy and responsibility.

Development and growth are continuous processes. While there are some global developmental expectations (for example, less capability for responsibility at younger ages), persons are not seen as developing through uniform time schedules. Thus, it is not assumed that chronological age is directly related to a characteristic such as responsibility. The direction of development is toward becoming who one is. Perls was fond of saying that a rose develops as a rose, a person as a person, and so on. Yet because there is always something new to be assimilated, development is never completed. New directions for growth are continuously emerging. Development is ended only with death.

Learning

It has been noted that according to Gestalt psychology the person's experience and relationship to the environment are something more than interrelated stimuli and responses. Rather, behavior is organized in terms of wholes or Gestalts. For example, hitting a golf ball is a Gestalt comprised of addressing the ball, swinging back, striking, and following through. Noticing the invariability with which behavioral units such as these are held together and repeated consistently attests to the organizational power of a Gestalt. How then does learning take place?

Learning occurs when Gestalts are formulated. The early Gestalt psychologists observed that a monkey in a cage tried to reach out for the banana that was just beyond his arm's length. At first he ignored the stick in the cage and kept trying to stretch his arm further. Finally, he picked up the stick and used it to bring the banana within his reach. At that moment he unified a Gestalt which included bringing environmental resources (the stick) into play to overcome barriers (the cage) in order to meet his need (eating the banana). His Gestalt was clear, creative, and functional. Learning had taken place through the formulation of a new Gestalt.

Sometimes learning takes place through formulating new Gestalts to replace old ones. Consider the golfer. He notices one day that he is hitting more slices into the rough than is usual, suggesting something in his Gestalt has been altered. Finally he becomes aware that he is using his new set of clubs, which happen to be a little shorter than his old ones. He moves an inch or so closer to the ball and begins to hit straight shots again. In this process he has formulated a *new* Gestalt to replace the previous one which was no longer functional.

Often new Gestalts formulated to replace old ones are much more dramatic and harder to achieve. For example, a person has a Gestalt comprising his body image as an obese person. The person then sheds 100 pounds and finds that he still has the obese body image. The older Gestalt has holding power, and the new one has not yet been integrated as it is still unclear and imprecise. As the person identifies more with his new body image and the way it fits into his total style his self-image changes.

The Nature of Problems

A common problem of many people today is a lack of awareness. A person may lose touch with the "what" and the "how" of his behavior, and be unable to achieve the sense of mastery and competence needed to live effectively. He tends to exist rather than to be, and he thus feels a sense of helplessness and despair in not realizing what he can do to serve himself.

Relatedly, a person can refuse to take responsibility for himself and his life, insisting instead on manipulating the environment to take care of him. He is then not able to be held accountable and can become an expert finger pointer in a blame game. This type of avoidance sets up barriers in his development and results in inappropriate behavior that is infantile in nature.

Losing contact with the environment is another perspective on human dilemmas. This can happen in two ways. First, the person's boundaries, that which differentiates him from the environment, may become so rigid that he permits no input into his system. He may cut himself off from other persons or resources in his environment that could be useful for meeting his needs. He becomes alienated and stagnant. Second, his boundaries may become disjointed and undifferentiated so that he experiences confluence. In such cases a person can invest so much of himself in others or incorporate so much from the environment into himself that he loses touch with where he leaves off and his environment takes over. The sense of self suffers in both cases.

"Unfinished business" or incomplete Gestalts is another type of problem. The person has an unfulfilled need, an unexpressed feeling, or some other uncompleted situation that is of significance to him. The most common among these are resentments, the bulldogs of unexpressed feelings in terms of retaining their bite. The unfinished task dominates the person's awareness and clamors for attention. Being "stuck" in this way severely retards the flow of attention and excitement required to cope with other needs yet to emerge out of the background. Resources for dealing with other needs are unproductively being sapped off.

Fragmentation may be another serious problem confronting a person. One form of this is disowning or denying. Suppose a person tries to disown his need to be aggressive, a common malady in our society. He loses three ways in his attempt. First, he has violated the integrity of his organism by thwarting a biological need. Second, he is losing the energy contained in the aggressive part of him which might be channeled into constructive behaviors. Finally, he is wasting valuable energy in the very process of holding a part of him in abeyance because the natural tendency of the organism will be to regain the loss.

A second mode of fragmentation occurs in dichotomizing continuous dimensions of the self. A person may consider himself as strong *or* weak, masculine *or* feminine, powerful or powerless, and so on. The full value of either end of the continuum is not realized as a result of denying its counterpart. For example, a person cannot feel the fullness of his strength unless he permits himself to experience enough of his weakness to be able to appropriate the contrast between the two. Perhaps the most famous split is what Perls has termed the "top dog" (You really should be better) and the "bottom dog" ("I'll try tomorrow, I promise).

Goals

In Perls's (1969) words, "We have a specific aim in Gestalt therapy and this is the same aim that exists at least verbally in other forms of therapy, in other forms of discovering life. The aim is to mature, to grow up . . ." (p. 26).

Since one of the key elements of development and maturation is becoming responsible, it follows then that being responsible for oneself is a significant goal of Gestalt therapy. Being responsible is not the process of carrying out duties according to someone's expectations. Rather, this "aim of therapy is to make the patient *not* depend on others, but to make the patient discover from the very first moment that he can do many things (*much*) more than he thinks he can do" (Perls, 1969, p. 29).

A second major goal of Gestalt therapy is achieving integration. In its literal sense, according to Webster's, to integrate is "to unite or become united so as to form a complete or perfect whole." This definition will serve here also. A person who is more integrated functions as a systemic whole comprised of feelings, perceptions, thoughts, and a physical body whose processes cannot be divorced from the more psychological components. When the person's inner state and behavior match, there is little energy wasted within his organism and he is more capable of responding appropriately (for him) to meet his needs. The less-well-integrated person has voids or splits in his self that inhibit full mobilization of his resources.

The content of the integrations can vary considerably within and across persons. For one person it may be important to integrate memories of the past with the present so that he is in one place and not two. Finding an appropriate relationship between bipolarities such as masculinity-femininity may be a significant area for integration. Similarly, there are ambivalences to be integrated such as loving and hating the same person. Integration of muscles, sensations, fantasies, thoughts, feelings, and perceptions are of tantamount importance. Reclaiming and owning needs and wants that have been denied are two significant dimensions of integration. Also, to function adequately the organism needs to be at one and integrated into contacts with the environment. Completing "unfinished business" is a means of integrating energy lost through the lack of closure. Further, contributions to integration are made by reclaiming parts of the personality that are projected onto others or into dreams.

In sum, the goals of Gestalt therapy are to teach persons to assume responsibility and to facilitate integration. These goals, however, are achieved only in approximation. "Now there is no such thing as total integration. Integration is never completed; maturation is never completed. It's an ongoing process for ever and ever. . . There's always something to be integrated; always something to be learned" (Perls, 1969, p. 64).

Change

In Gestalt therapy change is not planned, programmed, or coerced. It is allowed. Trying to be a "should be" or a "would like to be" denies what is and thereby disrupts integrative processes. As a person becomes more aware of and accepting of who he is, changes become possible that were thwarted by denying or disowning parts of himself.

Perls (1969) was adamant about how awareness related to change:

and I believe that this is the great thing to understand (*that awareness per se—by and of itself—can be curative*). Because with full awareness you become aware of this organismic self-regulation, you can let the organism take over without interfering, without interrupting; we can rely on the wisdom of the organism. . . . (p. 16–17).

Organismic self-regulation takes place on several levels. One of these is awareness of corrections needed in the body. For example, take the person who wakes up in the middle of the night and experiences numbing and tingling in an arm on which he is resting. The flow of blood has been interrupted and this is potentially dangerous to his limb. He takes the arm out from under his body and goes back to sleep. His self-regulation processes were at work. Pain which serves as a signal of hurt and vomiting up bad food are other examples.

Such self-regulation can also take place in relation to the environs. The person who is not attuned to his will not have the wherewithal to remove himself from potential danger. The person who is aware of a need for other people will be able to focus energy to meet the need. The person who feels thirst will, if left to trustworthy indicators and regulators, find and drink water.

The same processes hold for internal events. Suppose the person who needs others does not seek them because he imagines the outcome to be catastrophic. If he can stay with the awareness of how he scares himself with these fantasies he may then find the risks not so great and thus initiate some interpersonal behaviors. If on the other hand he feels the fear of his fantasies and does not experience the awareness of how he creates them, then he feels at the mercy of a bogus. The result is that change cannot take place because the reaction cannot be approached. Thus awareness must not only be present to clarify the emergent need which dominates the moment, but it must also be available to the problem-solving, often self-defeating processes required to meet the need.

Functions of the Gestalt Therapist

Consistent with the theory of change, the function of the Gestalt therapist is to facilitate the person's awareness in the now. The extreme importance of the concepts of awareness and now requires further discussion.

On awareness, Simkin (1970) has stated:

> Gestalt therapy uses as a tool awareness. Now, awareness is the capacity to focus, to attend. Thinking is not awareness, feeling is not awareness, sensing is not awareness. I need awareness to be in touch, to know that I am sensing or feeling or thinking. . . . If I am unaware of what I am doing, I am not responsible for what I am doing.

As stated earlier, awareness can be experienced only in the now. Further, it is not possible for a person to be aware of any experience that is not occurring in the now. This does not mean that the past and the future are not legitimately entwined in living. It does mean that both the past and the future are rooted in the now. A memory is experienced now. Sensations, thoughts, and feelings from the past are experienced only in the immediate present. In the same way a person may have predictions about the future. However, he can experience only his predicting. He cannot be aware of that which he has not lived.

One of the most salient points about the concept of now is that it is not a moment but a continuous stream. Roughly speaking, now is a series of infinitesimally small "new" nows that appear as an unbroken stream, an ongoing event, that cannot be stopped. "The" now is over in a flash and followed by yet another, into infinity. The sweeping second hand of a watch is constantly in the now.

Just as the now flows, so must the awareness of it. The blinking eye cannot be aware of the flow of water. Rather, it sees a series of jerky thrusts. Similarly, being aware of one's now means staying aware of one's flow. To glance at it momentarily does not afford the opportunity to get close enough to experience it in process.

The key, then, to becoming aware of what one does is through becoming aware of what he is *doing* now and remaining in this awareness, letting it flow with the stream of experience. Interruptions or avoidances in awareness diminish experiencing now, thereby eliminating the "knowing" of which Simkin speaks.

Gestalt Approaches

To enhance the person's awareness of his now, the therapist engages him in a relationship. Thus, the therapists's most potent tool is himself and his awareness in the now.

He must be able to enter into the person's now and react to it from his vantage in the relationship, perhaps by sharing his observations and experience at the moment. He does not interpret behavior, but rather focuses on the "what" and "how" of the person's now, the assumption being that the most pressing need will eventually emerge to be dealt with. Thus, the therapist's presence and approaches are geared toward enhancing the person's present awareness.

The therapist's personal responses may serve as potent interventions. He may share with the person his reactions to the material being worked on. Sometimes he will direct awareness to discrepancies or avoidances which the person is living and of which he is not aware. The therapist may offer himself as a screen for the person's projections, or he may engage himself as part of the person's dialogue. He will often suggest a lead sentence to communicate his awareness of which direction the work might take. Sometimes the therapist will offer his hunch about what the person is doing, taking care to note it is his guess and not necessarily a valid interpretation. The therapist does not restrict spontaneous responses such as self-disclosure, confrontation, offering support, or in some way "touching" the person who is hurting to convey an understanding.

The therapist will employ many different approaches for enhancing the person's awareness. Usually these are presented as experiments for the person to try. Awareness can be illuminated by repeating statements and gestures, sometimes exaggerating them for clarification. The person may be asked to do to someone else what he does to himself. Ploys that the person uses to avoid his awareness can be approached through similar methods.

The therapist assists the person to note discrepancies between his words and body expression by asking the person to be aware of both. For example, voice tone and gestures may not match what the person is verbally relating. The focus then is on enhancing awareness of the dominant message of the two modes of expression.

Imagined dialogues are an important tool in Gestalt therapy. The person may write and act out a script between two dimensions of a situation such as parent and self, two sides of a decision, two conflicting parts of self, or self and a particular difficulty, to mention just a few. Dialogues between various parts of a dream (the assumption being that each part of the dream is a projection of the person) is one of the most fascinating uses of this versatile method. There are no limits to what the two sides of the dialogue can be, except for the imagination of the person and a minimal degree of willingness to identify with them.

While fantasy is essential in dialogues it also has other uses. The person can fantasize situations to see how he reacted or may react to them. For example, a person who predicts a catastrophe that will render him helpless may play the situation through and see ways that he could cope and adapt. Similarly, the person might act out a past situation as though it were going on now in order to check the validity of his current reactions to it.

Considerable attention is also given to the person's verbal expressions. He is asked to use personal pronouns instead of the customary "you" or "they" when expressing his opinion. The therapist may ask him to change "can't" to "won't" to feel the proactive elements of his behavior. Also, an experiment of changing "but" to "and" can serve to connect seemingly disjointed or contradictory statements.

This brief discussion is by no means a comprehensive overview of what Gestalt therapists do. It may serve to communicate some of the flavor of the methods involved in practicing Gestalt therapy. Hopefully, it demonstrates the congruence between the theory and practice of Gestalt therapy. Case studies and specific examples of possible applications of approaches will serve to flesh out this skeletal introduction.

Summary

Gestalt therapy was developed by Fritz Perls, a Freudian analyst who was strongly influenced by Gestalt psychology. Principles of Gestalt psychology evident in Gestalt therapy include closure, projection according to current needs, behavior as a whole which is greater than the sum of its parts, behavior viewed in the person's environmental context, and the relationship between figure and ground.

The presuppositions about the nature of man state that he is (1) a body, emotions, and thoughts functioning in union; (2) an integral part of his environment; (3) a proactive being; (4) capable of awareness of his sensations, thoughts, and emotions; (5) able to make responsible choices; (6) capable of self-regulation; (7) able to be aware of himself only in the present; and (8) neither intrinsically good or bad.

Man is primarily motivated toward self-actualization. Biological and social needs also are present. At any given moment the most emergent need becomes figure and demands attention from the person. Upon gratification the need recedes into background, thus allowing the most pressing need in the "new" now to emerge from the background.

Development and growth take place as the self formulates and becomes the person's system of creative adjustments in his environment. The part of the person which identifies with or tries to alienate him from his self is the ego. Development is a continuous process which ends only with death. Maturation is defined in terms of self-support and responsibility.

Learning occurs when Gestalts are formulated into holistic relationships between events and phenomena. A person may formulate a unified Gestalt between his need, his means for coping with his need, and environmental resources available to him. Similarly, learning occurs when changes or adjustments are necessarily included in reformulating existing Gestalts.

The nature of personal problems may be viewed from several perspectives. Among the most common problems are a lack of awareness of the "how" and "what" of one's behavior, refusing to take responsibility for oneself, poor contact with the environment either through rigid boundaries or confluence, unfinished business which constantly clamors for attention, fragmenting or disowning part of oneself, and dichotomizing oneself by identifying with one side of a bipolarity and excluding the other.

The overall goal of Gestalt therapy is growth toward maturation, which is related to the degree of responsibility the person is willing to assume. Another goal is working toward integration of the person such that he functions as a systemic whole comprised of feelings, perceptions, thoughts, physical movements, and sensations. Integration includes filling gaps, claiming parts of the self which have been fragmented, and finding new centers in bipolar splits.

Change is not forced or programmed but rather is allowed. Change occurs as self-awareness is enhanced because this permits organismic self-regulations to take place.

The function of the Gestalt therapist is to raise awareness, which is defined as knowing what one is sensing, feeling, and thinking. Such awareness can be achieved only in the now, which is the continuously moving time that lies between the immediate past and the future. Thus the therapist assists the person to become aware of "what" and "how" he behaves in the present.

The therapist employs a broad range of interventions to assist the person in enhancing his awareness, the assumption being that in the spontaneity of the now, problems which need to be dealt with will emerge. Some of the basic interventions include exaggeration, focusing on the relationship between verbal and nonverbal behavior, acting out both sides of a dialogue, playing fantasies to their conclusion, and doing to others what the person does to himself as a means of clarification.

REFERENCES

English, H. B., and English, A. C., *A Comprehensive Dictionary of Psychological and Psychoanalytical Terms.* New York: David McKay Company, 1958.

Fagan, J., and Shepherd, I. L., *Gestalt Therapy Now: Theory, Techniques, Applications.* Palo Alto, Calif.: Science and Behavior Books, 1970.

Perls, F. S., *Ego, Hunger and Aggression.* New York: Vintage Books, 1947.

Perls, F. S., *Gestalt Therapy Verbatim.* Lafayette, Calif.: Real People Press, 1969.

Perls, F. S., *The Gestalt Approach and Eye Witness to Therapy.* Palo Alto, Calif.: Science and Behavior Books, 1973.

Perls, F. S., Hefferline, R. F., and Goodman, P., *Gestalt Therapy: Excitement and Growth in the Human Personality.* New York: Dell Publishing Company, 1951.

Polster, E., and Polster, M., *Gestalt Therapy Integrated: Contours of Theory and Practice.* New York: Bruner/Mazel Publishers, 1973.

Pursglove, P. D. (ed.), *Recognition in Gestalt Therapy.* New York: Funk and Wagnalls, 1968.

Simkin, J. S., *Individual Gestalt Therapy.* Philadelphia: American Academy of Psychotherapists Tape Library, No. 31, 1970.

3

Gestalt Approaches

in Counseling

Something as complex as Gestalt therapy is difficult to communicate. Thus, it is necessary to look further into what practicing Gestalt therapists do to identify components which can be specified, concretized, and communicated. Levitsky and Perls (1970) have recognized that there are certain specific behaviors which have found their way into the response repertoire of many Gestalt therapists. Some of these have been enumerated in their article "The Rules and Games of Gestalt Therapy." The authors immediately, however, state two important points about the rules and games they have identified. First, "They are definitely *not* intended as a dogmatic list of *do's* and *don'ts*; rather they are offered in the spirit of experiments that the patient may perform." Second, "Seen in this light, any particular set of techniques such as our presently used rules and games will be regarded merely as convenient means—useful tools for our purposes but without sacrosanct qualities" (p. 140).

Added to the qualifications of Levitsky and Perls is another message: *Gestalt therapy is more than the techniques which are identifiable in it.* This is a given which is consistent with the holistic tenets of Gestalt psychology. The message, however, has no dampening effects on the purpose of this book, which is to communicate some Gestalt approaches for use by counselors who have no intention of doing Gestalt therapy. A counselor can employ Gestalt approaches in an endless stream and still not be doing Gestalt therapy. Thus, while the counselor may adopt some Gestalt approaches into his work, he is not a Gestalt therapist. Rather, he will be a counselor who is using Gestalt approaches. While this point has perhaps been oversimplified, it cannot be over-stressed.

Appropriateness of Gestalt
Approaches in Counseling

Three main factors must be considered in weighing the appropriate-ness of Gestalt approaches in counseling. These are the relationship of Gestalt approaches to various counseling theories, the nature of Gestalt approaches, and the counselor's personality.

Gestalt and Theories of Counseling

From a theoretical point of view Gestalt approaches are well suited for applications in counseling. Currently, there are counselors who align themselves with theories such as Client-centered, Behavioristic, Rational-emotive, Transactional Analysis, Reality therapy, Adlerian approaches, psychoanalysis, and Existentialism. There is also a large contingency of counselors who consider themselves eclectic. How is it then that Gestalt approaches can be considered appropriate for use by counselors subscrib-ing to such a wide range of theoretical postures? One answer to this question lies in the values of the various theories. While each theory states its goals differently, most of them subscribe to values of self-direction, independence, self-knowledge, and responsibility. Gestalt ther-apy also embraces these values and is thus basically aligned with the other theories.

The differences among theories are more clearly delineated when the language of the theories is translated into goals and operations. From this perspective the means to the goals, which are expressions of the values, are different. Counselors who ascribe to different theories respond differently to their counselees even when their respective theories share values. For example, a Client-centered counselor and a Behavioristic coun-selor will both place a high value on their counselee's being able to make decisions. They will, however, approach their counseling task differently.

It can be stated that all theories of counseling would be dysfunc-tional without self-knowledge and self-exploration on the part of the counselee. In short, self-awareness is a core ingredient in any theoretical approach. Where the awareness is focused and how it will be enhanced will differ. The Rational-emotive counselor will try to enhance aware-ness of self-defeating or "insane" sentences the counselee feeds himself.

The Transactional Analysis counselor will tend to facilitate awareness of whether the counselee is behaving as Child, Parent, or Adult.

It is in the enhancement of awareness that counselors from various points of view can apply Gestalt approaches. Gestalt therapy places a premium on awareness. In fact, most Gestalt approaches have been devised to enhance and facilitate awareness. Thus, counselors of diverse theoretical postures may find Gestalt approaches useful. A Behavioristic counselor, for example, might be working with a counselee on reducing anxiety through desensitization. The counselor may find that some Gestalt approaches employing fantasy are appropriate for setting up the stimulus situations comprising the gradations of anxiety. An eclectic counselor may be involved with a counselee who has a decision to make. A simple dialogue between the part of the person who is "pro" and the part of the person who is "con" may lead to greater awareness than listing the reasons for and against an alternative. A counselor who employs Transactional Analysis might use some Gestalt approaches to explore the relationship between his Child, Parent, and Adult and how he relates to others. Some Gestalt approaches are particularly useful for awareness work in nonverbal behavior, which has a significance that transcends theoretical lines. In sum, there do not appear to be theoretical contraindications to these kinds of uses of Gestalt approaches.

The Nature of Gestalt Approaches

Another point regarding the appropriateness of Gestalt approaches has to do with the mystery and magic that is often imputed to Gestalt. Since I began working on this book a number of people have asked me, "How can counselors use Gestalt when it is such a powerful approach?" These statements have come from persons who have attended Gestalt workshops and from persons whose experience with Gestalt consists of viewing films and reading about Gestalt therapy. The first group has observed how persons in Gestalt workshops can quite rapidly get into heavy material such as unexpressed grief, sexual feelings and fantasies sometimes involving parents, expression of deep rage through physical behaviors such as pillow smashing, and identification with grotesque figures presented in nightmares. The second group, having been exposed to a carefully selected group of printed transcripts and films of Gestalt sessions, also does not feel that counselors will be able to do that kind of work. Both groups are properly concerned about the appropriateness of Gestalt approaches for counselors. I am in basic agreement with them and here is how I respond.

You are right that there is a great deal of Gestalt work that is not appropriate for counselors, and I'm not going to discuss this work in the book. I am not suggesting that counselors get into deep material using advanced Gestalt methods. As such, I will not be including these in my writing. Let's not throw out the baby with the wash, though, as there is much in Gestalt that counselors and teachers can use. I have seen evidence of this in training counselors and consulting with practicing counselors.

There are a few points implicit in your question that I want to respond to. First, you seem to imagine that there is tremendous power inherent in Gestalt approaches. I see you talking about them as if they had destructive power like hand grenades or razor blades. I think this is ascribing too much power to the interventions themselves. The interventions are merely words and experiments designed to enhance awareness; they have no power of their own. The power you speak of lies in the person who is using them. It is simply not true that the use of a Gestalt approach will automatically result in expression of rage, psychoses, or frenzies of physical activity or sexual intimacy.

You intimate that some counselors push counselees into situations, expressions of feelings, and encounters for which the counselees are not prepared and that negative results can occur. That is undeniable. However, doesn't this question have more to do with the ethics and judgment of the counselor than with the nature of the interventions he uses? The counselor who chooses to use his power to manipulate counselees to his own end will find ways to do so. If someone hits me with a club, do I place the responsibility for my bruises on the club? Hardly. These people do exist, and it is true that they might add some Gestalt approaches to their arsenal. However, they will soon be disillusioned when they find that the power they fantasized to be in the approaches is either not present or is overshadowed by the resistances and defenses of the counselee. The attempted use of any approach without trust, respect, understanding, and support is bound to result in failure.

I share your concern about the persons just mentioned. Most counselors, however, are not prone to take counselees into deep emotional material. If anything, many of them sell themselves short in terms of their competence to deal with such material and sometimes treat their counselees more gingerly than necessary or beneficial. Indeed, sometimes these counselors will not permit counselees to express something that could if expressed be constructive and growth producing. Often the counselor is afraid the counselee will be hurt or get into something that neither of them could handle. My work as a consultant in a mental health clinic serving approximately thirty schools has made it clear to me that one of the first approaches used by counselors when they feel reticent about working with a counselee is to reach for the telephone! In many of these cases, a supportive consultation coupled with a joint interview will result in the counselor going ahead with the counselee. In other instances referrals are made to therapists, although the inclination for this is often felt too quickly by the counselor.

So, an opposite problem exists with the majority of counselors. They needn't worry about their misusing Gestalt approaches to take counselees too far, because they are not inclined to do so regardless of their theoretical tendencies or the approaches they use. Rather, the problem is to help counselors understand that using Gestalt approaches does not convert counselees into fragile china dolls. Counselors, too, attribute too much power to Gestalt approaches, but their reaction is avoidance, at least, until they experiment with a few approaches and see that the expected casualties do not occur. I believe that working with counselors to overcome the initial awe that unfortunately Gestalt therapy elicits in them is necessary before the richness of Gestalt can be disseminated beyond the practice of the therapy itself.

The Counselor's Personality

The counselor's personality is a primary determinant in integrating Gestalt approaches into his counseling style, as Fagan and Shepherd (1970) have noted:

> Both the techniques that a therapist devises and those that he adopts from others must have some degree of congruity with his own personality make-up before he can use them effectively. The therapist who is able to use Gestalt techniques effectively generally prefers activity to passivity, accepts power but does not need it for personal gratification, acts with firmness and assurance, enjoys improvising rather than following a fixed plan, is not unduly afraid of intense emotional explosions, and can utilize himself and his emotional reactions without great fear of exposure. Persons who have high investments in cognitive or "computer" processes, who prefer emotional distance, who tend to be conservative, who prefer to reflect or "follow" the patient's responses, or who lack awareness of their own experience have more difficulty with Gestalt techniques. (p. 81)

Few counselors will permit counselees to explore or express themselves in areas where they themselves are limited. In one Gestalt weekend I attended there was very little expression of anger, which was quite unusual. At the end of the weekend one of the workshop participants commented on this unexpected phenomenon. The therapist stated in response that he had not been aware of the lack of expressed anger and *then* became aware that he had been checking his own anger for the previous six months! The same holds for other modes of expression. The therapist who has not experienced and enjoyed his own joy will not let others confront theirs.

A parallel dynamic is involved with counseling approaches. In general, counselors who do not like to be confronted will not confront counselees. Counselors who do not like to disclose themselves will not use approaches that may elicit disclosure on the part of counselees. Counselors who like to be told answers to their questions will be more prone to answer questions for counselees. Counselors whose own fantasy life is sterile will not be inclined to engage his counselees in fantasy.

In light of the interplay between the counselor's reaction as a recipient of interventions and the interventions he will see fit to apply, numerous self-exercises are interspersed throughout this book. If the counselor engages himself in the exercise, he will be able to sort out those approaches which feel "right" and avoid applying those which elicit dissonance in him. The counselor who finds that trying an opposite feeling leads him to some new awareness and excitement may then attempt this approach with his counselees, keeping in mind, of course, that they may not respond as he did. On the other hand, the counselor who is insulted by being asked to do this will probably not be inclined to believe that there could be advantages in it for his counselees. Even if he were to try it, the likelihood is that his own doubts and ambivalences would be communicated to the counselee in a nonfacilitative fashion.

Thus, the reader is encouraged to experiment with himself prior to his attempts to apply the approaches presented in this book. Some of the approaches will deserve working through several times, especially those where blockages and resistances are immediately encountered. Also, the counselor might note in persons around him the behaviors described in the examples. He may become aware of a new framework for observing nuances in language and nonverbal behaviors. With persons he knows well he might discuss his own or their behavior in light of the exercises and approaches. By asking some of his colleagues, friends, or family members to "play" with some of the approaches the counselor will be able to see how various persons can fruitfully use them. This can be a particularly enlightening experience when the next person's reaction is, "What do you mean, say 'won't' instead of 'can't'! That's the dumbest thing I've ever head of!"

The expected net result of the "trying on for size" processes is a wide divergence among counselors on the approaches they choose to employ. On this point Polster (1968) commented:

Some people are more kind than others, some more verbal, some more permissive. Some make broad strokes, describing grand life processes and stimulating patients to awareness of large sections of their natures such as fear of death, gross lechery, noble generosity. Others may face tiny details of existence such as the way a patient uses the word "wish" rather than "want" in asking for a promotion or the way a particular position of his musculature affects his expressiveness. Clearly, variations in style must exist, theory notwithstanding. (pp. 13–14)

In sum, no two readers of this book are going to respond to it the same way or take precisely the same things from it. I expect and appreciate these differences.

Integrating Gestalt Approaches into Counseling

The counselor who decides to use some Gestalt approaches will find numerous questions arising. How will I orient counselees to these different approaches? When should I begin using Gestalt approaches in a counseling relationship? What kinds of approaches are the most appropriate to start with? How are different counselees going to respond? What uses for Gestalt approaches will I find in the broad range of my functions as a counselor? The section which follows offers some suggestions which are geared toward answering such questions.

Orienting Counselees to Gestalt Approaches

The counselor should keep several points in mind in connection with orienting counselees to Gestalt approaches. One is by adopting and communicating to the counselee an experimental attitude such as, "Let's give this a try and see how it goes." This approach has advantages for both the counselor and the counselee. The counselor who works from an experimental framework will have less investment in the counselee's response being "right." He will be aware that some approaches will connect with and illuminate the counselee's awareness and some will not. His expectancies of the counselee will be loose enough to allow the expression of whatever the response may be. There will be less need to "thread the needle" with each utterance, which can eliminate much of the frustration counselors sometimes feel.

On the other hand, the counselee will not feel that a hoop has been set which he must jump through. Sensing the open-endedness and experimental nature of the approach, the counselee may experience less of the fear of failure which is often a function of trying to please the counselor or be a "good" counselee. In this spirit the counselor and counselee can be colleagues in a process of discovery which is more likely to occur in the absence of limited expectancies.

Some counselees may be puzzled by Gestalt approaches when they are asked to do some things they have not done before. For example, a counselee may be quite surprised by the counselor's asking him if he can accept responsibility for a certain feeling, thought, or behavior. The counselee may feel that the counselor is blaming him and feel rejected. What is missing is the counselee's understanding that upon assuming responsibility he is permitting himself the capability for choices and changes. A brief explanation at this point may eliminate enough of the strangeness from the counselor's question that the counselee will be willing to attempt a few experiments on responsibility. Additionally, these brief explanations may serve to establish trust in the counselor. The counselee can feel that the counselor has an understanding of what he is doing. Further, the counselor does not appear to be trying out secrets and tricks that are alien to the counselee and that can result in establishing his inferiority in the relationship. While this approach can result in the benefits just mentioned, the counselor needs to be aware of when an explanation becomes a lecture. Overintellectualizing on these topics can be counterproductive, especially when the explanation evolves into extensive talking about or a list of "shoulds."

Often a brief description of the purposes of an approach will not be sufficient for the counselee to know how to respond. In such cases the counselor may engage in modeling behavior to help the counselee bridge the gap from "what" to "how." For example, a counselee may not grasp how he frustrates himself. The counselor, offering an example from his own life, may say

> I frustrate myself sometimes, too. Here is an example of how I do it. "Look, Bob, I'm letting you want to save up some money to go on a trip. And then just when you are getting some money saved, I'm going to tease you into buying something else to keep you from getting the amount you need for your trip." That's just one way I do this. You're different and have your own ways. How do you do your frustrations?

This example on the part of the counselor can clarify how the counselee can go about exploring his frustration. It is also sharing and self-disclosing on the part of the counselor. Accordingly, the counselee-counselor relationship may be deepened and broadened to the point where the counselee will feel the safety and trust necessary to disclose himself.

As the counselee begins the experiment he may offer a comment or two and then feel as though he has said all he has to say. The counselor can be facilitative at this point by helping the counselee to unravel tightly knit semantics and experiences which have been encoded into brevity by the counselee's rehashing of them. A counselee, for example, may be exploring how he can expand his feelings of worth and competence. He might be making an imaginary list to give to someone, and after saying one or two things he might stop. The counselor might then ask the counselee, "May I feed you a sentence here?" Based upon observations on what he has heard, the counselor might suggest that he say, "I am able to build transistor radios very well." One sentence thus interjected by the counselor will often unfreeze the counselee in his elaboration of certain points. Provided the sentence is accepted by the counselee, it will indicate to him that the counselor has been observing and hearing and is developing an understanding of him. After this approach becomes established, the counselor will be able to feed sentences without having to ask each time. Also the counselor will be able to raise points which may seem new to the counselee, such as confronting him with strengths he has demonstrated but with which he has not identified.

Timing in Applying
Gestalt Approaches

The counselor needs to be aware of the timing of introducing Gestalt approaches. With a new counselee it is a good idea to start early in the relationship when the counselee's expectancies are being established. The counselee will then recognize that the counselor will be responding to him in ways different from those he encounters in his everyday interaction. He may also, through his own experience, be able to see the potential for discovery in responding to Gestalt approaches. By participating in some of the simpler experiments and approaches, for example, language changes and some basic awareness work, the counselee will be developing tools that can be used in approaching more stressful concerns.

Introducing Gestalt approaches into already established counseling relationships must be handled carefully. If, for example, the counselor has been responding to the counselee with a consistent style and then one day introduces a Gestalt approach calling for a behavior which is far afield from the counselee's expectancies, the counselee may become confused and wonder how well he really knows the counselor. This could hamper the relationship. There are times when upending a counselee's expectancies can be therapeutically productive. However, if this is carried too far the dissonance experienced by the counselee can outweigh the advantages. The implication is that the counselor should work Gestalt approaches into his own style so that he does not appear radically different to the counselee. Giving the counselee a brief introduction to the approach may alleviate this potential problem and help the counselee realize that the counselor is the same person but is trying something different which may be to the counselee's advantage. The transition to some regularly used Gestalt approaches can then be smooth.

One counselor I know became impressed with the communicative power of nonverbal communication and decided to start working with it in his counseling. One day he was particularly attuned to the discrepancies between the verbal and nonverbal behaviors of a counselee. He was accurate in his perceptions of the discrepancies and brought these into the counselee's awareness. To his surprise the counselee became defensive and somewhat hostile. In discussing this interchange with the counselor several points became apparent. First, the counselor had not previously responded to the nonverbal behavior of the counselee. Second, he did not preface his approach so that the counselee could have at least some understanding of what he was attempting to do. And third, the counselor introduced the awareness of nonverbal behavior at a time when the counselee was broaching a topic which was new and not easy for him to relate.

Related to the timing of introducing Gestalt approaches into counseling is the number of them to be initiated. A certain degree of "phasing in" will be beneficial to the counselee until he acquires an understanding and feel for Gestalt approaches. This means that the counselor is ill-advised to bombard the counselee with several Gestalt approaches in rapid succession, especially in the early phases of counseling or with counselees who have had no prior exposure to Gestalt. Suggesting to the counselee that he attend to certain nonverbal behavior, change certain words, try a new fantasy, and speak of the past as if it were the present might overload and confuse him. His awareness of one thing might be enhanced—a certainty of not returning to the counselor!

A preferable begining is to start with a few approaches the counselee seems able to assimilate. For example, a counselee may rarely use the word "I" or make self-references. The counselor might suggest the use of "I" to replace words such as "it," "you," or "one." This does not mean, however, that the counselor will suggest the pronoun every time he hears an impersonal remark from the counselee. Rather, the suggestions should be temporarily spaced with support offered when the counselee works with the substitutions. Occasional refreshers or reminders might help. After all, the counselee is learning a new behavior and cannot be expected to reverse life-long speech patterns instantly. If the counselor expects to hear a flow of appropriate "I" remarks after once introducing the intervention, he is setting himself and the counselee up for frustration.

Gradations in Approaches

The idea of gradations in counselee responses to an approach is important for the counselor to keep in mind. A counselee may not be able to respond immediately to an approach. Consider a counselee who is afraid to make eye contact with people. Suggesting that he look directly at the counselor may be asking too much, but he may be able to do the task by gradations. He may first look at the counselor's foot or hand. A further step might be to look at the counselor's face. Several such steps may have to be repeated before the counselee will venture a brief look at the counselor's eyes with the provision that he can look away as he wishes. Finally, he may be able to look at the counselor's eyes. It is therefore important to watch initial responses to an approach and, if needed, to change the counselee's task within the framework of the approach.

Gradations within an approach being used with a counselee can also be changed according to the counselee's readiness. Sometimes too little may be asked and he is ready to do more. One counselee, for example, was asked if he could let himself be aware of the anger he seemed to be feeling. His response was, "Sure. It's my father I'm mad at. I might as well get into that with him." He was obviously primed to do more than just be aware of his anger.

The counselor will also be aware of the gradations between approaches. Imagine a counselee who finds difficulty in expressing himself. The counselor should not assume that the counselee will immediately be able to become aware of how he holds himself back and then decide not to. It may take some time before the counselee can understand and experience this blocking. He may come slowly into the idea of accepting responsibility for it and has to move at his own pace. He may then have some unfinished business with the person who taught him this behavior. Finally, as he comes to accept the behavior as part of himself he can explore alternative behaviors.

One girl I worked with had things she wanted to say to her brother who had been killed in an auto accident two years earlier. At first there was no chance of her doing this in dialogue fashion because the mere awareness of her brother touched off her grief. She did not even bring up the topic until after we had met in several sessions and even then could not mention his name. Her fear was that if she let herself feel the grief she might not recover. Ever so slowly she worked up her strength to talk about him. "Talking about" in this case was very appropriate as a gradation moving toward expression of feeling. Eventually she permitted herself to grieve and express feelings which she had held in abeyance for two years. Only then and after several sessions of grief work could she permit herself to fantasize an image of her brother. Finally, she was able to venture a few words to him about the impact he had had on her life and how much she had appreciated him. There were also some resentments she had been harboring about his untimely death, as it occurred at a time when he was one of her main sources of support. After this work the girl expressed her desire to her family to speak with them about her brother, a topic that had been taboo since his death. Her initiative broke the ice—the other family members had wanted to speak about him and had all been keeping quiet to "protect each other's feelings."

This girl had to move slowly, as many counselees do. Strength had to be built and withdrawals permitted before she could move ahead. Working with gradations allows counselees to build strength and to sense movement in their work. Often counselees will realize what they need to do and may feel frustrated when they don't do it immediately. However, when they can sense the gradations in their work, they can realize the movement.

The notion of gradations can also be useful for the counselor. Sometimes the counselor will be able to identify correctly the direction a counselee's work will take. This is well and good except when the counselor's timetable is different from that of the counselee. When the counselee's movement does not keep pace with the counselor's expected pace, the counselor can feel frustrated. With his eyes set on the end product, the counselor may then measure progress against what is yet to be done. From this perspective it is easy both to lose sight of what *is* being done and to recognize its significance as a step or movement.

In and Out of Counseling

A final point on the appropriateness of Gestalt approaches for counseling has to do with their use in and out of the counseling session. Certain approaches are applicable in both places. When, for example, a counselee is learning how to become aware of himself, it can be appropriate for him to spend some time each day working with himself on being aware of behaviors, thoughts, and feelings. In fact, such "homework" assignments are consistent with one of the aims of Gestalt work, which is for persons to be able to "be their own counselors."

Some approaches, however, are best experienced only in what Perls has referred to as the "safe emergency" of the counseling session and not worked into everyday life. Consider, for example, a counselee who is always bending to the will of others. An experiment he might work on in counseling could be to say "Go to hell" to everyone who he feels puts undue demands on him. Through the experiment he may learn how he gives himself up and how to stand up for himself. This learning can then be channeled into appropriate and constructive ways of not being everyone's patsy. Imagine the counterproductive consequences if he immediately began directing "Go to hell" statements at parents, teachers, and friends every time he felt put upon by them. Thus, the counselor will want to discuss with the counselee the difference between in-counseling and out-of-counseling behaviors.

Individual Differences
among Counselees

Counselees will vary considerably in their reactions to Gestalt approaches. One area of difference will be in the ability to relate to a range of experiments and use them productively. Some counselees will be able to focus on several dimensions of awareness fairly early in their exposure to Gestalt approaches. Others may be able to connect with awareness of fantasy, for example, but find difficulty relating to the significance of their nonverbal behavior. Thus, the counselor will use his judgment in exploring the kinds of approaches which may be beneficial for each counselee. The use of other approaches can wait until the counselee has spent some time with those with which he can work.

Counselees will also vary widely in their responses to any single approach. This point is well documented in *Gestalt Therapy* (Perls, Hefferline, and Goodman, 1951) through written responses to the self-exercises. The responses for the exercises usually range from a "This is worthless!" all the way to "What a great experience!" This range will also be noted in face-to-face contact with counselees. The counselor should expect this variation and thus not judge the worth of an approach after trying it with only a few counselees. What has been useful with some counselees will fall flat with others, and vice-versa. In fact, a counselee might work very well with a particular approach during one session and want nothing to do with it during the next.

The counselee's age is another dimension of individual differences which needs to be taken into account in using Gestalt approaches. While there are Gestalt approaches which may be used with counselees of all ages, some are more or less appropriate for counselees at different developmental levels. Children, for example, are able to use fantasy quite productively to express and accept feelings. They also have free access to imagination for "being" other people to understand how they feel. At a very young age children are able to tell the difference between "can't" and "don't want to" and thus are capable of becoming aware of their ability to make choices. Body and sensory awareness can be very useful in working with developmental tasks involving motor coordination.

On the other hand, children are less able to understand the dynamics of the projections. To them a person who "makes" them feel bad is a mean person. They may not be able to realize they are imputing some meanness to the person. Similarly, a child may not be able to accept the responsibility for how he makes himself feel happy, frustrated, or envious, until the capacity for this type of responsibility develops. This development varies among children such that chronological age may have little meaning. Some adults never develop adequate responsibility! Given these developmental limitations, there is considerable work that can be done with children to raise their awareness of their own behavior and feelings.

With older counselees several factors need to be taken into account in judging the appropriateness of Gestalt approaches. One of these is the counselee's current level of awareness. As Gestalt work is based on awareness, it is a prerequisite for the effective use of many interventions. With many counselees it is necessary to work on enhancing a sense of awareness before other approaches can be used.

A second factor is the degree of responsibility the counselee is willing to assume for his physical, emotional, and cognitive behavior. As with awareness, building responsibility is both an end and a means for growth. That is, it can be of significance in its own right, and certain levels of it are assumed for approaches such as those which focus on the owning and creating of feelings.

The counselee's willingness to change is a third significant determinant in judging the appropriateness of certain Gestalt approaches. The counselee who is resistant to change, and that includes most of them at one time or another, will be less willing to experiment with new behaviors. He will be reluctant to part with familiar behaviors even though they may be counterproductive. Thus, approaches geared toward change will have to wait. Instead, all approaches should be used that will enhance the counselee's awareness of his steadfastness and ambivalences about changing. Too often these important dynamics are not focused upon or are approached as barriers to be hurried over, around, or under in order to make "progress."

Finally, the person's overall level of psychological functioning must be considered. Sometimes a counselee may want and be willing to change but not be in enough command of his resources to encounter and work through his problems. As with the girl whose brother had died, the counselor will have to judge readiness. Often counselees will be unaware of their current capacity for changing. Some will overestimate and plague themselves with "should" and "ought." Others may choose not to recognize their resources and harass themselves with "can't," "but," and "if only" postures. In any case an important task for the counselor is to help the counselee to experience how he is functioning at the time. Until this is recognized and accepted there is no solid base from which to grow and change.

Gestalt Approaches
in Group Counseling

Just as counselors of various theoretical persuasions can use selected Gestalt approaches in working with individuals, so can counselors who work with groups. With the increasing popularity of films showing Fritz Perls, it is important to distinguish between a Gestalt group and a counseling group in which Gestalt approaches are employed. In these films one person interacts with the therapist and much less frequently with the group members, unless they are engaged in the person's experiments. While this model is fairly typically but not exclusively used by Gestalt therapists, it is not the one recommended here.

The recommended model is a counseling group in which Gestalt approaches are utilized. Such groups differ from Gestalt groups in several ways. First, not all of the interventions or approaches used by the counselor will be of a Gestalt nature. Instead, the counselor will selectively use Gestalt approaches as they are appropriate in the development and focus of the group. Second, the counselor will not be the principal figure in the group such that the majority of interactions will be between the counselor and a single counselee. The counselor will at times engage a counselee in a Gestalt approach. This will, however, take place no more frequently than when the counselor is not employing Gestalt approaches. Finally, the counselor will be concerned with facilitating interaction among the group members.

From this perspective Gestalt approaches in group counseling can serve a dual purpose. The approaches can be used to help individuals attain greater awareness of their own behavior. This awareness is reinforced in the group setting where the individual is in the midst of other individuals who are also becoming more aware of themselves. Group members can serve a catalytic purpose for each other's self-explorations as well as provide support and encouragement. Enhancing self-awareness on the part of the individual, however, is not the only purpose that Gestalt approaches can serve in a group.

A second important element in group counseling is the interaction among the group members. As will be noted below, Gestalt approaches can be used to facilitate learning and experience in interpersonal perception and communication. The approaches contribute to facilitating the development of the group process and encouraging trust, cohesion, understanding, acceptance, and respect to emerge among the group members.

All of the points raised in this chapter about the use of Gestalt approaches are applicable in working with groups. One of them deserves extra attention because of the group setting. That is that no counselee should be forced to participate in any individual or group experiment. It is important that this be clearly communicated to the group members as early as appropriate. If a counselee refuses to engage in an approach suggested by the counselor, the choice is to be respected. This holds also for experiments which the counselor may suggest for the total group.

The counselor may on occasion suggest that each member of the group focus awareness on a specific concern. A counselee who does not wish to participate should be under no pressure to conform. Other counselees may explore their awareness which can be beneficial to them in its own right. The counselor may then ask the group members to share their awareness. At this point some counselees may not wish to disclose themselves. They are not to be forced. The counselor may ask them to share their experience as they explored the awareness (for example, "I got confused." "I found it difficult.") without their having to disclose the specifics of their awareness. Again this is done at the discretion of the counselee.

Through this process the counselor is creating a situation which teaches respect for the rights of the individual. As the reticent counselees see that they are not going to be forced to do anything that they don't want to do, they will feel freer to participate. They may, for example, first decide to try some of the focused awareness experiments without disclosing themselves. Later, as they notice how other counselees can share their experience safely they may begin to participate at that level. It is expected that counselees will move at different paces in their participation. The counselor's demonstration of respect for these differences will serve as an important model for the counselees and act as a deterrent to the forces of conformity that sometimes emerge in groups.

Summary

Certain approaches are often used by many Gestalt therapists. The identification of some of these makes the process of Gestalt therapy more communicable even when it entails taking them out of context.

Further, there are many approaches utilized by Gestalt therapists which can be used by counselors. It should be kept in mind, however, that using Gestalt approaches is not synonymous with doing Gestalt therapy.

Several factors are important in considering the appropriateness of Gestalt approaches in counseling. First, the theory of Gestalt therapy shares the values of counselee self-direction, independence, self-knowledge, and responsibility with most theories of counseling. Relatedly, the *sine qua non* of most theories of counseling is awareness, and thus Gestalt approaches whose main function is to enhance and facilitate awareness can be used by counselors of different theoretical persuasions. Second, the frequent objection to employing Gestalt interventions in counseling is based on the false assumption of inherent power in the approaches themselves, such that regardless of who uses them, they will "open" a person up. Rather, the case is made that Gestalt approaches have no more impact, positive or negative, than the person who is using them. Third, the counselor's own personality is a primary determinant in which Gestalt approach he will use in working with his counselees. In short, the counselor who finds responding to a particular approach objectionable will be unwilling and unable to use that approach effectively.

As the counselor begins to integrate some Gestalt approach into his counseling, he will want to keep in mind some of the following points. Counselees can get more out of responding to Gestalt approaches if they are oriented to them. Second, the timing of introducing one or more Gestalt approaches to a counselee can affect their usefulness to him. Third, certain Gestalt approaches and experiments can be practiced both during counseling and between sessions while others are best worked with only during counseling. Fourth, the counselor will be alert not to suggest experiments or expect responses which are beyond the capacities of the counselee. Fifth, there will be wide ranges among counselees on ability, willingness, and productivity in responding to a single Gestalt approach.

Gestalt approaches employed in group counseling can serve a dual purpose of enhancing individual self-awareness and promoting interaction among the group members. It is important that counselees not feel compelled to participate in group exercises or activities.

REFERENCES

Fagan, J., and Shepherd, I. L. (eds.), *Gestalt Therapy Now: Theory, Techniques, Applications.* Palo Alto, Calif.: Science and Behavior Books, 1970.

Levitsky, A., and Perls, F. S., The rules and games of Gestalt therapy, in Fagan, J., and Shepherd, I. L. (eds.), *Gestalt Therapy Now: Theory, Tech-*

niques, Applications. Palo Alto, Calif.: Science and Behavior Books, 1970, pp. 140–149.

Perls, F. S., Hefferline, R. F., and Goodman, P., *Gestalt Therapy: Excitement and Growth in the Human Personality.* New York: Dell Publishing Company, 1951.

Polster, E., A contemporary psychotherapy, in Pursglove, P. D. (ed.), *Recognitions in Gestalt Therapy.* New York: Funk and Wagnalls, 1968, pp. 3–19.

4

Present-Centeredness

and Awareness

A person's life may be viewed from at least three perspectives. First, there is the "what" of his life. "What" includes all of his internal and external behaviors. What does he eat? What work does he do? What clothing does he use? What values does he hold? What does he do in specific situations? These are but a few of the myriad of behaviors that may be part of a person's life.

A second perspective on a flowing life is "how." "How" describes the forces, the means of the "what" in life. Take the example of eating. How is the food procured? How is it prepared? How is it gotten to the mouth? How is the food chewed? How is the waste material from the food dealt with? Thus for each "what" of behavior there are several parallel descriptions indicating the "how," which are means to the end.

"When" is a third life perspective. "When" describes the timing of the "what" and "how." Time itself, however, can be viewed from several vantage points. There is time in relation to the age of the universe, time in terms of man's history, and then there are more specific indications of time, such as years, months, weeks, day, hours, minutes, seconds, and fractions thereof. These indicators of time are present regardless of the person.

"When" also has relevance to points within the person's past, present, and projected future. It can refer to age, such as "When he was just four . . ." "Now that he is sixteen . . ." and "After he turns 21. . . ." "When" can also indicate a developmental phase which may or may not be age related: "When he was crawling. . . ." "He is just learning to drive" and "Someday he will be a father." Similarly, "when" can be of importance in relation to significant events that occur and which have an effect on the person's life: "His father died when he was nine" "He is now very happy with his new baby brother" "He will have a great time when they move across the country."

The ways that theories of psychotherapy and counseling view the significance of the "what," "how," and "when" of a person's life are key factors that differentiate them. Each could merit its own discussion. However, among the three, beliefs about "when" seem to enjoy the widest divergence of opinion among theories and is the topic of the following section.

Present-Centeredness

As discussed in Chapter 2, Gestalt therapy focuses neither on the past nor the future. Instead, emphasis is placed on the now. In Perls's (1947) words:

> Whatever is actual is, as regards time, always in the present. Whatever happened in the past *was* actual then, just as whatever occurs in the future *will* be actual at that time, but what *is* actual—and thus *all* that you can be aware of—must be in the present. Hence the stress, if we wish to develop the feeling of actuality, on words such as "now" and "at this moment." (p. 32)

There are several reasons for the pivotal position of the now in Gestalt therapy. The main one was covered in the above quote. That is, it is not possible for a person to experience anything other than what he is doing at the moment. Regardless of the type of experience, whether it is feeling, thinking, or sensing, it can be lived only in the now.

A second reason for the importance of the now is that changes in the person can occur only in the present. Any adjustments or self-regulations the person makes can occur only during the now. He cannot redo his past or change that which he has not experienced, the future. Thus, changes in values, feelings, thoughts, physical behaviors, and the like, can emerge only in the present.

Feeling the actuality of the present also results in clearer contact with the real environment. The person who has one foot out of the present, whether it is aimed backward or forward, is dividing his attention and is not fully with what he is doing at the moment. This means that he cannot be bringing his full resources to bear on the problems which confront him. Necessarily, then, the interest, excitement, and attention are curtailed. On the other hand, when the now is contacted the person is capable of using his awareness to discover what he needs and how to go about getting it.

The sense of self is also enhanced by being in the now. Upon noticing that "This is me doing this right now" the person gains a sense of self as one who feels, thinks, and does. He is less likely to live in a fuzzy world wherein he is not aware of doing something until he is half finished with it.

The Gestalt point of view does not deny the significance of the past and the future in a person's life. However, these time dimensions are treated as present experiences. That is, the person can experience his memory of the past and can explore how he lives in relation to it. Likewise, the person can experience that he is planning and futurizing. In Chapter 8 this process of "presentizing" will be further elaborated.

Awareness

In Chapter 2 the relationship between present-centeredness and awareness was discussed. Polster and Polster (1973) have stated the following on this topic:

> At its best, awareness is a continuous means for keeping up to date with one's self. It is an ongoing process, readily available at all times, rather than an exclusive of sporadic illumination—like insight—only at special moments or under special conditions. It is always there like an underground stream, ready to be tapped into when needed, a refreshing and revitalizing experience. Furthermore, focusing on one's awareness keeps one absorbed in the present situation, heightening the impact of therapy experience, as well as the more common experience in life. With each succeeding awareness one moves closer to articulating the themes of one's own life and closer also to moving towards the expression of these themes. (pp. 211–212)

There are several important points to be made about awareness. First, awareness is different from introspection. Awareness is the process of noticing and observing what you do, and what your feelings, thoughts, and body sensations are. Importantly, these processes are not subject to interference, but rather are viewed as a passing, flowing panorama which is your now experience. Introspection, usually limited to looking inward for a purpose, such as trying to learn something or figure something out, is thus a more obtrusive means of noticing self and is more likely to have an interrupting effect on what is being experienced. Further, introspection is usually evaluative while being aware is not.

A second point about awareness is that it is not possible to simultaneously attend to two things with the same degrees of awareness. Try this simple experiment. Tap your foot in a rhythm and then snap your fingers intermittently. Notice what happens when you attend to both. In the same vein, try looking intently at something and hum a song at the same time. Can you attend to both with equal levels of clarity? The inefficiency in divided awareness can be quite costly, especially when new areas of awareness are being approached. Gestalts cannot be formulated with partial attention.

Third, you have the power to focus your awareness. For example, right now you are probably not aware of what is going on with your right foot. Now that I have mentioned it, I imagine that you are aware of it. Now I am imagining that there are several background noises in your environment on which you can focus your awareness. Further, you may now be feeling some excitement or curiosity about this idea of awareness. Focus on that. Experiment with this further until you get the feel of your awareness as a useful tool for illuminating aspects of your experience.

Fourth, the absence of awareness is usually associated with avoidance. Feel, for example, how you can choose not to be aware of something if you so desire. I would imagine that you find much more ease in being aware of and focusing on the satisfying or pleasing parts of yourself. Most likely you can also be aware of felt deficiencies. However, if you are like most people your awareness of these is probably limited to their discomforts and inconveniences. If the deficiencies had been permitted full awareness, chances are they would no longer be present. Some adjustments or acceptances would have been made.

Since awareness is the essence of Gestalt therapy, this chapter includes several self-experiments designed to assist you in enhancing awareness in your now. Hopefully the experiments will provide some experiential data which will illustrate the intent of present-centered approaches to counseling. An understanding of the importance of the now is necessary for employing some of the now-centered approaches.

Much of this section is modeled after portions of experiments and discussions from *Gestalt Therapy* by Perls, Hefferline, and Goodman (1951). Readers who are interested in a fuller treatment of these and more advanced self-experiments will profit from reading that source.

Your Now

For the next several minutes be aware of your present experiences. Put this awareness into a stream of sentences beginning with "Now I'm aware of . . ."; "Here and now I am. . . ." Notice that the ending of each sentence places you in a new now in which you may be aware of something different. As such, keep the sentences flowing with whatever words that come. Continue this for several minutes.

Now that you have worked with this experiment there are several questions I would like you to ask yourself. What areas of your now were you most aware of? Your body? thoughts? feelings? Did you choose what you wanted to be aware of or did you stay with noticing the full range? Did you find the experiment more or less complex than you expected? Did you discover any new awareness? Did you experience any blockages in which you had to search for what you were aware of? Did you notice any areas of awareness that demanded attention repeatedly? Did you find that there were some areas of awareness which you resisted or which you wanted to avoid?

Now do the experiment again, keeping in mind some of the questions just raised. See if you can feel how you try to avoid certain awareness. Don't force yourself into these awarenesses, rather just notice what you do to censor them. Do the experiment the second time before proceeding.

Awareness of Self

A basic tenet of Gestalt psychology is that a person is inseparable from his environment. In fact, a person is considered a self-in-environment. This means that for a person to live effectively he must have sufficient awareness of both himself and his environs.

Since Gestalt psychology views a person as an organismic whole, there is much of which he can be aware. He is a body with several complex structures and parts. He is movement in his body. He is numerous body processes. He is sensations in his nerves and muscles. He is emotions that are anchored in the psychological and the physical components. He is a complex of thoughts and a constellation of fantasies.

The person is each of these components, and in being all of them is something more than a ledger of them. He is the only one who can experience their entirety. No one can be aware of them as he can. However, experiences and observation teach that he can also not be equally aware of one or more of these dimensions simultaneously.

What follows, then, is a series of self-experiments on awareness which have three purposes. First, they briefly introduce some major dimensions of self-awareness. Second, you can use them for explorations and discoveries in your awareness. Also, you can selectively use some or portions of the experiments with counselees. It will be to your advantage to take the time to participate fully in the experiments. You may want to find a room where you can be alone to do them.

Body Structure

Start by becoming aware of the totality of your body. For the purpose of this experiment, don't do anything with your body except to observe. Feel your overall size and the amount of space you occupy. . . . Now try to be aware of your weight and the density of your body. . . . If you have a full-length mirror, stand in front of it and observe your total body. . . . What do you become aware of as you do this? . . .

Now concentrate on parts of your body. Approach this as if you were taking an inventory. Feel your large limbs, your legs, and your arms. . . . Now focus your awareness on your neck and head. You might try feeling them with your hands. . . . Now move your awareness to your central body, including your chest, abdomen, and pelvic area. Explore these areas. See if there are new discoveries you can make here. . . .

Move now to smaller parts of your anatomy. Focus on your hands and fingers. Your feet and your toes. . . . Now be aware of the smaller details of your face, such as your eyes, nose, mouth, tongue, and teeth. Feel them there. Again a mirror might be helpful. Notice also your hair and ears. . . .

Now that you have reviewed your outer body structures individually, notice their interrelatedness. . . . Consider your body again as a whole. . . . Do you find any difference in doing this now as compared with your attempt at the beginning of this experiment? . . . What differences do you notice as you examine a part of you separately as opposed to being in the context of your total body? . . .

Do you find that there are parts of your body that you have skipped over or avoided all together? . . . If so, return to them and just simply observe what is there. Can you do this without evaluating? . . .

Movement

Now that you have reviewed your body structures, let's go back and explore their movements. Start by wiggling your toes, slowly and then rapidly. . . . Now flex them tightly and hold them that way. . . . Now release them and see what you experience there. . . . Now rotate your ankles back and forth as if you were tapping your feet. . . . Flex the muscles in your calf and feel them. . . . Move to your knee. What kinds of movements are available there? . . . Flex your thigh muscles and release them, noticing there is no direct movement in the thigh. . . . Now stand and take a few steps. Notice how the lifting comes from the hip. . . .

Stand on one leg and let the other swing freely to experience the joint where your leg connects to your pelvis.

Now bend at the torso and feel your lower back and pelvis as a hinge. Go forward and backward and to both sides. . . . See if you can move your pelvis by itself. Keep your thighs and spine as still as you can and experiment with rotating the pelvis or making whatever movements you can with it. . . . Tighten and release the group of muscles around your anus and genitalia. . . . What do you experience as you do this?

Now experiment with moving, flexing, and releasing the muscles in your abdominal and chest areas. . . . Pull your stomach in and out, holding it in each place and then releasing. . . . Notice what kinds of movements you can make around your rib cage. . . . While keeping your pelvic area still, experiment with upper body movements involving the spine. Make big circles with your shoulders and bend in all four directions to experience the flexibility of your spine. . . .

Now explore your arms. Start by moving your fingers and opening and closing a fist. . . . Work up your arm using the same exercises as with your legs, noticing muscles, joints, and connections to your shoulders. . . .

Turn now to your shoulders and neck. Try moving each shoulder independently. . . . Move them forward and backward and squeeze them in toward the middle of you. . . . Feel how you can tighten these muscles and release them. . . . Rotate your head to experience the movement afforded by your neck. . . . Now make your neck rigid, focusing particularly on the muscles in the back of it. . . . Feel anything familiar? Now release them. . . . Do this also with your throat.

Now go to your head. Here you have one of your most powerful muscles in the jaw. Try some biting motions. . . . Clamp your jaw shut and then let it hang open. . . . Feel how you can move it laterally also. . . .

Now experiment with moving the muscles that are connected to your nose. . . . Feel now how you can open your eyes wider than usual. . . . Now squint. . . . Now clamp your eyes shut. . . . With your eyes open and your head still roll your eyes and imagine making x's with them. . . . Now try to move the eye muscles around your skull. Experiment with flexing and releasing them. Tightness here is the cause of many headaches.

As you do these experiments what do you observe about your movements? . . . Are there certain muscles you can move which you were not aware of? . . . Are your movements fluid or jerky? . . . Do you notice how movements in one part of your body result in sensations and movements in connected parts? . . . Are you making demands on parts of your body which do not fit that structure, for example, lifting with the wrist when the elbow would be more appropriate? . . . Are there some parts of your body which you do not seem to be using, such as your pelvis? . . .

Body Processes

Now let's explore some of your body processes. Start with breathing. Feel how you draw air in. . . . Do you inhale by using the muscles in your lower abdomen, or is most of your breathing done with your chest muscles? Use your hands to explore this. Is there any movement or expansion in your rib cage? . . . Fill your lungs and experience the air going in. Keep it there and feel the fullness. . . . Empty your lungs now and notice that exhaling is not an effort but rather a release, the opposite of effort. . . . Try running in place for a minute and feel what changes you notice in your breathing.

Become aware of your heartbeat. If you did the running you can probably experience or "hear" your heart without having to feel your pulse. Focus on the beat. . . . What changes do you observe as you stay with this? . . . When your heart has resumed its normal pattern, can you feel it without touching your chest or your wrist?

Find something to eat and let's explore that. . . . Go ahead and take a few bites. . . . Do you experience your teeth cutting and crushing the food? . . . Be aware of how much you chew something before you swallow it. . . . Try to experience just what you do when you swallow. . . . Is swallowing easy for you or is it an effort? Are there times when you can be aware of your digestion? . . . Do you experience your stomach working on food? . . . How about your intestine? Do you ever experience any activity there? . . . When you eliminate, do you force the process or do you yield to the involuntary muscles and allow them to do their work without interference?

Sensations

Feel your body now and see what sensations enter into your awareness. Try to observe and concentrate on them without interfering with them. . . . Do you feel any internal sensations such as hunger or dryness in your throat? . . . Explore your skin. Do you notice any itches or scratchy sensations? Are there any places where you feel some moisture such as sweating palms? Are you aware of any places where you experience more warmth or coldness? . . . Now be aware of your genitalia. Do

you experience any sensations in them now? Compare this with sensations you have when sexually aroused. . . .

As you explore the sensations in your body do you find some areas
which are more "alive" than others? . . . Try concentrating on these
areas. What happens when you do this? . . . Do you experience any
emotional feelings or fantasies? . . . Try concentrating on these areas of
your body in which you sense little. What do you experience? Do you
notice any difference when you do concentrate? . . .

Feelings

Now observe the feelings you are experiencing at the moment.
Notice again how different feelings move into your foreground and then
recede into background as others emerge. . . . See if you can stay with
one of these feelings. . . . As you do this do you become aware of any
physical sensations related to the feeling? If so, attend to this. If, for
example, you are feeling a bit angry and are aware of some tightness in
your hand, go ahead and clench the fist. . . . As you become aware of
this feeling do you feel an urge to do or say something? Experience the
mobilization power of the feeling and see if you can allow yourself to
follow through with it. . . .

What is the range of your feelings? Do you experience happiness,
joy, and peacefulness and accept those as feelings which are as real
and as important as sorrow, anger, and frustration? . . . Consider some
situations in which you have positive feelings and see if you can let yourself have them. What do you do? . . . Now see if you can get in touch
with some negative feelings. . . . Do you become aware of any unfinished
business? What is it that you can do to express this feeling and finish the
situation. . . . If you find this feeling objectionable see if you can become
aware of what you do to avoid it. Do you push it down in favor of other
thoughts? Do you find something in your surroundings to look at and
focus upon? Feel how you move your awareness away from the feeling
and thus prohibit experiencing it. . . .

Thinking

Let yourself free associate for a moment and be aware of your
present thought processes. Don't try to change them. Just observe the
panorama. . . . How many different things did you think of in that short
amount of time? . . . Did you think of something that you hadn't

expected would come in? . . . Did you find that there were one or two ideas that were recurring? . . . In order to feel how difficult it is to stay with a single thought, close your eyes and start counting subvocally. How far can you get before a thought flashes across? . . .

Now try some purposeful thinking. Be aware, for example, of the thinking you do when you divide 74 by 4. . . . Consider the similarities and differences between a piece of coal and a puppy. . . . Now try to think of as many words as you can which rhyme with "boat." . . . See how many uses you can think of for a brick. . . . What is the first four-letter word you think of which starts with "f"? . . . Was it fork, ford, food, fool, fowl, or foul? . . . Now, see if you can make your mind go "blank" or think of "nothing." Is this possible for you? . . . Consider the cognitions that enter into a decision that you are pondering? . . . What other kinds of purposeful thinking do you do? . . . What do you experience in these ways of purposeful thinking that are different from each other? . . . How do they compare with the free associating? . . .

Fantasy

Through fantasy you are able to go beyond your senses and body experiences and relate to things which may or may not exist. For example, can you get a visual image of a horse that has an elephant's trunk, dressed in a green vest and hat, and roller skating in a parade? Can you do this? . . . Now can you fantasize yourself as doing something you have always wanted to do? What do you feel as you do this? . . . How often do you catch yourself daydreaming about how you would like things to be, or what would have happened "if," or what's going to happen "when" or "if"? . . . Put on a piece of music, close your eyes, and go with the music. Experience the musing and fantasies that come up. . . . Can you recall some of your dreams and the things that happened in them which may not be possible in reality?

Environmental Contact Awareness

To round out the self-in-environment constellation the person must not only be aware of himself but he must also be in tune with conditions which surround him.

"Your sense of the unitary interfunctioning of you and your environment is contact. . ." (Perls, Hefferline, and Goodman, 1951). Interactions between the person and his environment, then, are dependent upon his awareness of that environment. The person who has a dull or fuzzy awareness of his environs will experience contact which is correspondingly unclear. Such contact renders the person less competent and effective to cope with the environment to meet his needs. Similarly, the person misses out on the stimulation and excitement in his environment which if contacted could contribute to his interest and growth. Thus, being aware of the environment is a necessary component for contact.

The five basic senses of seeing, hearing, touching, tasting, and smelling are receptors which serve to orient the person in the environment. The extent to which these senses are adequately functioning determines the person's awareness of what is in the environment and thus sets limits on contact. One of the ways that contact can be facilitated and enhanced is by augmenting the acuity of the receptor senses.

Seeing

Give your eyes liberty and let them explore your current surroundings. . . . Let your eyes rest on any object which has some interest for you. Attend to this object. Notice its shape and form. Be aware of how the object is foreground as opposed to the visual background. . . . Now let your eyes roam once more. This time choose a color and remain with it. Do you notice any changes in it after a while? . . . Pick out another object and regard it carefully. Keep looking at it until you move your eyes away. Repeat this and be aware of what occurs in you that you look away. . . . Pick out a dull, uninteresting object. Examine carefully its shape, size, and color. Do you feel any difference in attitude toward the object? . . . Now close your eyes for several minutes. When you open them be aware of the first thing you focus on. Feel the sharpness of your vision due to the slight rest. . . . Feel the control you have over focusing your vision. Alternate between directed seeing and letting your eyes wander. Compare and contrast your experiences as you do this.

Hearing

What are you most aware of hearing right now? See if you can sharpen your attention to that sound? How do you do this? . . . Stay with the sound a little more. Do you notice anything new in it? . . . Listen for cycles, rhythms, speed, loudness, pitch, intensity. . . . What other dimensions can you discover in hearing the sound? . . . Now choose a sound that you can't help but hear such as an air conditioner. With your hand make some sort of noise like banging a pencil on the desk. Attend carefully to that noise. What then happens to the air conditioner?

Again this is the figure-ground shift. . . . Now close your eyes and listen. See how many different sound stimuli are present in a few minutes' time. You may discover that there is more going on around you than you imagined. . . . Now put your hands over your ears and see if you can block out all sounds. When you remove your hands what do you experience in your hearing? . . . Is it possible for you not to hear without your hands over your ears?

Touching

At this moment what are you most aware of in your world of touch? Explore those things with which you have bodily contact without changing your position. Start with the obvious things such as this book, a pencil you may be holding, the chair supporting you. What other tactile sensations can you be aware of? Can you feel your clothes? Can you be aware of your sock? Try to bring some of the less obvious things touching you into the foreground. What do you notice?

Now try some touching experiences. Pick up an object. Close your eyes and feel its shape, size, and texture. What can you discover through touching? . . . Set up some touching contrasts. Feel something smooth and then something rough. . . . Find something warm, touch it, and then touch something cold. Find a corner and compare touching it with touching something round. . . . Touch something big. Touch something small. . . . Touch an object for a long time and reach out and touch it for a short duration. . . . Touch something that you touch everyday and then touch an object that you have not touched for quite some time. . . . Touch something moving (swing your leg back and forth if nothing else is available). Now touch something which is stationary. . . . First touch an object with your hands. Now touch it with various parts of your body such as your tongue, shoulder, hip, foot, and so on. . . . Touch a single object. Now touch several objects simultaneously. . . . Touch an object purposively. . . . Now be aware of an object touching you.

Tasting

Are you aware of any tastes at this moment? Before you answer "yes" or "no," explore your taste by focusing on your mouth, particularly on your tongue. Any taste remnants? . . . Now go into the kitchen and try some taste experiences. Choose anything you wish. Put a morsel of it in your mouth. Chew it, let it remain there, and experience the taste. What happens to the taste as you let the food remain in your mouth? . . . Now try some other tastes. Alternate tastes which are sweet, sour, bitter, and salty. Compare and contrast them. . . . Try different combinations such as vinegar and jelly. Can you differentiate the tastes when they are ingested simultaneously? . . . What other taste experiences can you try? The next time you have a meal notice whether you taste your food.

There are probably many objects in your environment that you have never tasted in a literal sense (at least not since you were an infant). Select a few objects that you are willing to taste and sample them. What do you discover in doing this? . . . Recall how many things in the world you taste which are not foods, for example, stamps, medicines, nails, soaps. What others can you be aware of in one day of living? Try keeping track of them for a day.

Smelling

Until this moment I imagine that you have not been aware of scents or odors, that is, unless you are smoking, drinking coffee, or if there is some cooking or other scent-producing activities going on around you. Smell what is to be smelled without searching. . . . What do you notice that you were not aware of before?

Sample some of the smells you experience daily—aftershave, various foods, flowers, gasoline, and so on. Stay with one of these scents. Attend to it and see if you can discover something new in it. You may take your sense of smell for granted. . . . Look around you and smell some objects in the room that you normally do not attend to. . . . What do you discover?

These sensory awareness exercises, serve to increase awareness of what is to be seen, heard, touched, tasted, and smelled. The person, however, is not a passive recipient of external stimuli. Rather, he is an individual actively "sensing," albeit at various levels of alacrity. The difference here is between "I see" and "I am looking at." The second statement is more purposeful, active, and suggests that the person is in the process of doing something. He is attending and engaged, thereby more likely to discover. Enhancement of the awareness of the self "sensing" is the purpose of the following experiment.

In a previous experiment you finished the sentence fragment "Now I am aware of." In this experiment modify the same sentence by completing it with a report of what you are sensing in your environment. For example, "Now I am looking at the words I am writing." "Now I am listening to the cars going by outside." "Now I am attending to the pencil in my hand and the paper." "Now I am tasting the tobacco from my pipe." "Now I am smelling the cup of hot coffee in front of me. . . ." Continue the experiment, adding "This is me doing this" after each sentence.

Talking and movement are two other important contact functions. They differ from the contact functions of the receptor senses in that they are processes through which the person expresses himself and acts on the environment to meet his needs. It is possible for a person to express himself with the organs of the receptor senses, for example, by looking away or refusing to touch. However, expression is a tangential function of the receptive sensory mechanisms.

Voice

Listen to yourself in a conversation. Do you normally listen to what you say as you are talking? What do you hear? . . . Do you say what you mean or do you tend to ramble, hoping the message will get across? . . . To what extent is your language personalized and an expression of yourself? Listen for the times when you say "it," "you," "they," or some other pronoun other than "I". . . . Listen to the range of your vocabulary. When was the last time you learned and used some new words to express yourself? . . . How much do you hear yourself prefacing or qualifying in advance what you have to say? . . . Do you hear a predominance of either active or passive words as you speak? . . . When you speak are you emitting words as if broadcasting or do you direct them to persons? . . . What changes do you make in your language when speaking to a child as opposed to an adult, a friend as opposed to an acquaintance, a professional colleague as opposed to someone in another profession or occupation? . . . What difference in your language are you aware of when you are in different settings, such as a church, a picnic, a business meeting, or a supermarket? . . . What adjectives would you use to describe your language? . . .

In addition to the words you use, there are several other important expressive elements in your voice. Do you tend to speak slowly or rapidly? . . . Listen to the volume of your voice. What do you hear? . . . How much does your voice vary in inflection? . . . Would you say that your voice tends toward being lively or dull? . . . How much breath is in your voice? Can you talk with a lit match in front of your mouth? . . . If your voice were to be converted into a musical instrument, what would that instrument be? . . . a bass drum? a piccolo? a violin? an organ? . . . How much does your voice vary with your mood or feelings? . . . What do you sound like when you laugh? . . . When you cry do you make sounds? . . . From the viewpoint of others would you say your voice is settling? unnerving? . . . What do you feel are the most distinguishing qualities of your voice? . . . When you hear your voice on a tape recorder, what do you experience? . . . Are you aware of conditions in which you purposively vary or regulate some of these nonverbal dimensions of your voice?

Movement

Right now could you be aware of your posture? How does your posture relate to what you are doing at the moment? . . . Can you think of times when your posture reflects your openness or closedness in contacting the environment? . . . Can you be aware of the support you are receiving from the couch, chair, or floor? . . . When you move about can you feel the differences in the tentativeness or the assurance in your movements? On what in the environment do these depend? . . .

Now can you be aware of your gestures? Do you use your hands when you are talking or expressing yourself? . . . In what ways do you use movement in your head to relate to the environment? . . . Focus on your mouth. What do you experience there? . . . Are smiles, frowns, smirks, and kisses available to you? . . . How about your eyes? How can you use them to communicate where you are or what you are feeling? . . . Consider your face as a whole. Would you say your face leans toward being impassive or expressive? . . . To what extent are your body posture and gestures "matched" with your inner experience? . . .

Now let's explore the dimension of purposefulness in your movements. Compare and contrast your movements in situations such as getting a glass of water when you are thirsty, playing a musical instrument, shaking a fist at someone when you are angry, taking a leisurely stroll, applauding at a ballet, running away from a snake, or stretching after a nap. . . . During which of these behaviors do you experience the most and the least contact with your surroundings?

Approaches for Enhancing Present Awareness

Several approaches can be used for enhancing awareness. An important point to keep in mind in applying the approaches is that they are not bound to any particular area of awareness. That is, each could be used for increasing awareness of the environmental contact functions or the self-awareness functions.

Now I am Aware . . .

Some counselees function at low levels of awareness. They are living and functioning but often are not connected with what they are doing. Their behavior lacks an element of involvement—they are merely going through the motions. The counselor might try asking such a counselee to do some "Now I am aware" sentences.

Ce: There are times when I find that I am uninvolved with what I'm doing. I sort of come out of a trance to find that I'm shining my shoes or something.

Cr: Let's do some work that might help you to become more aware of what you do.

Ce: What good will that do me?

Cr: Well, for one thing you won't feel like you're in a trance if you're aware of what you're doing. Shall we try some of the awareness work I mentioned?

Ce: What is it about?

Cr: What I want you to do is take the sentence fragment "Now I am aware" and finish it and immediately do another one. Make them a continuous flow. Just let whatever words occur to you come out. For example, Now I am aware of looking at you. Now I'm aware of the noise in the hall. Now I'm aware that I want to stop so you can try this. O.K. You try a few.

Ce: Now I'm aware that I'm not sure how to do this. . . . Now I'm aware that I don't know what I should be aware of. I'm aware of the birds chirping outside. Now I'm aware that you are nodding your head.

Cr: Change that to "Right now I'm watching you nod your head."

Ce: You're not nodding it now. Right now I'm watching you smile. Right now I feel my back hurting from the way I'm sitting. Right now I'm changing the way I'm sitting.

Cr: Do some more of these, focusing on yourself.

Ce: Right now I'm wiggling my foot and I'm looking at it. Now I'm looking at my hand.

Cr: Continue. You're doing fine.

Ce: Right now I feel a little funny doing this because it's new to me. It's easier now, though, than when I first started.

Cr: O.K. Let's stop this for now. Try this with yourself a little bit each day. While you're walking along or eating or doing something try some of these "Now I am aware" and "Right now I" sentences. Just a couple of minutes several times a day will be good to start.

The counselee may experience more of himself through this experiment. He may find that his perceptions and environmenttal contacts become clearer when he becomes aware of his feet touching the sidewalk and his teeth cutting through food. Further, because each of the sentences requires an "I" statement he may become more aware of himself in the process.

What Are You Aware of Now?

A counselee may be functioning at different levels of awareness during a session. Sometimes he may be connected with what he is experiencing. Other times he may be sitting and talking, unaware of his now experience. Thus, there may be some occasions when the counselor will want to try to direct the counselee's awareness into the present. One way of doing this is to ask the counselee, "What are you aware of now?

Self-Experiment

Try this with yourself. Take a few minutes and get involved with something other than reading this book. You might empty the trash or something. At some point in your involvement ask yourself, "What am I aware of now?" Spend a few moments with that awareness and then continue with your task. . . . Do this with yourself several times during a day at unspecified times. For example, you might try it while you are brushing your teeth, talking with another person, walking down some stairs, eating, or daydreaming. Notice what asking yourself this question does to your awareness at this moment? . . . Do you feel any difference in the sharpness of your awareness?

Counseling Applications

Ce: I enjoyed watching that welder. He took these pieces of steel and his torch and made this joint that two bulldozers couldn't break.

Cr: You like what he was doing.

Ce: Sure. It is an important part of making buildings.

Cr: What are you aware of as you are telling me about him?

Ce: I feel kind of excited. Like maybe this is something that I would like to be.

Cr: What else are you aware of?

Ce: I'm good with my hands and like doing physical work. I know that. I've been worrying about what I'm going to do after graduation and this might be something for me. I need to have some sort of goal.

This counselee experienced an expansion of his awareness which included some excitement over discovering a possible vocation that would fit his interests and aptitudes. He also noted that he needs to have some sense of direction. Thus, through stimulating his current awareness the counselee went beyond describing what the welder was doing.

Ce: It seems that every time I call Betty we have neat conversations. I wish I could get up enough gumption to ask her out.

Cr: That's what you want to do and don't.

Ce: Yeah. Maybe someday.

Cr: Bill, what are you aware of now?

Ce: I like being able to talk with you about these things. You know what I mean and don't make fun of me.

This little example shows how the counselee's awareness after hearing the question is not always predictable. The counselee may have been aware of impatience with the counselor, frustration, or nonchalance. Instead, what he became aware of was how much he enjoyed conversing with him. Thus, the counselor has to stay flexible and keep open his expectations of how a counselee will respond.

Can You Be Aware of . . . ?

Sometimes the counselor will notice behavior on the part of the counselee which the latter does not seem to be aware of. The counselor may feel that the counselee could benefit by bringing this behavior into awareness. Further, the counselor may want to suggest this direction of awareness without imputing the meaning of it to the counselee. One way to do this is to ask the counselee, "Can you be aware of . . . ?" or "What do you experience . . . ?"

Ce: After I leave here, then I have to go to two more classes. There is a meeting of my club after school, too. When I get home I have all kinds of things to do.

Cr: Sue, can you be aware of what you are doing in your chair.

Ce: What do you mean? I'm just sitting here.

Cr: Can you be aware of what you are doing while you are sitting?

Ce: I guess I'm fidgeting around a lot, aren't I?

Cr: Feel how you do this.

Ce: Well, I keep crossing and uncrossing my legs. My fingers are usually tapping. I have a hard time sitting still.

Here is a counselee who resembles the mad hatter in Alice in Wonderland. She has to keep moving. Being accustomed to the busy schedules she sets up for herself, she is not aware of her rushing and continually having to be on the move. By experiencing and becoming aware of some of her fidgeting she will be able to explore its place in her life.

I'm Aware that You . . .

In the previous experiment the counselor asked the counselee if he could be aware of a certain behavior. Implicit in that intervention was the counselor's awareness of the specific behavior. Another approach in helping the counselee to become aware of certain behaviors is for the counselor to state explicitly his awareness to the counselee. In this way the counselor is becoming more confrontative and personal in the relationship. For example, the counselor might say to the counselee, "I'm aware that you. . . ."

Ce: I'm still having trouble making friends. When I'm around other people I just feel funny.

Cr: Do you feel this now?

Ce: A little bit. Not as much as I used to.

Cr: One thing that I'm aware of is that you don't look at me when you talk.

Ce: That's one of the hardest parts for me. I find it very difficult to look at people when I talk to them, even though I want to.

Cr: You mean like right now?

Ce: Yeah. I keep looking away.

By bringing up a relevant interpersonal behavior that is presently taking place between the counselor and the counselee, a here-and-now situation can be used to explore the counselee's behavior in the relationship. This may then result in exploring how he behaves in other relationships.

Ce: Hi, Mrs. Jones.

Cr: Hello, Johnny. Come in.

Ce: How're you?

Cr: I'm well, thanks. I'm also aware of something about you.

Ce: What?

Cr: This is the first time that you've gotten here on time for our appointments.

Ce: I know. I guess I have been doing that a lot more lately instead of always letting things slide by.

Cr: What are some other examples?

In this case the counselor put her finger on a behavior which allowed the counselee to expand on his awareness of an emerging change. An important point about the interchange is that the counselor has chosen to focus on what appears to be a positive behavior. Too often these are ignored as the counselor is set to perceive and react only to the counselee's deficits.

I'm Aware that I . . .

The counselor can serve as a powerful facilitator of the counselee's awareness by sharing with the counselee what he is aware of in himself. Being faced with what the counselor is experiencing at the moment can open new areas for the counselee. Such disclosures can also be helpful models of self-disclosing behavior and add an element of trust in the relationship.

Ce: (*After a five-minute monologue*) So there it is. What do you think?

Cr: I'm aware of feeling tired.

Ce: What do you mean?

Cr: You go on and on and on and I get tired trying to keep listening.

Ce: I always talk that way.

Cr: Do you have many listeners?

Ce: No, I guess I don't and when someone does listen I try to get it all out. Are you saying other people might get tired listening to me, too?

Cr: I wouldn't be surprised if they did.

In normal, everyday discourse this counselee might never get feedback about his being difficult to listen to. A counselor can provide such feedback through sharing his own awareness without judging or incriminating the counselee. In this way the counselee may feel free to explore the impact of his behavior on others.

Repeating

Repeating a behavior can help a counselee to explore and expand awareness of the meaning of the behavior to him. What may seem like a behavior made in passing or an inadvertent behavior may carry a message that the counselee misses. The Gestalt of the message is not clear or sharp and its meaning is thereby cloaked. Repeating the behavior can result in more energy and excitement being invested in it which can serve to clarify and illuminate its meaning.

Self-Experiment

Try repeating some behavior of yours. Select something that you are doing. It could be a body movement or a thought you are having. Repeat it and don't try to interpret or force an understanding of it. Just experience it. . . . What do you become aware of as you do this? Is there some message that you were not getting before? If nothing comes, continue the repetition a bit more and see what happens. Try repeating some other behaviors. . . . You might try repeating the statement you are making to yourself about the worth of this exercise and see if there is any expansion of that awareness.

Counseling Applications

Cr: Jim, I notice your grades are dropping pretty rapidly. What's happening?
Ce: I dunno.
Cr: Would you say that again?
Ce: I said "I don't know."
Cr: Once more.
Ce: I don't know!
Cr: Again.
Ce: I don't know! Dammit will you stop pushing me. You're as bad as those teachers who keep pushing all kinds of crap at me.
Cr: Tell me more.

In this instance repeating the "I don't know" got the counselee in touch with frustration that he had been feeling in his classes and transferred onto the counselor. Repetition can serve as a means to bring a feeling more fully into awareness. Until such time as the feeling is experienced, it cannot be explored, accepted, and integrated.

Exaggeration

Exaggeration serves the same purpose and is similar to repeating. It is actually an extension of repeating. The difference is that in repetition the counselee is not asked to change the behavior, while exaggeration calls for a repetition but with a purposefully higher investment of energy and excitement.

Self-Experiment

There are probably some feelings you are aware of having but which are somewhat vague to you. A common feeling is for a person to refuse to do something and not to be fully aware of his objections to it. See if you have such a situation. . . . Now, try to exaggerate your refusal by making the "no" more and more emphatic. . . . What do you experience as you do this? Do your objections become any clearer to you? Are there any other feelings with which you can try this? If so, then exaggerate some aspect of them. . . . Now try exaggerating a nonverbal behavior. . . . Will you permit yourself to do this? If not, try the suggested work with your objections and you might make a discovery.

Counseling Applications

Cr: How are you doing in your English class?
Ce: O.K., I guess.
Cr: What are some examples?
Ce: Well, we had a test last week and I got a B+.
Cr: No kidding!
Ce: Yeah.
Cr: Tell that to me again.
Ce: I got a B+ on my English test.
Cr: Now what do you feel as you say that?
Ce: Sort of good, a little proud.
Cr: I'd like to try something. Boast to me about the test. Tell me how great you did. You might feel a little phony at first. Try it a little; let's see what would happen.
Ce: O.K. Well, I studied real hard. It was important to me and when I set my mind on something I can do it. I'm not as dumb as some people think. I showed that by cooling that test. I'm a pretty smart guy actually!
Cr: Tell me more about how smart you are.

The example presented depicted the use of exaggeration in the expression of the feeling of pride and accomplishment. A similar method can be employed for feelings of anger, hurt, disgust, or any other feelings at which the counselee affords himself only a glimpse. Since exaggeration may call for a little staging, the counselor may want to offer the counselee support by letting him know that "You may feel a little phony at first."

Not all exaggerations need be on verbal expressions. Sometimes exaggerating nonverbal behaviors can amplify the feeling.

Ce: . . . and then Saturday morning I spent two hours practicing the piano. (*Head shaking from side to side, slowly*)

Cr: While you are saying that I noted you were shaking your head. Would you exaggerate the head shaking a little? Don't talk, just shake your head. (*Ce does so*)

Ce: I don't understand this. I've always. . . .

Cr: Try a little more. (*Ce does*) Now what is the feeling that goes with this shaking?

Ce: No, no. no!

Cr: And what is this "No" about?

Ce: Wasting all those mornings banging on that damned piano! All the rest of the kids are playing ball . . .

Staying With

A counselee may have a feeling he is only faintly aware of. He keeps himself from attending to the feeling and in so doing prohibits himself from expressing it and making discoveries related to it. This leaves him with another unresolved or unfinished situation which may become an impediment to his spontaneity and growth. The counselor can assist the counselee in expanding his self-awareness by asking him to "stay with" his experiences in the now.

Self-Experiment

Take a few moments and be aware of the many things you are doing, thinking, and feeling. Notice how motor behaviors, sensations, feelings, and thoughts seem to move in and out of your awareness. . . . As you notice a feeling that flashes in and out, see if you can stay with it. This doesn't mean to capture and pin it down like a butterfly for inspection. Just see if you can let yourself experience it. . . . What happens to the feeling when you let yourself be open to its emergence into your now? What do you notice about the clarity of the feelings. Is there any difference in its intensity? Try the experiment again, perhaps with a different feeling, and see what you discover.

Counseling Applications

Ce: I used to enjoy visiting my Aunt Claire. Now that she's moved, though, I don't think about her very much.

Cr: What do you feel as you mention her now?

Ce: Well, I miss her and that makes me a little sad. Oh well, like I said, I usually don't think of her very often.

Cr: Can you let yourself stay with this feeling of sadness?

Ce: I don't like to feel sad.

Cr: I know· Who does? But you seem to have quite a bit of it here. Just try staying with this sadness.

Ce: I do feel a little sadness.

Cr: "I'm sad right now."

Ce: Yes. I am sad.

Cr: "I have things to be sad about."

Ce: I do. She was the only one around that I could really talk to. I miss her so much it hurts. I didn't realize how much she meant to me.

By staying with this feeling the counselee is able to let it come to the foreground. She may then be able to discover that it is possible to think about her aunt without having to be sad. This may also enhance the counselee's awareness of her need to have someone with whom she can talk. Without being aware of this and accepting the aunt's absence she stands little chance of mobilizing to fill one important void.

In this example the counselor "fed" some statements to the counselee to facilitate her awareness. In one instance the counselor suggested the counselee say "I'm sad" as opposed to "I feel sadness." Try this difference with one of your own feelings to see if you can discover the rationale behind that difference.

Awareness Approaches in Group Counseling

There are several ways that awareness approaches can be used in group counseling. First, it can be a means through which individuals can come to a better understanding of themselves. Second, vicariously experiencing the present awareness of others can expand the counselee's understanding of them and himself in relation to them. And finally, occasionally focusing on the present awareness of individuals or the group as a whole can serve as a means to facilitate interpersonal contact and movement within the group.

Self- and Environmental Awareness

Self-awareness can be a contributor to the growth and development of the group members and to achieving the goals of the group. A group may be set up to assist counselees with study problems, vocational planning, interpersonal relationships, family problems, or other concerns. For the counselees to work effectively on these concerns they must be aware of who they are and the "what" and "how" of their behavior. Orienting themselves through self-awareness–enhancing situations can be a good place to begin. In other types of groups self-awareness may be the goal for its own sake.

After some orientation on the nature of the present and its importance in understanding behavior, the counselor can introduce the group to the concept of awareness. An important first step lets the counselees demonstrate how they can focus and shift their awareness. This can be done simply by having them become aware of different parts of their body, things about them, internal processes, and each other. What is used as the focal point of this initial awareness work is less important than getting across the idea that each person has the ability to select and concentrate his present awareness.

A second step might then be to have each group member complete the sentence fragment "Now I am aware of . . ." several times in succession. This will help them to experience how their awareness must move from one focal point to another because their now is fluid and constantly changing. This simple exercise will also serve to assist learning how to report on current experience as it is happening.

After some of this preliminary work with present awareness the more detailed awareness exercises in this chapter may be used. The counselor will select the exercises and when they will be used according to the purposes of the group. The exercises can be used in such a way that each counselee does them, with discussion following the completion of the last group member. For groups oriented toward self-awareness this would be appropriate and could cover the course of several meetings. In another type of group the counselor may choose to use a few of the exercises which seem most relevant to the goals of the group. For example, in a group whose purpose is to assist counselees in making vocational plans the exercises on thinking, feelings, and fantasy would be most appropriate. The counselor may choose to introduce the exercises when he feels that they will contribute to what is going on in the group at the time rather than according to a plan. Also, the counselor may note that the group members could profit by having some of the exercises be done outside of the group as "homework" assignments.

Present Awareness and the Group

In addition to contributing to the group of individual group members, present awareness work can also be used as a means of facilitating the movement of the group. There are several ways to use the "Now I am aware of . . ." sentence fragment which counselees complete with their current experience.

One of the most significant places for this approach to be used is at the beginning of the group session. Counselees and, for that matter, the counselor can arrive for the group meeting at the end of or in the midst of a busy day. "Now I am aware of . . ." can be a natural opener which can be very helpful for getting the members in touch with what they are experiencing in the present. It can help focus wondering and busy awareness antennas on the here-and-now situation, which can be quite valuable for groups which may meet for short times.

Cr: To start today, I'd like each person to finish the sentence "Now I'm aware of. . . ."
Ce₁: Now I'm aware that that is our signal to start.
Cr: I'm aware that you're on to my number. (*Laughter*)
Ce₂: Now I'm aware of my biology test this afternoon.
Cr: What feeling do you have now about that?
Ce₂: I'm a little nervous.
Ce₃: I'm trying to remember what we did last week.
Cr: So then right now you are aware of yourself remembering.
Ce₄: Now I'm aware that there's something I want to talk about.
Cr: You're experiencing some anticipation?
Ce₄: Yeah.
Ce₅: I'm aware of wondering what Judy (Ce₄) wants to talk about.
Cr: You are aware of your curiosity.

This approach can serve several purposes as a session opener. First, it requires each person to focus on the present, which can help get the counselees tuned into what is occurring in the group. Second, the counselor has a chance to help clarify present awareness. Third, each person has an opportunity to speak, which serves to affirm his presence in the group. Fourth, the presence of agendas for the session can be alluded to, as in the case of Ce₄ and Ce₂. Finally, as Ce₁ noted, the approach can serve as a signal to begin.

A second significant place for using this approach is at the time when a group member has disclosed and dealt with something which may also be of significance to the other group members.

Cr: Now that we have heard about Tom's situation with his mother, I'd like to hear what the rest of you are aware of now.

Ce: I'm aware that I often have the same difficulty with my own mother, but I never thought of it that way.

Cr: You've gotten in touch with something new for you.

Ce: Yeah. I guess I always thought everything was her fault.

Cr: And what do you feel about this now?

Ce: Now I'm not so sure.

Cr: Care to share this with us?

This counselee, upon listening to Tom's situation with his mother, apparently came into some new awareness about her situation with her mother. She had sat quietly while Tom and the group were focusing on his concern. However, when asked to share her awareness she revealed that she was now aware of something of importance. Thus, the counselor, instead of continuing around the group, offered her a chance to explore her situation.

The counselor may find that checking the present awareness of the group members can be beneficial at other times during the group sessions. For example, there may be a time when the group is involved in a long silence, the meaning of which may be explored by finding out what the counselees are experiencing during it. Another example might be when the members of a group single out a person and inappropriately respond to that person en masse. One way for the counselor to deal with such a situation is to ask the persons involved to share what they are aware of as they engage in the behavior.

Yet another way that present awareness can be used is for the counselor to introduce a topic to the group members and then ask them what their immediate awareness is upon hearing the topic. Consider, for example, this group, whose purpose is to deal with academic habits and skills.

Cr: There's a topic that we've kicked around some in the group and yet haven't spent much time on. I'm going to introduce the topic and then I'd like each of you to tell us what you are aware of. Everybody ready? (*Group indicates affirmatively*) The topic is homework.

Ce_1:   What I'm aware of is "ugh."

Ce_2:   I can't be with my friends because of it.

Ce_3:   That's something that my parents and I fight over all the time.

Ce_4:   All I know is that they keep giving us more and more of it. And it seems to be getting harder to do.

Ce_5:   My homework grades are lousy. I hate having to lug all that stuff home all the time.

Ce_6:   My teachers are always giving me a rough time about homework. It seems like they single me out more than other kids who don't do theirs.

During this kind of exercise each counselee has the occasion to state what he is aware of in relation to the topic. At this point there is no delving or interpreting of what is said. Rather, the purpose is for each person to attend to his own awareness and to be able to hear what others are aware of with respect to the topic. To this end, the approach can serve as an effective opener on a topic which can be further developed within the group.

Interpersonal Contact

An important aspect of awareness has to do with contacting the environment. Within the environment one of the most significant types of contacts is with other persons. The group can serve as a valuable place for counselees to learn about how they make and avoid contact with others.

Often group members may be reticent about speaking for fear that they may not be heard or understood. Then, one of these counselees may make some comments as a trial balloon. Such comments are often not connected to another person in the group. Contact is not made and the chance of response is lowered. To try to prevent this and to facilitate contact among the group members, the counselor can ask the counselees to speak directly to a group member.

Ce: I don't know what to do about my shyness. I'd like to be having as much fun as other people but . . . (*eyes are wandering*)

Cr: Sue, who are you talking to right now?

Ce: No one I guess.

Cr: Pick out someone in the group and say what you have to say to that person.

Ce: O.K. I'll tell Shirley.

Cr: Fine. Try looking at her while you do.

Ce: Shirley, I'm awfully shy and I don't know what to do about it. You're lucky because you're not shy.

Part of Sue's shyness is that she has trouble making contact with others. By asking her to speak directly to someone she can benefit several ways. First, she has an opportunity to disclose her difficulty. Second, her choice of the person to whom she wishes to speak is a type of reaching out which could enhance that relationship. Third, by speaking to someone she is engaging that person and is thus more likely to get a response from her than when speaking to no one. Finally, by addressing herself to Shirley, Sue is in a here-and-now interpersonal contact situation which encourages exploring how she approaches others.

The "speaking to" approach can also be used in other types of interpersonal contact situations. One of these may be to check out the perceptions or feelings of a group member.

Cr: Jim, you appear to me to be wanting to say something.
Ce: I do, but it wouldn't do any good.
Cr: Would you clarify that?
Ce: I don't think anybody here wants to listen to me.
Cr: Want to test that out?
Ce: How?
Cr: Ask someone here if they want to hear what you have to say and let's see what happens.
Ce: George, do you want to hear what I have to say?

This counselee has been behaving "as if" no one wants to hear him out. Having established this as a truth within himself he has not ventured beyond it. The experiment the counselor suggested for him may reveal that someone in the group does want to listen to him. If not, the situation may yield some feedback about difficulties others have in listening to him.

One of the most common barricades to interpersonal contact in a group occurs when one member talks about another group member rather than relating to the person directly. This type of "gossip" can be converted to contact through the "speaking to" approach.

Ce: I thought what Larry had to say was really important. I'm glad that he said it.
Cr: To whom are you saying this?
Ce: To you, I guess.
Cr: Now could you say what you have to say to Larry.

Interpersonal contact is prevented when one person's response to the other is directed to yet another person. "Speaking to" can help to establish the contact where it belongs.

Summary

A person's life includes a past, a present, and a future that has a bearing on current living. Based on what we have seen in this chapter, Gestalt approaches focus on the present. Reasons and advantages to this thrust include the impossibility of experiencing anything except in the present, the tenets that change can take place only in the present, that experiencing the present can enhance contact with the environment, and that the enhancement of self-awareness comes from living in the now.

Awareness is a valuable tool for being in contact with oneself and the environment in the now. Awareness differs from introspection in that the former is observing without judgment while the latter is peering with a purpose. A person cannot simultaneously attend to two things with the same degree of awareness. Awareness can be focused and guided by the person onto himself or the environment. The absence of awareness is usually associated with avoidance.

A person is a self-in-environment. To live effectively in his environment he must have sufficient levels of self-awareness in the areas of body structure, movement, body processes, sensations, feelings, thinking, and fantasy.

To orient himself within his environment the person relies on his receptor senses of seeing, hearing, touching, tasting, and smelling. To express himself in the environment and to act on it to meet his needs the person uses his voice and his movements.

Several approaches can be used for facilitating awareness. The counselor can direct the counselee's own awareness of himself, or the counselor can share with the counselee his current awareness of the counselee or himself. Other methods for enhancing awareness are repeating, exaggeration, and staying with.

Awareness approaches in group counseling can serve to promote self-awareness and interaction among group members. Stating present awareness can be used to begin a group, to allow a counselee to share something which may be of significance, to remove the focus of the group from one person, and to explore commonalities around a specific topic. Interpersonal contact in the group can be facilitated by asking group members to "speak to" another person rather than "gossiping about" that person.

REFERENCES

Perls, F. S., *Ego, Hunger and Aggression.* New York: Vintage Books, 1947.

Perls, F. S., Hefferline, R. F., and Goodman, P., *Gestalt Therapy: Excitement and Growth in the Human Personality.* New York: Dell Publishing Company, 1951.

Polster, E., and Polster, M., *Gestalt Therapy Integrated: Contours of Theory and Practice.* New York: Brunner/Mazel Publishers, 1973.

5

Language Approaches

Man's capacity for and use of language differentiates him from other forms of life. While animals are able to communicate, none can do so with the completeness and specificity of human speech. As such, one of the means for understanding man is to study his language.

In the same vein languages differentiate nationalities and tribes. Eskimos, for example, have seven or more words for different types of snow. The preciseness of the German language reflects the methodical industriousness of the German people. In our current society one of the ways that subcultures differentiate themselves is by developing a language that is particularly related to their behavior. This is true for craftsmen, drug users, neurosurgeons, and minority groups, to mention just a few. A person entering one of the subgroups must learn its dialect or jargon to relate to the persons in it. Similarly, studying the subgroup's language patterns can provide some understanding of its social order, mores, and uniqueness.

The same relationship holds for an individual. An individual's way of speaking reflects his personality. On this subject Perls, Hefferline, and Goodman (1951) have written:

> From one angle, it is useful to define "personality" as a structure of speech habits and consider it as a creative act of the second and third years; most thinking is subvocal speaking; basic beliefs are importantly

habits of syntax and style; almost all evaluation that does not spring directly from organic appetites is likely to be a set of rhetorical attitudes. To define in this way is not to belittle or explain away personality, for speech itself is a profound spontaneous activity. (pp. 320–321)

This relationship between speaking and personality has powerful implications for counseling. It suggests that an individual's speech patterns are a means to understanding his inner thoughts, feelings, and attitudes. From a Gestalt approach, then, working with overt speaking habits is one way to increase a person's awareness of himself.

There are two main components of speaking that can be the focus of awareness. One of these is the manner of speaking or how the person speaks. These "how's" include such nonverbal cues such as pitch, speed, intensity, volume, and voice modulation. The spoken words are often of less import than the characteristics and style of delivery. Chapter 6 in this text will be devoted to working with nonverbal behavior.

A second major component of speaking is the content or the choice of words used to convey a message. This is the world of signs ("There is a red light") and symbols ("The red light is on a street corner. Thus, I have to stop my car."). That different persons will use different words and combinations of words to describe a situation or an experience demonstrates how speech patterns are reflective of the total person. This is also noted in how the same words can have different meanings for different individuals.

A person's language is not necessarily spontaneous. In fact, speaking is one of the means of expression over which control is most easily exercised. Speech can be manipulated so that what the person is trying to say is masked or couched in words which convey a different meaning. Some of these manipulations are unique with individuals, and others have become a part of idiomatic English.

The focus of the approaches in this chapter is on speech patterns common in today's society and which are manipulations that keep the person from expressing himself. In fact, they are often used so habitually that they reduce the speaker's self-awareness. The intent of the approaches is to experiment with changing certain speech habits as a means of enhancing the person's awareness of his inner dynamics.

Personalizing Pronouns

English often tends to be depersonalized, especially in the use of pronouns. When two people encounter each other on the street an exchange such as the following is not uncommon "Hi. How's it going?"

"O.K. How are things?" The conversation may continue in a similar vein and then end in a mutual "Take it easy."

This type of idiomatic expression carries over into the pronouns used when a person is referring to himself or supposedly expressing himself and does not employ self-references in his speech. Some of the most commonly used depersonalizing pronouns are "it," "you," and "we."

Changing "It" to "I"

It-talk is heard among counselees who live in a world in which depersonalized language abounds. This sort of speech represents one more habit which keeps them from expressing themselves. It also sets up barriers to their awareness of self. Perhaps the more that a person relates to the world through it-talk, the more that person will experience himself as an "it." This is an undesirable and deleterious developmental direction for any person. Working with it-talk, then, is a means whereby the counselor can help the counselee match the "what" of speech with the "what" of experience. In the process the counselee's awareness of experience may become clearer.

Self-Experiment

Try saying some examples of it-talk that are common in everyday discourse. "It's good to be here with you today." "It is aggravating when you do that." "It's beautiful, isn't' it?" Do any of these sound familiar to you? Can you think of some of your own speech patterns that are similar? . . . Notice the difference between these kinds of it-statements and others such as "It's raining today"; "It is a big house"; "It is now half past five."

Now change some of the original statements and say them this way, "I'm glad to be here with you today"; "I am aggravated when you do that"; "I think this is beautiful." Compare and contrast the "it" and "I" approaches to the same statement. . . . Can you feel the difference in the degree of yourself that you invest as you do each? Or does "*it*" feel different?

Counseling Applications

Ce: It is very dull in here today. There's no excitement or activity.
Cr: What is the "it" you are referring to?
Ce: The mood. It's heavy and tedious.

Cr: Cathy, say the heavy and tedious thing again, only change the "it" to "I."

Ce: I'm heavy and tedious?

Cr: I don't know. Are you?

Ce: No. Actually, I'm bored and not interested in what we are doing.

Ce: That's a great class! It's smart and likes to work!

Cr: Great! Now try saying this another way like "I'm smart. . . .

Ce: I am! And I like to work in there. I'm actually one of the leaders in the class . . .

Ce: I didn't have very many dates this year. Next year it will be different.

Cr: It will be different? Who are you talking about.

Ce: Me. I'll be different.

Cr: What will you do differently?

Note how these students tended to project the feelings onto situations. They could then comment on the situations as partial expressions of what they felt. Working with the form of it-statements resulted in stating their own feelings about these situations.

Changing "You" to "I"

You-talk is no more or less common among counselees than in our society in general. A counselee may use "you" to tell you how he feels. He may also use "you" to tell you how he imagines you will react in a particular situation which is, in essence, another way of telling you how he feels. The counselee may not be aware of how he is diluting his expression of self through this approach or how he is generalizing to others. The counselor can enhance awareness in these areas by working with "you" and "I."

Self-Experiment

Here is a person responding to the effects of a drug he had taken: "Well, you got kind of dizzy. Then you felt the pain go away. Finally you didn't care what was happening." Do you recognize anything in this that is familiar in your speech patterns? . . . Experiment with this by making up some comparable you-statements. . . .

Now change your you-statements to sentences which begin with

"I". . . . Can you feel and hear the differences between you saying something about yourself as compared with announcements about someone in general?

Relatedly, what do you feel when someone tells you what you'll do or how you will feel about something? "You'll love this person. He is so funny." Such statements assume a great deal. Can you recall the reactions you have when someone speaks for you? If you haven't been aware of this, try noticing this you-talk and attend to what your feelings are when you hear it. What do you feel about the speaker?

Counseling Applications

Ce: When you go skiing you feel healthy and vigorous. You have this sense of excitement.
Cr: Sue, try saying the same thing only substituting the word "I" for "you."
Ce: Why?
Cr: Because I believe you're saying something about yourself except you're not sounding that way.
Ce: When I'm skiing I feel healthy and excited.
Cr: Do you hear the difference?
Ce: Yes. The second one is what I really meant.

This counselee obviously enjoys skiing. Her expression of her enjoyment, however, was somewhat camouflaged in her "you" statements. Stating "I" can afford her even more of a sense of "This is me who is enjoying skiing."

Ce: You'll love that movie. There is so much good music and the acting is great.
Cr: How do you know I will like it?
Ce: Because it's such a great movie.
Cr: Then, what you mean is you liked the movie a lot.
Ce: Yeah.
Cr: Then try saying it that way. That "I liked the movie and so on." Neither of us knows how I will like it until I see it.

This counselee may come to see that his feeling may not be the same as the counselor's. This does not mean that his feeling about it has to change in any way other than to be owned as his.

Changing "We" to "I"

Counselees identify and relate to their peers. The sense of belonging to a group is important to their interpersonal development because peer groups are a primary reference source for the formulation of beliefs, attitudes, feelings, and overt actions. Thus, the use of "we" is to be expected, and the counselee's relationship with the peer group is to be respected.

Certain counselees, however, use the term "we" in ways that mask expression of themselves. In order to help these counselees become aware of what they are experiencing in relation to what they are saying the counselor may suggest substituting "I" for "we."

Self-Experiment

Reflect on how you use the term "we". . . . Are you validly reflecting the feelings of the others for whom you are speaking? . . . Do you sometimes say "we" to bolster support for something you want to say and will not say alone?

Take a few sentences about yourself and cast them into we-statements. . . . What is your experience when you do this? . . . Now restate them as I-sentences. . . . Compare the two experiences. Note the differences for yourself.

Counseling Applications

Ce: We are always being told what to do and we don't like it. It seems like every time we move there is someone there watching.

Cr: Who are the we you are talking about?

Ce: All of us kids. The whole school.

Cr: I'd like you to say what you feel about this.

Ce: I feel just like everybody else does.

Cr: Try saying what you feel in your own way. Say "I" instead of "we."

Ce: I'm sick of being spied on. The other day I was on my way to the office and two teachers stopped me to ask me where I was going. I felt like some kind of criminal.

In this particular instance the counselee started by stating the feeling of the total student body as perceived by her. When asked to express herself, she related a specific instance bothering her. She was then expressing herself rather than serving as a spokeswoman.

Ce: We hate the part-time jobs in our work-study programs. None of them are working out.

Cr: Who else feels this way?
Ce: Well . . .
Cr: You're not sure.
Ce: Not exactly, but I'm pretty sure there are others.
Cr: Tell me about your job. Only be sure to say "I" when you're talking about it.
Ce: I don't like my job. They never let me do anything except sweep the floor.
Cr: "I'm frustrated there."
Ce: Yes! I want to learn how to work on cars.

This counselee demonstrated a common use of "we." He had something to relate which he was reluctant to say unless he could build up a case by stating there were others who felt as he did. Through this approach he may learn that he can have and relate "his" feelings without having to couch them in an anonymous "we." Further, he may become more responsible for his feeling, regardless of others.

There are numerous other examples of pronouns which are used in the ways described above. "One," "some people," "no one," "everybody" are just a few more. Can you think of additional ones? If so, then listen for them in your counselee's speech. You might try approaches with them that are similar to those presented in the examples of "it," "you," and "we." Better yet you may invent some of your own.

Changing Verbs

Many verbs in English have similar meanings and are used interchangeably. "Listening" and "hearing" is one example; "seeing" and "looking" is another. Right now I am "hearing" rain as background. When I shift my attention to the rain then I am "listening" to it. The difference is in my awareness—my knowing when I am listening or seeing.

Several other verbs often arise in counseling which have counterparts that distract from awareness and thus responsibility. Four of these which will be discussed in this section are "can't," "need," "have to," and "know." The passive voice is also related and will be mentioned.

Changing "Can't" to "Won't"

"Can't" is commonly heard among counselees. Sometimes their use of the word is appropriate. A counselee may have certain limitations that are reflected in real "can't's." Assistance in realizing and accepting real restrictions can be a source of growth for a counselee.

Quite often, however, a counselee will say "can't" when the felt restrictions are within the realm of "can-if-I-choose." The counselee actually experiences the impasse of the "can't" and feels unable. He may not be aware that his saying "can't" is more a statement of "I won't" or "I am not willing." Asking the counselee to substitute "won't" for "can't" is a way of enhancing the awareness of his responsibility for the refusal or fear that is at the base of the "can't."

Self-Experiment

Try to recall some of the "can't" statements that you often use. Repeat a few of these slowly and attend to the feeling that accompanies them. . . . You may recognize that there are some things which you actually cannot do. See if you can differentiate between the types of "can't" statements. Which are impossible? . . . Could you do some of them if you chose to invest in the time and energy it might require?

Now focus on the other "can't" statements. Repeat them a few times. . . . Now try substituting "won't" where you previously said "can't". . . . Do you feel any difference? Repeat one of the "won't" statements again and be aware of the feeling that accompanies it. . . . Are you taking the responsibility that is in "I will not"? Try to get in touch with the nature of your refusal. Allow the refusal to expand and feel the strength that is in it. . . . Compare what you feel when making "won't" statements with your experience when making "can't" statements. The difference is your sense of responsibility for your behavior.

Counseling Applications

Ce: Every day I just sit there and feel like a stooge. I just can't speak up in that class.

Cr: You say you can't.

Ce: That's right. I've tried and I know I should. I mean I know the stuff, that's not the problem. I just can't get the words out.

Cr: Try saying "I won't talk" instead of "I can't talk."

Ce: I won't talk in that class.

Cr: Let yourself feel how you are refusing to talk.

Ce: I guess I am holding myself back a little.

Cr: What are your objections to speaking up?

Ce: Well, everyone else in there seems to be talking just to talk. I don't like doing that.

Ce: English essays are due and I can't do mine.

Cr: Judy, try saying that a different way. For example "I am unwilling to write my English essays."

Ce: I am unwilling! Heck, I'm not doing anything but staring at the paper.
Cr: What would happen if you wrote it?
Ce: I'd probably get another C. Essays are hard for me.

Many counselees experience a sort of relief when they can experience their "can't" as "won't." They feel both more in control and ready to examine their fears. Further, a "won't" is often a manifestation of defiance. It is important to help counselees experience and integrate the strength that is evidence in defiance. Owning and accepting this strength is necessary for reclaiming it and using it constructively.

Changing "Need" to "Want"

Sometimes a counselee will impute a sense of necessity to something desired. The outcome is that he begins to feel as though he needs it in order to survive. Such being the case, the counselee can put himself into a panic if he feels the "need" is not being met. Helping the counselee differentiate between wants and needs can assist him to become aware of anxieties he produces in approaching some of his wants as needs.

Self-Experiment

What do you need in order to live? Imagine a list of these things. You might even make one. . . . Now look at each item and silently say to yourself "I need this in order to survive." Then ask yourself whether the statement you just made is true or false. Note how there are probably fewer things you need than you imagined.

Now take the remaining items and try recognizing them as things you want. Try alternating back and forth with one of them, stating, "I want this," then, "I need this." . . . Do you feel any difference? In doing this exercise have you gained any new awareness about your wants and needs? . . . Can you give yourself permission to have your wants?

Counseling Applications

Ce: If I don't get into that crowd, I don't know what I will do!
Cr: Sounds pretty important to you.
Ce: It is! They are such groovy people. I need very much to be in with them. There's no one else I like.
Cr: Sharon, what do you need in order to live? Like things you can't do without.

Ce: Well, let's see. Water. Air. I have to eat. And you can't live without sleep. When it's cold out I have to wear clothes to keep me warm.

Cr: O.K. There are things you must have, that you actually need because you couldn't live without them. Now, what are some things that you want to have or be?

Ce: I want to be smart. I want to live a happy life. And I want to get along with my parents. I would like to have some new clothes and records. Also, I want to be popular, particularly with that crowd. That's important.

Cr: Uh huh. So there are a number of things you want. Now, do you feel that you could live without some of these things?

Ce: Well, I suppose so.

Cr: Then there are things you want and things you need. Where does being in with the crowd fit?

Ce: It's something I want.

Counselees may feel a sense of less urgency upon realizing that they will, in fact, continue living if they do not have what they want. This may result in less anxiety about the want and thereby afford a greater openness to exploring alternatives for getting what they want or recognizing how other alternatives may substitute.

Suppose that Sharon had concluded that being in the gang was something without which she could not survive. The counselor then may have asked her to carry out the fantasy of life without being in the gang. It is almost certain that she would have come to a realization of how she could cope with not gaining her entrance to the gang. In fact, this intervention could have been used with Sharon had she had the previous experience of differentiating between her wants and needs.

Changing "Have to" to "Choose to"

Counselees will often present themselves as persons who "have" to do things. Certainly within the structure of most schools there are many "have to" conditions which are real. Attendance, certain assignments, and conduct specifications are not always open to choosing, or at least they do not appear to be. As a result of these restrictions many counselees develop a "have to" mentality. They feel like rules and regulations are coming at them from every direction. Even situations in which they are making choices begin to feel like there is no real choice. Asking these counselees to substitute "I choose" for "I have" or "I must" may help increase their awareness of the freedom of choice and responsibility they can exercise.

Self-Experiment

Try to be aware of all of the things you feel that you "have" to do or must do. . . . Go over each one slowly, concentrating on the "have" or "must" of each statement. . . . Now go over each one again and repeat "Who says so?" after each one. See if you can locate who is calling the shots for you.

Now try the statements again, only this time say "I choose to" where you said "I have to." Emphasize and savor the "choose" in your statement. . . . Can you feel the responsibility in "choosing" as opposed to "having" to do something? There may be some excitement in this for you. You are capable of acting rather than reacting.

Counseling Applications

Ce: Well, I have to take French again this year. What a drag.
Cr: Who says you "have to"?
Ce: Everybody I've talked to has said that if you want to get into foreign service work you have to take French.
Cr: Who says *you* have to?
Ce: The people who would hire me.
Cr: I'm aware of that. The question, though, is who says you have to take French this year?
Ce: I guess I do because I do want to work overseas.
Cr: Then try saying "I am choosing to take French".
Ce: Actually I am choosing to. I would not take it if I didn't want that job.

Ce: I have to always be funny when I'm around Sam and the other guys. They really seem to dig my jokes.
Cr: Bob, can you feel the choice that you have here?
Ce: What do you mean?
Cr: I'll show you. Try saying "I choose to always be funny."
Ce: I choose to be funny and crack jokes for Sam and my other friends.
Cr: Can you accept the responsibility for this?
Ce: Not entirely. They've more or less told me that's why they let me hang around.
Cr: Whose choice is it whether or not you hang around?
Ce: Mine. I want to hang around with them.
Cr: So you choose to do what?
Ce: Be the funny man.

Some counselees may try to avoid the fact that they are responsible for putting themselves in discomforting or inconvenient situations. Yet until they can recognize and accept how they are behaving in accordance with their choices, they will not feel their power to generate alternatives and do otherwise. Increasing awareness of "choosing" as opposed to "having" to do cannot be done selectively. Rather, to be effective the counselee will have to realize and accept the full range of choices.

Changing "Know" to "Imagine"

Some counselees live in worlds of untested assumptions and hypotheses. They feel that what they imagine is what they know and act accordingly. Not being aware of the differences between knowing and imagining, who could expect them to do otherwise? The counselor can note a counselee is behaving according to imagined facts, information, or events. An important task to perform is assisting the counselee to differentiate between what is known and what is imagined. (The topic of fantasy and imagining will be further developed in Chapter 7.)

Self-Experiment

Focus your awareness on the things that you know, those things about which you are certain and of which you have a clear understanding. What do you know of yourself at this moment? of others? of situations and events that are outside of your immediate experience? . . . Investigate for yourself what has to occur before you feel that you know something. . . . What feelings, thoughts, and body sensations are associated with your knowing?

The other side of knowing is imagining or fantasizing. Test this out for yourself by pretending that you are imagining some of the things you feel that you know. . . . You can imagine what you would be like as a member of the opposite sex. You cannot know it. Examine the lines of demarcation between what you know and what you imagine. . . . How do you decide which is which? What cues or data do you use? Can you feel the difference between the two experiences? Are you willing to relinquish knowing for imagining in some cases?

Counseling Applications

Ce: I'm not going to get to the circus with the rest of the kids.
Cr: Oh?
Ce: I just know it's not going to work out.
Cr: How do you know this?

Ce: I know. Everytime I plan something fun like this something comes up to spoil it.
Cr: Then what you're doing is imagining that your plans will not work out.
Ce: I'm not imagining it. I know it!
Cr: It hasn't happened yet. You can only imagine how it will be. And you are imagining that you'll miss out.

Ce: The school work here is just too difficult for me. I'm not surprised, though, because I know I have a low I.Q. How can a dummy like me do this kind of work?
Cr: How do you know you have a low I.Q.?
Ce: Well, my grades have never been very high and my parents and friends have told me this must mean I have a low I.Q.

This student has not received valid feedback on his academic abilities. He has been told of his limitations, imagined that this input was true, and has lived out the self-fulfilling prophecy. As the counseling proceeds the counselor may provide some information so that what the counselee knows about himself can supplant what he has been imagining as truth.

Ce: I think I'd like to go into pharmacy. My uncle owns a drugstore, though, and he says it can be tough sometimes.
Cr: You know what your uncle does in his store.
Ce: Yeah. I sometimes visit him.
Cr: What else do you know about what pharmacists do?
Ce: Well, they all make up medicines. That means they work in drugstores.
Cr: This is what you imagine about pharmacists. Sounds like you imagine they are all like your uncle.
Ce: Well, he's the only one I know.
Cr: So let's see if we can get you some more information about pharmacy. That way you can check out some of these things you imagine about it.

Changing Passive Voice
to Active Voice

One of the chief processes that counselees employ to avoid responsibility for their behavior is to use the passive voice. Speaking "as if" they are reacting rather than acting in life is both a cause and an effect of their view of themselves. They may speak that way because they feel controlled and manipulated. Likewise, passive verbs tend to stamp in that view. The counselor may intervene at the language level and suggest changing some passive statements to active assertions or declarations. In this way the counselee may regain or attain awareness of powers he has not been using.

Self-Experiment

Go back to when you first got up this morning and trace your activities through the day up to this point. . . . Take some specific behaviors and state them in the passive voice. "I was gotten out of bed. My face was washed. Breakfast was fed to me. My car took me to work." Cast away all volition and will in your behavior. Imagine yourself the pawn in a completely predetermined day in which all of your behaviors were prescribed. . . . Now reflect upon this experience.

Reverse this process now. Replace all the passive verbs with active ones. . . . Do this with all of your activities, even if you have to exaggerate some. Assume that you have complete mastery over what you do. How much responsibility for your activities are you willing to take? . . . What means do you use to avoid responsibility when it is to your convenience? . . .

Counseling Applications

Ce: It's graduation time now. Would you believe I ended up in the top fifteen percent of my class? The list was printed this morning and they put me down as forty-second.

Cr: Did you have any part in this?

Ce: Sure. I'm the one who got the grades.

Cr: Oh? Tell me how you did it.

This student was not giving herself credit for her accomplishment although she probably felt it. The counselor attempted to have her take the responsibility for the success. In this way the counselee can learn to give herself support and encouragement for her behavior as well as assume the responsibility for it. Learning to be responsible for positive outcomes is just as important as learning to be responsible for negative outcomes. In essence, the responsibility does not change.

Ce: I'm in trouble because my newspapers didn't get delivered last night.

Cr: Someone didn't deliver them?

Ce: Yeah. And people were calling the house—"Where's my paper?"

Cr: Terry, who didn't deliver the papers?
Ce: Me.
Cr: So what you mean when you said the papers "didn't get delivered" was . . .
Ce: I didn't feel like doing it last night. I get tired of that route. Every day, seven days a week.

In this case, as in others, when the counselor focuses awareness on the counselee's responsibility for her behavior the feelings involved in the situation tend to emerge. Confrontation, when appropriate, will usually result in further self-exploration.

Changing Sentences

The choice of words is not the only language manipulation that can dampen awareness. Sentence structure can also contribute to confusion or making a message sound like something different from its intent. Two examples of this behavior are the use of "but" and the asking of questions.

Changing "But" to "And"

"But" is a commonly used conjunction which is usually employed to mean "except that" or "on the contrary." "I like your dress, but it would be prettier in green." "I want to lose weight, but I just keep on eating a lot." As such, the latter part of a "but" sentence qualifies the former clause. In some cases it completely irradicates it. A person who is serious about losing weight will alter his eating habits.

Sometimes a counselee will use the word "but" and not be aware of its qualifying and erasing power. He may not experience both sides of a statement such as "I want to go to college, but I don't want to go through all the hassels of applying." In such cases the counselor may ask the counselee to substitute "and" for "but." "And" is a connector, usually meaning "in addition." This slight change may guide the counselee to an awareness of the contradiction in his thoughts.

Self-Experiment

In this experiment I want you to produce a series of "but" sentences, such as, "I like chocolate candy, but it gives me pimples." You can either say these to yourself or write them down. Now go over them, repeating each a few times. Carefully note what the "but" does to the relationship between the thoughts on either side of it. What does the second thought do to the first? and vice versa?

Now go over the "but" statements you have made. In each case where you have used "but" replace it with the word "and." Compare the total message of the sentence when "and" is used instead of "but." Is there any difference in your awareness as you contrast the two?

Counseling Applications

Ce: I want to go out of town this weekend, but I don't want to miss Susan's party.

Cr: Sam, say that again only this time substitute "and" for "but."

Ce: I want to go out of town this weekend, and I don't want to miss Susan's party.

Cr: How does what you said sound to you now?

Ce: Like maybe I want them both.

Cr: Sounds that way to me, too. Where does that leave you?

Ce: Maybe I'd better try to decide which I want more because I can't do them both.

Ce: I've been preparing myself for this race all season, but I'll probably blow it.

Cr: Try that sentence again, Sally. Only this time say "and" instead of "but."

Ce: I've been preparing myself for this race all season and I'll probably blow it.

Cr: Your preparation has been good?

Ce: Yes.

Cr: And you'll probably blow the race?

Ce: Yes.

Cr: My hunch is that you believe one of these statements more than the other.

Changing Questions to Statements

There are several ways that a counselee can employ questions. They may be used to gain information about course selections, test results, job applications, college requirements, or some other concerns.

There is, however, another class of questions used by counselees comprised of pseudo-questions. Such questions are actually declarations. For example, the question, "Don't you think it's warm in here?" is likely to be a declaration something like "I am warm" or "I would like the heater turned down." Yet instead of expressing this the speaker throws out a general inquiry, and if somebody picks up the hint, the person will get what is wanted without the risk involved in directly stating the desire. Counselees will sometimes employ this nonquestion so that the counselor will take the responsibility for the statement that conveys the counselee's feeling or experience. The counselor can assist the counselee in self-expression by helping to change such questions to statements.

Self-Experiment

Imagine that you are in a conversation with someone who is asking you a number of questions. Now listen carefully to each one. Assume for the moment that the concept of the question no longer exists and you have to help the person change the questions into declaratory sentences. If the question were "What is to be done now?" you might suggest the sentence be "I don't know what to do now."

Now focus your awareness on how you use questions. . . . Do you sometimes ask questions which are really a way for you to state what you want to say? (Try changing the question just asked into a statement.) Ask yourself some questions about what you are doing right now, that is, "Am I learning anything?" . . . Now try changing some of these to statements. . . . See if you can imagine a question that does not have a statement in it. In your next conversation listen to how you use questions.

Counseling Applications

Ce: You know me, don't you think I'd be better off if I didn't go to school next year?

Cr: You may have given your own answer. Change that question around to a statement and let's see what you have to say.

Ce: Going to school next year is not right for me. Not now, anyhow.

Ce: That math test coming up is really going to be difficult.

Cr: From what you've said I would agree with you.

Ce: Do you think I can pass it?

Cr: Joe, you seem to be implying something by asking me whether I think you can pass the test. I'd like to hear what you feel about that.

Ce: I think I can pass it. I'll have to work hard though.

Ce: So Bob said we were through. Then he called me up and asked me out. What am I supposed to do?

Cr: Try saying what you're "supposed" to do rather than asking about it.
Ce: Well, I'm not supposed to be a yo-yo for him, that's for sure!
Cr: Then say what you want to do.
Ce: I want to be through with him.

This type of work is based on the assumption that the vast majority of verbal behavior is of a declaratory nature. However, the declaration or statement is often veiled behind the format of a question. The speaker feels that he is asking rather than saying. Thus, the message to himself and others often remains implicit. By helping the counselee to ferret out the statement in the questions, the counselor offers another means to enhance awareness of what is being experienced and said.

Other Language Approaches

Asking "How" and "What" instead of "Why"

There is little disagreement that self-understanding converted into change is an important goal in counseling. However, too often the counselor and the counselee will pursue this goal through the labyrinth of trying to find out why the counselee acts a certain way. There are several difficulties with "why" questions. One problem is that they smack of causality and lead to a search for the prime cause, the supreme insight that will unlock the mysteries of behavior and effect instant and effective behavior change. This path leads to quicksand. Second, "why" is too easily answered by "because" responses that place responsibility on external or unknown loci of control. These "because" responses may indicate rationalization, explanation, justification, excuses, and so on. A third problem with "why" questions is that they often lead the questionee into "figuring things out" in a cognitive, problem-solving fashion that rarely enhances the experiencing and understanding of emotions. Fourth, "why" questions are usually accusatory. One way that counselors can help to break the "why" chain is by asking "how" and "what" instead.

Self-Experiment

For the sake of this experiment try to get in touch with one of those parts of yourself that you understand least. . . . Now ask yourself a series of "why" questions about this. See where these questions take you. . . . Now answer these questions. Take note of the number of "because" answers and answers that are in turn "why" questions. Did you come to any further understanding? any new awareness?

Now take the same situation. Ask yourself questions again except leave out the "why." Rather, focus on the "how" and "what" of your situation. . . . More specifically, approach yourself with "How do I . . . ?" and "What do I . . . ?" statements. Try a number of these. . . . How do you experience these questions? What is different about them in contrast to the "why" questions? My guess is that you may have found them more difficult to duck or answer with excuses.

Counseling Applications

Ce: I'm always late for my first class. Everyone is there and I come crashing in. Miss Jones has a fit.

Cr: What are you doing when you come in late?

Ce: Arriving late. (*Laughs*)

Cr: Besides that, what are you doing?

Ce: Causing some confusion.

Cr: What else?

Ce: All of the kids notice me.

Cr: What else?

Ce: Make Miss Jones mad.

Cr: What do you get out of doing all these things?

Ce: It seems as though I'm one way around strangers and another way around my friends.

Cr: What do you do differently?

Ce: It seems like I'm always getting myself into jams around here. No matter what I do I get into a mess.

Cr: How do you do this?

Ce: Every time I get ready to call somebody I fink out and don't do it.

Cr: How do you stop yourself?

Asking "how" and "what" invites the counselee to experience his behavior. The words presuppose he is doing something and facilitate his awareness of the content and structure of the processes of doing it. Asking "how" and "what" demonstrates respect for the person's ability to become aware of his motivations. "How" and "what" inherently include "why" by examining the experience. Thus, the person is assisted in realizing and accepting responsibility for his behavior.

Listening to Self

Counseling is based on the assumption that by talking out problems, some understandings and solutions may be discovered. Often, though, it appears that counselees are talking "at" the counselor or broadcasting into the universe. The person who most needs to listen to what the counselee is saying—the counselee himself—may not be listening! The counselee who does not listen to himself is exhibiting a dynamic that makes meaningful self-exploration highly unlikely. Sometimes the counselor may want to ask the counselee, "Are you listening to what you are saying?"

Self-Experiment

The purpose of this experiment is to explore the extent to which you hear what you say when you talk. The first step is for you to attend to your current thoughts and feelings without verbalizing them aloud. Just let them be as they are and observe them. . . . Feel how you listen to your internal vocalizations. You might try closing your eyes while you do this. . . . What do you most notice about the language of your subvocalizations?

Now begin to speak of some of your current thoughts. As you do this listen carefully to what you say. . . . Compare the vocalizations with the subvocalizations. What difference and similarities do you note?

Now try speaking aloud without listening to what you are saying, as if you can reduce your words to noises you hear but do not fully attend to. . . . Are you able to feel the gap? Now once more speak aloud and listen carefully. . . . Contrast your experiences of speaking with and without listening. . . . What have you become aware of? . . . The next time you are in a conversation try this experiment with yourself and see what you discover in an interpersonal situation.

Counseling Applications

Ce: Then I came home and went to my room. . . . The radio was on and I just fooled around a while. . . . There wasn't much to do.

Cr: Jim, are you listening to what you are saying?

Ce: No, I guess I'm not.

Cr: To whom are you speaking?

Ce: I dunno. You, I guess. Who listens to himself talk?

Cr: People who want to know themselves a little better.

Ce: It isn't something I normally do.

Cr: What do you normally do when you talk?

This counselee may become a little more aware of the lack of attention he receives from himself. Working with him on listening to what he says is one dimension of enhancing his total awareness. It may come out that he does not listen to others either, thus contributing to a sense of alienation from them.

Ce: My schedule is so busy I can't believe it. I have classes and study periods during the day. There's my part-time job later in the afternoon and on weekends. At nights I have club meetings and homework. Also I like to make my own clothes. I just don't enjoy these things as much as I used to.
Cr: Judy, are you listening to what you are saying.
Ce: Yes.
Cr: What are you hearing?
Ce: Like I'm into a lot of things; I hadn't listed them all off like that before. I sound like a merry-go-round.
Cr: What is the merry-go-round like for you?

This counselee through listening to herself came in contact with what she does to cram her time with activities. Having received her message she can now go on to explore her feelings and responsibility for the "merry-go-round." Alternatives for adjustment and changes will then be possible.

Ce: There is just nothing that I'm interested in. Everything is such a drag.
Cr: There's nothing that you like.
Ce: Yeah. My life is really dull.
Cr: Not even one thing that you like?
Ce: Well, music sometimes. Depends on the songs.
Cr: What else?
Ce: Walking in the park, especially when there are children playing and I can watch them.
Cr: Anything else.
Ce: Sometimes I enjoy talking with my friends.
Cr: Judy, are you listening to these things you're saying?
Ce: Sounds as though there are a few things I like, doesn't it?
Cr: That's a question. What's your answer?

Omitting Qualifiers

Qualifiers are used by counselees to deal with ambivalences and decisions. "May," "possibly," and other similar words are dual edged, suggesting "possibly won't." Some counselees are not aware of the sides of the ambivalences. This makes clarifications of feelings and decisions difficult if not impossible. Other counselees may use qualifiers in order to avoid making decisions. In either case the counselor can augment the counselee's awareness by noting his use of qualifiers.

Self-Experiment

Focus your awareness on the degree to which you employ qualifiers. Some examples are "Maybe I feel a little sad about that"; "It is possible that I'll come over this afternoon"; "I guess that this is O.K. with me." Find for yourself the ways that you put qualifications on what you say.

Now try some of these statements without the qualifiers. . . . What do you notice about how they serve you? . . . What difference in feeling do you have when you eliminate these qualifiers?

Counseling Applications

Ce: Our teacher is trying some new methods with us. Instead of lecturing he puts us in small groups and we discuss topics. Sometimes we play games.

Cr: What do you feel about these new methods?

Ce: I guess they're all right with me.

Cr: Can you drop the "guess" from that and say it again?

Ce: They're all right with me.

Cr: True or false?

Ce: True. His lectures are usually a drag and we have to write like mad to get everything down.

Cr: Anything on the false side?

Ce: Well, I feel a little funny in the discussions sometimes.

With this counselee "guess" and "all right" reflected ambivalences which required further clarification. So that both sides of the "all right" were dealt with, the counselor did not assume that one side of the true or false question covered the range of feeling.

Language Approaches
in Group Counseling

The language approaches in this chapter were presented in the context of counseling with individuals. They are no less relevant to the individuals within a group. In fact the personalization and responsibility objectives of the language approaches may become group norms consistent with the goals of the group. In one instance a group of persons in an extensive counseling program were exposed to some of the language approaches. Several weeks later one of the persons was brooding and stating, "I can't do it." Another member of the program, upon hearing this, stated, "You mean you won't do it." The counselor had initiated the approaches, the members of the group were accepting the responsibility for making them operational.

Personalizing

One of the advantages of a group is that the counselee is allowed the opportunity for learning in a social situation. Thus, there are chances for testing the validity of statements made by the counselee. This can be particularly important when generalizations are being made by a counselee.

Ce_1:   We're not getting anywhere in this group. The kinds of things that we talk about are silly.

Cr: Silly to whom, Joan?

Ce_1:   To the whole group. I mean, who really cares about getting better grades. We don't or we wouldn't be here.

Cr: Let's see how other people feel about this. I'd like to hear what you have to say.

Ce_2:   I've been finding the sessions helpful, especially when we've talked about taking tests.

Ce_3:   The way that we talked about taking notes on books we read has been interesting for me.

Ce_4:   I like the sessions because I thought I was the only one having these kinds of problems.

Cr: Joan, could you change what you were saying to "I" instead of "we"?

Ce_1:   O.K. I think that what we're doing here doesn't make sense.

Cr: This is how you feel.

Ce_1:   Yes.

Cr: O.K. Now let's hear what you want to be doing here.

This counselee was experiencing the group as not meeting her needs and was projecting this experience onto the other members of the group. ("How could anybody be getting something out of this group if I'm not?") The work with her "we" statement revealed how she was generalizing dissatisfaction, which once owned could be converted into an exploration of what she was expecting from the group and not receiving.

There are advantages in having counselees personalize their statements. They learn to take the responsibility for what they have to say. The other group members are more likely to respond to the counselee who is speaking personally. The personalized statement comes off as more authentic and clear. Also, some counselees may dislike being clumped into statements which purportedly are speaking for them and respond to that rather than what the person is trying to say about herself. Personalizing can prevent this.

Changing Verbs

The main growth objective of the verb changes dealt with in this text is to enhance the counselee's sense of responsibility. There are few groups in which this would not be important. These approaches can be used in a group with individuals as presented above. They can also serve as a useful exercise for a total group.

Changing "can't" to "won't" can serve as a prototype for how the verb changes can be used as a group exercise. To start, each person in the group can be asked to relate a few "I can't" statements and then change them to "I won't" statements. Discussion of the exercise can take several directions. It may focus on the difference in the feelings of responsibility of the speaker when making the two types of statements. Each of the group members will hear some of what the other group members consider possible or not possible for them. The point may be made that there are, in fact, some things which genuinely can't be done by an individual and how these relate to expectations and the acceptance of limitations.

Changing Sentences

A group can be an excellent situation for counselees to experience and learn about the canceling power of "but" sentences. One way to work with this is to have the group members make up some "but" sentences (for example, "I like your hair, but it could be a little shorter") and to explore the meaning of this message when the first clause is left off. Also, the same message could be changed by substituting the word "and" for "but." These approaches can be discussed in the group both from the viewpoint of the person saying the sentence and from the perspective of the person being spoken to. The counselor may also ask the counselees to be aware of their use of "but" in the group interactions and ask for occasional clarifications.

Many of the questions that counselees ask each other in groups are not really questions at all. Rather, they are declarative statements about the other person or about self which are phrased in a question form designed to camouflage their true intent. Changing questions to statements makes their message more explicit.

Ce$_1$: Well, the next time I call Alice I'll try talking with her in a different way. I guess I have been a little short.

Ce$_2$: Are you serious about trying this?

Cr: Jim, what are you trying to say to Bob?

Ce$_2$: Just what I said. I'm wondering about how serious he is about trying something different.

Cr: Say what you have to say to him in a statement instead of a question.

Ce$_2$: Bob, I don't think that you're going to do it.

Changing questions to statements is advantageous to both the questioner and the questionee. The questioner learns to take the responsibility for explicit expression, which increases his awareness of what he has to say and how he says it. The questionee is less likely to be confused by the innuendoes of the false question, can respond more directly to a statement, and does not have to figure out what the questioner is trying to say.

There is a group exercise that emphasizes how every question has a declarative sentence at its base. The exercise consists simply of having group members ask questions and then having other group members make the question into a statement. This exercise can be extended by having group members try to think up some questions which cannot be changed to statements. The group may be surprised to find out that there are none and that language and interpersonal communication could survive quite well without questions.

Summary

The words a person chooses to express himself are a reflection of his personality, his self-awareness, and the extent to which he assumes responsibility for himself. Assuming that changing certain behaviors can enhance self-awareness and increase responsibility suggests that experimenting with language changes can be growth producing.

One way that Gestalt therapy interventions can be used to enhance self-awareness is by changing statements which employ impersonal referent pronouns (that is, "it," "you," and "we") to statements with a self-referent such as "I."

There are also numerous verbs which are often used interchangeably such that the shades of difference between them are lost. In this chapter the author suggests that verb changes such as "can't" to "won't" may enhance awareness, purposefulness, and responsibility. Another method is to ask the counselee to experiment with changing selected verbs from the passive to the active voice.

Two changes in sentence structures may be used as language awareness approaches. One of these consists of changing "but" sentences to "and" sentences so that the counselee can become aware of both components and their relationship to each other. Second, the counselor might ask the counselee to change questions to statements. In this way the counselee can find that the answers being sought are often present in the statements cloaked in question form.

Three other language approaches may be employed. One is that the counselor avoid the pitfalls of asking "why" questions, and instead pose questions which center around "how" and "what." Second the counselor can facilitate the counselee's awareness simply by asking the counselees to listen to what they are saying. Third, the counselor can ask the counselee to omit using qualifiers to minimize risks and commitments.

Personalizing statements to self-references, changing verbs to make responsibility explicit, and changing "but" sentences and questions can contribute to the growth of individual group members. They also add significantly to more authentic and direct interpersonal contact among group members.

REFERENCES

Perls, F. S., Hefferline, R. F., and Goodman, P., *Gestalt Therapy: Excitement and Growth in the Human Personality.* New York: Dell Publishing Company, 1951.

6

Nonverbal Awareness

A person's observable behaviors can be classified as either verbal or nonverbal. Verbal behaviors are what the person says or the content of his language, as discussed in Chapter 5. Body posture, voice inflections, facial expressions, and gestures are examples of nonverbal behaviors. At any given moment a person may be exhibiting both verbal and nonverbal behaviors.

The importance of enhancing awareness of nonverbal behaviors is based on theoretical principles basic to Gestalt therapy. First, every behavior emitted is an expression of the person at the moment. In fact, regardless of what a person is doing, it is impossible for him not to be expressing himself. Thus, minute gestures and extensive locutions are similar in that they are means of expression. On this subject Perls (1973) has written:

> But consider for a moment this fact: Everything the patient does, obvious or concealed, is an expression of the self. His leaning forward and pushing back, his abortive kicks, his fidgets, his subtleties of enunciation, his split-second hesitations between words, his handwriting, his use of metaphor and language, his use of "it" as opposed to his use of "you" and "I", all are on the surface, all are obvious, and all are meaningful. (p. 75)

Second, in most cases a person is less likely to be aware of his nonverbal behavior than of his verbal behavior. Most words usually follow thoughts in the form of interval verbalizations. Words, then, are thought, spoken, and heard by the person. Further, there is a heavy emphasis placed on expressing and communicating through words. Thus, a person seems more attuned to listening to what he is saying than he is to noticing what he is doing with the rest of his body.

Third, nonverbal behaviors are generally more spontaneous than verbal behaviors. Words can be selected and monitored prior to being emitted. It is quite easy to falsify words to fit what "should" be said, to avoid what is actually being experienced, or to achieve some expedient end. Nonverbal behaviors, on the other hand, are not as easily subject to control. In many cases they are expressions which are due to "leakage." That is, they are often expressions of aspects of the person's current experience which find no direct outlet and thereby work themselves into nonverbal behaviors. Because these expressions often take place in spite of the person's attempts to control them or without his awareness of them, they are likely to be more valid indications of the present experience than what is being said.

Fourth, the person who is functioning in an integrated fashion will have verbal and nonverbal expressions which match. For example, an angry person who is registering a verbal objection which is accompanied by a jutting jaw, a clenched fist, a rather loud voice, and a flushed face is expressing himself with integrated or matched verbal and nonverbal behaviors. Conversely, consider the person who is stating that he is happy about something and does so with a flat voice, a slouched body posture, tight lips, and eyes that are fixed on an object across the room. The verbal and nonverbal expressions do not match, as the words are saying one thing and the overt behavior is saying another. This person's expressions clearly are not integrated.

Finally, exploring nonverbal behavior can be a valuable means for the counselee to enhance his overall awareness of himself and to make new discoveries about how he lives. Researchers have indicated that as much as two-thirds of interpersonal communication is relayed nonverbally. As such, one way to enhance interpersonal communication is to increase awareness and sensitivity to nonverbal messages. There are also powerful and significant nonverbal messages that are intrapersonal. Intrapersonal communication consists of the continuous messages that the person is both sending and receiving. Many of these messages are verbal in thought or in actually "talking to oneself." Enhancing awareness of the existence and meaning of these nonverbal messages can be a valuable tool for growth and self-understanding.

Nonverbal Behavior in Counseling

There are four basic ways that a counselor can respond to the non-verbal behavior of a counselee. One way is to indicate how the counselee's nonverbal behavior is congruent with and validating what is being said. A counselee who is stating that he feels pleased and who experiences his smile and excitement may be attaining a greater awareness of his pleasure. He will also be able to experience a match between his verbal and nonverbal behavior which can help him to understand the connection between the two modes of expression. Until he experiences such a match he will have no basis for understanding the meaning of a discrepancy between his words and his nonverbal behavior. Consequently, responding to a match is an appropriate way to introduce a counselee to the significance of nonverbal behavior.

The counselor may then proceed to respond to discrepancies between the counselee's verbal and nonverbal behavior. In this way the counselor is confronting the counselee with two dimensions of his behavior which seem to be in contradiction. The self-exploration which usually follows such confrontations can be of value to the counselee. Through exploring the discrepancy he may become aware of how he splits himself into verbal and nonverbal dimensions which may or may not be integrated. He may realize how he confuses himself by trying to say and believe words which are counter to the rest of his experience. He might upon working with the discrepancy make some discoveries or experience some messages that he had not been letting through. Finally, he may come to realize that being aware of and trusting his nonverbal behaviors can be a powerful means of knowing himself.

Sometimes the counselor will respond to nonverbal behaviors which are exhibited when the counselee is not speaking. Sullenness, boredom, fear, and withdrawal are quite often expressed nonverbally. Through responding to nonverbal behavior the counselor will communicate to the counselee that when he is not speaking he is doing "something" rather than "nothing," which is often the word to describe a person's behavior during silence. This opens up a vast array of obvious here-and-now behaviors to which the counselor can respond by feeding back to the counselee what he observes, his own awareness, and perhaps some hunches. The counselee will be given the opportunity of being received and understood on the basis of behaviors not usually responded to openly. Through this the counselee's awareness of his present behavior can be augmented.

Often a counselee will reach a point where he cannot find the words to express what he is experiencing. In such instances the counselee might be able to express his experience nonverbally. Encouragment to follow through on some present gestures or other nonverbal behaviors and carry them to their conclusion may help the counselee to become more aware of the experience. Also, the counselor or the counselee may devise a non-verbal experiment to enhance his awareness of feelings which are only vaguely accessible. Connecting words with experiences attained through nonverbal expression may or may not need further exploration through verbalizing.

In working with nonverbal expressions there are several considerations the counselor should keep in mind. One of these is the difference among different persons and situations in the meaning of nonverbal behaviors. For example, two persons might behave in precisely the same way and be expressing completely different feelings. Two people may get up and leave a movie during the same scene. One may be disgusted by the movie, the other may have to go to the bathroom. Conversely, two persons may both feel very happy and one of them will become physically active and the other more still. Furthermore, a single person may perform a single behavior in two contexts and the behavior could have a different meaning in each place. He may, for example, stamp his feet in frustration over flunking a test or in excitement over winning a lottery. Tears can come during sadness and happiness.

The implications of these differences for working with nonverbal cues in counseling are clear. Care should be taken in imputing meaning to nonverbal behaviors. Generalizations are tempting, as there are certain patterns of meanings in nonverbal behaviors. However, these are risky and are best offered as hunches, since incorrect interpretations can lead a counselee away from the flow of his experience. If, however, the counselor facilitates the counselee's own awareness of the meaning of the nonverbal behavior, the chances for interpretive errors are curtailed. Furthermore, the counselee is permitted to make the discovery personally rather than have it offered.

A second noteworthy consideration is the changes in a counselee's nonverbal behavior. Very often the data for changes in counselees are verbal self-reports on behaviors. The counselor, however, who is aware of the counselee's nonverbal behavior patterns will note and explore differences in them as they occur. For example, a counselee who normally becomes quite fidgety and restless during the counseling session may show behavioral changes by becoming less fidgety and less restless. Another counselee may develop a particular posture each time a topic comes up. Nonverbal behaviors, then, can change, disappear, and begin patterns, all of which can be fruitful input into the counseling session.

The counselor should also be aware that responding to nonverbal expression can be somewhat disturbing to the counselee if the rationale behind the responses is not understood. Some preliminary work on what nonverbal expressions are can usually alleviate this difficulty. One way to approach this is by indicating some gestures the counselee uses and how these gestures and facial expressions add to what is being said.

A fourth and related consideration in responding to nonverbal behaviors is that the counselor can distract or interrupt the counselee. Such distractions can be productive or unproductive. They can be productive when the counselor's responses serve momentarily to upend the counselee's expectancies. For example, a counselee may be settling into relating his "case" the way that he has to numerous other persons. A response to nonverbal expressions can break the flow of this routine and bring him into contact with the present behavior. (In this way the counselee may be confronted with new ideas of awareness which can then be explored.) The idea is communicated to the counselee that this counselor will be trying to understand him totally rather than just attending to words.

On the other hand, some responses to nonverbal behaviors are interruptions which take the counselee away from his current flow of feelings or ideation. A counselee may be relating an experience and have a tone of voice and gestures which are congruent. Picking out a single nonverbal behavior that appears out of phase with other expressions can result in the counselee's unwillingness or inability to get back into the material being dealt with before the interruption. Sometimes, however, that single behavior which is the discrepancy can be used to open new areas of awareness. Unfortunately, whether the nonverbal response was germane or incidental to the total constellation of the counselee's behaviors will be known only after the fact. Experience, knowledge of the counselee, and intuition are all factors which figure significantly in the decision to respond to a nonverbal behavior.

There are times when the counselor may respond to combinations of nonverbal behaviors. For example, a counselee who is poised as though ready for a fight will demonstrate an array of behaviors which when taken collectively are a more valid cue of "fight" than clenched fists, red skin, or clamped teeth taken individually. In general, then, the counselor can be more sure of the importance of the nonverbal message when it comes through several behaviors in concert.

Body Language

This section focuses on the numerous gestures, movements, and other physical reactions which are the vocabulary of body language. The high degree of relationship between body language and emotions is throuoghly consistent with the philosophical tenets of Gestalt therapy, which assume that a person is a unified system of thoughts, emotions, and body. Thorough documentation from scientific sources is available. However, none is more graphic and illustrative than the presentation by Schutz (1967) in his book *Joy: Expanding Human Awareness* (pp. 25–26):*

> Implicit general recognition of the close connection between the emotional and the physical is evident in the verbal idioms that have developed in social interaction. Feelings and behavior are expressed in terms of all parts of the body, of body-movement, and of bodily functions. Following is a partial list of some of the terms in common usage that describe behavior and feelings in bodily terms:

lost your head	butterflies in the stomach
heads up	can't stomach it
sorehead	yellow belly
save face	bleeding heart
two-faced	broken-hearted
face up	heart in your throat
chin up	heartless
get in your hair	lily-livered
hair-raising	vent your spleen
grit your teeth	stiff upper lip
skin of your teeth	bare your teeth
give your eyeteeth	sink your teeth into
pain in the neck	eyebrow lifting
shoulder a burden	sweat of your brow
get it off your chest	catch your eye
lot of gall	starry-eyed
no guts	big mouth
get off my back	cheeky
no backbone	turn the other cheek
my aching back	shoulder to the wheel
spine-tingling	give him a hand
twist your arm	back of your head
open arms	get out of hand
put the finger on	knuckle down
tight-fisted	knuckle under
palm off	elbow your way
nose out of joint	get a leg up
nosey	watery knees
hard-nosed	stand on your own feet
bend your ear	put your toe in water
ear to the ground	tight ass

no balls	kiss off
you have your nerve	keep in touch
gets under the skin	shrug it off
thin-skinned	get a kick out of it
blood-curdling	got a kick coming
pissed off	itching to do it
choke up	sucker (pp. 25–26)

What follows are numerous examples of how the counselor can respond to various nonverbal cues to enliven the counselee's awareness of his current feeling. The examples demonstrate variations on the interplay between verbal and nonverbal behavior. It should be noted that the different styles of responding can be used with other nonverbal behaviors.

Self-experiments on nonverbal behaviors precede the counseling application examples, and the language of them may need some clarification. The experiments are written in the form of "You smile," "You blush," and "You grit teeth." This is done purposefully so that you can relate your own experience to the nonverbal behaviors. You can get the most out of them by actively doing the nonverbal behaviors which are available to you at the moment. On the other hand, you may not be blushing now but can remember when you last did and what you felt at the time. As you work with each experiment, pay close attention to the feelings and associations you have while you are experiencing them. You might find repeating and exaggerating the behaviors helpful to experiencing them more fully. For behaviors not at your immediate command try summoning up a recent experience and examining your feelings while exhibiting it.

Head

In comparison with other parts of the body the head has less movements available to serve as nonverbal expressions. This is not to say that those movements are any more or less expressive. Gestures of the head and how it is carried or positioned in relation to the rest of the body can be significant cues to the person's inner experience.

Self-Experiment

You raise your head into an erect position quite suddenly. . . . You nod up and down. . . . You point to someone or something with your head. . . . You hold your head erect and motionless. . . . You cock your head to one side. . . . You let your head hang with your chin on your chest. . . . You move your head in rhythm with some music. . . . You position your head so that your chin is pointing slightly upward. . . . You wag your head back and forth. . . . You turn your head rapidly in a certain direction. . . . You let your head hang backwards. . . . You are bowing your head to someone. . . .

Counseling Applications

Ce: (*Comes in and sits down in silence*)
Cr: Hello, Jim. How are you?
Ce: O.K. I guess. (*Sits with chin on chest*)
Cr: When I see you sitting there with your head hanging like that I imagine that you're not really O.K.
Ce: I'm not.
Cr: What's happening?
Ce: Failing English again.

When a counselee's head is hanging with his chin touching his chest, the chances are fairly good that he is not feeling "O.K." The counselor was fairly sure in this case that all was not well. In this way the counselor communicated enough understanding of the counselee for him to reveal what was troubling him.

Ce: So the results of this test indicate that engineering is a field that might be good for me.
Cr: Among other things, yes.
Ce: Hmm. (*Nods head in "no" gesture*)
Cr: You're nodding "no." Could you continue to do this a little more?
Ce: (*Does so*)
Cr: What feeling comes with this?
Ce: Disbelief. Surprise. I've always sort of been interested in engineering and building but I was always told it was only for boys!
Cr: And now you know differently.
Ce: Do I ever!

Had this counselor assumed that the "no" nod always meant something negative, the counselor might have misinterpreted this counselee. By letting her experience are gesture and then by telling the counselor what feeling went with the gesture she was not thrown off the track by having to explain an erroneous counselor remark.

Mouth and Jaw

If a large number of persons are asked which part of the body is the most expressive, one of the most frequently mentioned parts will be the mouth. Clowns, actors, ballet dancers, and other performers who wish to communicate nonverbally with audiences carefully apply cosmetics so that expressions of the mouth are accentuated.

The nonverbal behavior of the mouth and the jaw are of evolutionary significance. Teeth and their driving force, the jaw, were once primary instruments of self-protection and aggression. In his earlier writings Perls maintained that biting and chewing are crucial ingredients in personality development, especially as related to assertion. Thus, it is no surprise that many nonverbal mouth and jaw behaviors are associated with feelings of hostility, anger, and frustration, to mention a few.

Conversely, the mouth and jaw can express pleasurable feelings. The infant experiences and explores the world with the mouth. Fondness and caring are often related through kissing. The smile is usually associated with a positive feeling. Even persons who have been blind from birth will smile when experiencing pleasurable or satisfying things.

Self-Experiment

You lick your lips. . . . You smile slightly. . . . You grit your teeth. . . .Your mouth is dry. . . . Your mouth drops open suddenly. . . . You bite your lips. . . . You snarl. . . . You jut your jaw forward. . . . You grin broadly. . . . You clamp your jaw shut. . . . You spit. . . . You are kissing. . . . You stick out your tongue. . . . You move your tongue rapidly. . . . Your lower lip is quivering. . . . Your lips are drawn tight. . . .

Counseling Applications

Ce: This Friday night there is a dance that should be a lot of fun. Everyone will be going.

Cr: Sounds like you're looking forward to it.

Ce: I am. There's one problem, though. I've heard that my ex-boyfriend can't get a date.

Cr: Oh?

Ce: He's asked a lot of girls and they either already have dates or they don't want to go with him. I feel kind of bad about that.

Cr: I hear what you are saying and at the same time I see you clamping your jaw. Is there something else about this?

Ce: Well, sort of.

Cr: What do you mean?

Ce: He broke up with me for no reason at all. I told him if he did that I would make sure no girls would want to go out with him. It seems that my plan is working.

This girl was feigning concern for her former boyfriend. Actually she had plotted to sabotage him socially. By noting her jaw, which reflected determination to succeed with her scheme, the counselor opened the way for her to explore her feelings of hurt and resentment toward the boy.

Cr: I went to the doctor the other day. He had to run a bunch of tests on my kidneys because I've had a lot of trouble with them.

Cr: Sounds as though you are concerned about the tests.

Ce: Um hm.

Cr·   When you think about them your lip begins to quiver a little. My hunch is that you are upset.

Ce: (*Begins to cry*) I'm scared. I keep hearing about all of those people on kidney machines and getting kidney transplants. I don't know what's going to happen to me.

By noting nonverbal behavior the counselor was able to communicate awareness of how upset the counselee appeared. This can often serve as permission or license for the counselee to emote and reveal feelings which may have been held in abeyance.

Voice

Few people will deny that "how" something is said can be as significant as "what" is said. This can be demonstrated by taking a single sentence and repeating it, with variations on which word is emphasized and modulating pitch. For example, "Which way is the bathroom?" can be communicated as an inquiry, a plea, or a demand, depending on how it is said.

Nowhere are the nonverbal aspects of the voice more poignantly evident than in acting. When preparing for a play an actor will rehearse key lines several times to make sure that the pacing and inflections carry the full message of the line. It is the ability to breathe life and meaning into spoken words that separates actors who can "reach" audiences from technicians who are good at memorizing lines. The actor and the director both know that on the other side of the lights are sensitive receptors which resonate with nonverbal messages even though they may not always be fully aware of them.

While the nonverbal dimensions of the voice and speaking may be noticeable to others, the person expressing them may not be as aware of them. A person is more likely to be aware of what is being said than how it is being said. By learning to listen to the nonverbal aspects of the voice the person can develop a "third ear" for self-understanding.

Self-Experiment

You speak rapidly. . . . Your speech is fluent. . . . You speak in a high pitch. . . . Your voice is free and unrestrained. . . . You speak loudly. . . . Your voice is soft. . . . You sound whiny. . . . You vary the pitch and rhythm in your voice. . . . You speak slowly. . . . Your speech is halting and tentative. . . . You sound breathy. . . . You sound harsh. . . . Your voice is monotonous. . . . You restrain and control how you sound. . . . You speak in a low tone. . . . Your voice sounds resonant and full. . . . Your voice rises or falls as you speak. . . . You talk nonstop. . . . You sound choked. . . . You whisper. . . . You emphasize certain words as you speak. . . . You are silent. . . . You are gasping. . . . You make a grunting noise. . . . You release a sigh. . . . You growl. . . . You scream. . . . You are moaning. . . . You laugh. . . . You yell. . . .

Counseling Applications

Ce: If things don't change around that house I am going to have to do something!

Cr: Do you hear your voice right now?

Ce: Yes!

Cr: What are you hearing in it?

Ce: Anger and madness.

Cr: Let yourself feel it.

Ce: I am! How can I help it?

Cr: Who are you angry at?

Ce: My brother! I'm sick and tired of his always pushing me around. It's my room, too, you know!

With this counselee the nonverbal voice cues were congruent with what he was saying. There was a match between his intentional and unintentional behavior. Thus, it was appropriate for the counselor to inquire about the source of anger. A similar approach may be used also for nonverbal cues which appear to express happiness, pleasure, or contentment. In fact, trying this intervention at times when the counselee is expressing positive feelings may serve as a base for later interventions focused on negative feelings.

Ce: I'm in French only because they made me take it. So I'm not going to study in there!

Cr: Carol, do you hear your voice?

Ce: Sure.

Cr: What are you hearing in it?

Ce: Well, nothing in particular. It's just my voice.
Cr: Try saying the "I'm not going to study in there" part.
Ce: I'm not going to study in there.
Cr: Again.
Ce: I'm not going to study French.
Cr: Once more and listen to your voice.
Ce: I'm not going to study French!
Cr: Now what do you hear in your voice.
Ce: I sound determined. As though I mean it.

A counselee who is not aware of the communicative and expressive qualities of his nonverbal voice qualities may learn to attend to himself through repeating and listening to how he speaks. The counselor can assist in this process by giving support in the repetitions and listening to how the repeated statements match up with the first expression.

Ce: I didn't get into Smith High School. They said my marks and test scores weren't high enough.
Cr: And you feel how?
Ce: Disappointed. Everything was all set for me to go there. Both my brothers did. My parents were hopeful I would too. I'm really sorry about it.
Cr: Berl, how convincing do you sound?
Ce: Not very, I guess.
Cr: What do you feel about not going to Smith?
Ce: More relieved, actually. All my friends are going to Thomas High. I'll be with them in classes and clubs and things.
Cr: Now what do you hear in your voice?
Ce: More excitement. I'm looking forward to Thomas.

This student was able to use the miscatch between his words and voice intonations to realize that Smith High was not right for him. When he tuned into his feeling about attending Thomas, his statements and voice tone were unified. The match indicates the validity of his feeling as opposed to what he had been expressing while parroting his parents' disappointment.

Eyes

There is considerable evidence that eyes are an important means of expression. Poets have long referred to eyes as "windows of the soul" and "mirrors of the inner person." Novelists portray the nature of their characters by ascribing to them eyes which are "bright," "narrow," "laughing," "beady," "sad." Everyday language is laced with comments such as "Boy, was he staring daggers at me"; "I felt like he was undressing me with his eyes." A television commercial for eye make-up states, "She has eyes that say it all."

Researchers have also studied eyes and how they are related to communication, personal characteristics, and psychological states. Dominant persons will maintain eye contact more than those who are submissive. Maintaining eye contact can be a sign of readiness for interpersonal exchange. Lowering eyes may suggest a desire to withdraw from a topic or a situation. Pupil dilation and blinking are both indicators of organismic alarm or satisfaction. Rapid eye movements are directly associated with dreaming and anxiety. Brain states of tranquility (for example, alpha waves) are more likely to be attainable when a person's eyes are shut.

Self-Experiment

You fix your eyes on a spot. . . . You keep your eyes closed tightly. . . . You wink at someone. . . . You open your eyes widely suddenly. . . . You avoid looking at some person or thing. . . . You make your eyes dart around. . . . You raise your eyebrows. . . . You blink rapidly. . . .You are aware of moisture and tears in your eyes. . . . Your eyes are burning. . . . You close your eyes and there are rapid, small movements. . . . You sneak glances at someone, quickly and furtively. . . . You squint and furrow your brow. . . . You stare off into infinity with your eyes unfocused. . . . You look at something you enjoy. . . . You keep your eyes lowered as you speak with someone. . . . You maintain eye contact with a variety of persons ranging from some you dislike to those you love. . . .

Counseling Applications

Ce: I've been feeling much more comfortable around people lately and I feel good about that.

Cr: You're not feeling as self-conscious as you were.

Ce: That's part of it. I'm not sure of what's happening, but I'm just feeling more at ease.

Cr: Are you aware of what you've been doing with your eyes as you've been talking?

Ce: I've been looking at you.

Cr: Much more than you usually do, it seems to me. What do you feel as you look?

Ce: That I like looking and it doesn't hurt you either. You know I've been looking at people a lot more lately and I don't get all jumpy like I used to.

This counselee is learning that looking at people is not the scary experience that she once imagined it to be. The counselor noted and commented on this behavioral change. This was supportive and reinforcing for the counselee and helped her to become aware of something she had been doing differently which may be a component of her feeling more comfortable around others. Through this awareness she will be able to assume responsibility for the positive changes rather than experiencing them as something that is "happening."

Ce: I was sent down here because everybody says I should be doing better in my studies.
Cr: What do you say about that?
Ce: I dunno.
Cr: You don't know.
Ce: Yeah.
Cr: You know, as I'm sitting here I'm noticing your eyes. What kind of look am I seeing in them?
Ce: Probably something bad.
Cr: Something like "go to hell" maybe?
Ce: You've got it, man.
Cr: Who's bugging you?
Ce: Who isn't? I am taking gas from so many directions it's unbelievable!
Cr: Let's see if I can believe some of them.

In this case the counselor ventured a hunch about the nonverbal message in the counselee's eyes. The hunch was based in part on other cues such as his being sullen, relatively uncommunicative, and having been "sent down here." The accuracy of the counselor's hunch helped the counselee to feel understood even though he hadn't "said" much. The chances of the counselee relating and expressing some of his concerns were greatly enhanced through the response to the eye message. Empathic understanding is not limited to only verbal communications.

Nose

On first thought the nose is often not considered as a means of expression. Consider, however, some of these common clichés: "She is very snooty"; "He is always sticking his nose into other people's affairs"; "His nose wrinkled up in disgust"; "She's always looking down her nose at me." These examples are probably familiar and indicate that the nose does serve communication purposes.

Self-Experiment

You smell a scent you enjoy. . . . Your nose is bright red. . . . your nostrils are flaring. . . . You smell something which is repugnant to you. . . . You scrunch your nose and hold it there. . . . You exhale quickly through your nose. . . . You wiggle your nose. . . . You raise one nostril.

Counseling Applications

Ce: Well, this weekend we go visit my aunt in Smitheville.
Cr: Oh?
Ce: Yeah, we go there once a month. It takes up most of Saturday. (*Exhales rapidly through nose*)
Cr: Are you aware of how you exhaled through your nose?
Ce: Yes, I am.
Cr: Try it a couple more times.
Ce: (*Draws breath and almost snorts it out*)
Cr: What do you feel as you do this?
Ce: I feel impatient and frustrated. There's no way I can get out of it. My parents always make me go. All day long driving and sitting. I'm getting so damned tired of it!
Cr: Do they know how you feel?
Ce: No. We've been going for so long that everyone just accepts it as a habit.

This counselee was accepting the monthly visit as a habit that she detested. However, she was not mobilizing on her own behalf to try to change the situation. Focusing on her exhaling may have helped her to contact enough of her frustration that she might try to free herself from the obligation.

Ce: My puppy has been very sick and I'm worried about him.
Cr: You're upset.
Ce: Yes. (*Nostrils are flaring*) But then, he's going to be O.K.
Cr: You look as though you might cry any moment.
Ce: No, I'm not. Boys are not supposed to cry.

Here is a counselee whose nonverbal behavior reflected his tears of hurt and worry. However, he has learned to restrict his expression of these feelings and tears. Further counseling may help him to learn that expressing hurt through tears is not a weakness.

Neck and Shoulders

The neck and shoulders play prominent roles in the upper body. The neck supports the head, and the shoulders, while also providing support for the neck, help to provide leverage for moving the arms. Each is significant to nonverbal expression. The neck is one of the places where body tension is most likely to be experienced. Expressions such as "He's a pain in the neck" attest to this. Such colloquialisms also suggest that shoulders can emit significant nonverbal messages about the state of the person—for example, "He looked as though he had the weight of the world on his shoulders"; "With a casual shrug of his shoulders, he dismissed the whole idea."

Self-Experiment

You shrug your shoulders. . . . You feel tightness in your neck. . . . You have your shoulders forced back. . . . Your shoulders are brought up and forward. . . . Your neck is limber such that your head feels very heavy. . . . You feel as though there is a load on your shoulders. . . .

Counseling Applications

Ce: Every time Betty calls I get a little nervous and jumpy.
Cr: You've mentioned that before. I've also seen you start rubbing your neck when you mention her. Try saying, "I feel tight when Betty's around."
Ce: It's true. I do feel tight when she's around. I never know what she's going to pull on me next.
Cr: "So I stay tight."

This counselee identified his neck as an "it" that feels tight. By a simple language change the counselor was able to help him realize that "he" feels tight. What the counselor did was to help the counselee more fully identify with the tightness rather than leaving it as something in his neck. Exploration can now proceed on how the counselee keeps himself tight when in contact with the girl.

Ce: So now I have to make a choice between two summer jobs and they both want to know by next week.
Cr: And where are you with the decision?
Ce: (*Shrugs shoulders*)
Cr: Do that again.

Ce: (*Does*)
Cr: Do it a couple more times.
Ce: (*Does*) Damn it anyhow!
Cr: What?
Ce: I have such a hell of a time making decisions. Even on something like this. What's going to happen when I have to start making big ones?

This counselee's difficulty was not in the specific decision which confronted him but rather in the frustration he feels in making decisions. Staying with the shrugging may have gotten the counselee in touch with several other unresolved decisions which represent important unfinished business for him.

Arms

The part that arms play in expressions can be most clearly noted when it is either absent or inappropriate. Picture, for example, a person walking and talking with absolutely no arm movements. There is a stiffness and robot quality to such a person. Sometimes, however, arm movements are exaggerated and out of phase with the rest of the person's expression. This is often seen in the arm gestures of public speakers who have been cued to "get more arm movements in." The results can resemble marionettes dancing to music which the puppeteer is not hearing.

Self-Experiment

You have your arms hanging limply at your sides. . . . You are hugging someone. . . . You have your arms tightly folded over your chest. . . . You are waving your arms. . . . You are pushing something away. . . . You move your arms as if you were lifting something. . . . You are leaning on an elbow. . . . You are making reaching motions. . . .

Counseling Applications

Ce: The pressure is really on for getting into college. It seems like there's nothing I can do without college.
Cr: And how do you respond to all of this pressure?
Ce: I'm not as excited about college as everyone else is, so I'm not doing much about it. (*Folds arms across chest*)
Cr: Jo Anne, could you concentrate on your arms and hold them there.
Ce: O.K.

Cr: What do you feel in them?
Ce: They're kind of tight. Sort of like I'm holding on.
Cr: Holding onto what?
Ce: To me. If I don't they'll shove me all over the place. They don't know how I can hold on!

This counselee who stated she is "not doing much" about the pressures on her was wrong. She is, in fact, doing a lot. She is resisting the pressures for fear they will push her into directions she doesn't think are right for her. As she becomes aware of how much strength and energy she is investing in her resistance she may clarify just what it is she is objecting to. She may actually be wanting to go to college and yet be resisting the pressures as a statement of individuality. Also, spending so much time and energy warding off outside pressures does not leave her with full resources for exploring appropriate alternatives.

Ce: I'm having a lot of trouble with my friends these days.
Cr: What's happening?
Ce: I don't know. They just don't like being around me anymore. (*Makes pushing motions*)
Cr: Do you see what you're doing with your arms as you say that?
Ce: I wasn't noticing.
Cr: Try it again. You were going like this. (*Counselor mirrors pushing movements*)
Ce: (*Makes motions*)
Cr: A couple of more times. (*Ce does*) Now what kind of movement is that?
Ce: I look as though I'm pushing.
Cr: Exaggerate it a little. (*Ce does*) If you were pushing somebody, who might it be?
Ce: Some of my so-called friends.
Cr: So then you're wanting them to stay away from you.
Ce: As long as they're trying to get me to do drugs I am.

This counselee is feeling as though her friends are not accepting her. There is another side to the situation though. She is not wanting to be "around" them and may have been less aware of this than her feeling that they don't want to be around her. She probably has been communicating her feelings to them at different levels. By owning up to her feeling and her reasons she may be better equipped to deal with the dilemmas that can result from this kind of peer pressure.

Hands

How the hands can be used as a means of expression is most evident when watching two deaf-mute persons communicating. Through an assortment of signs and symbols they are able to convey descriptive messages, including facts and nuances of feelings. Of course, they do not rely solely on their hands, as facial expressions and other parts of the body are included.

Most people are not deaf or mute and vary in the degree to which they express themselves with their hands. Some of them say of themselves, "Tie my hands up and I wouldn't be able to say a thing!" Others will use their hands intermittently. Still others will scarcely use their hands at all. Enhancing awareness of the present and the absence of fist clenching, pointing, wringing, holding on to someone, waving, rubbing, and other expressive behaviors in the hands can contribute to the person's overall self-awareness.

Self-Experiment

You wring your hands together. . . . You let your hands rest on your lap. . . . You clench one or both of your hands into a fist. . . . You point at something with your index finger. . . . You hold tightly to your chair. . . . You stroke one hand with the other. . . . You keep your hands in a continuous fidgeting motion. . . . You sit on your hands. . . . Your hands are trembling. . . . You hide part of your body with your hands. . . . You snap your fingers. . . . You make your hands stiff. . . . You purposefully keep your hands still for several minutes. . . . You are touching someone with your hands. . . .

Counseling Applications

Ce: Tonight is the big game against Franklin. We've been looking forward to this one all season. They beat us pretty bad last year.
Cr: So you want to get back tonight.
Ce: You bet! I just hope we'll be able to do it. I think we will.
Cr: Do you notice what you are doing with your right hand as you say that?
Ce: I've got it made into a fist and I'm pounding on the arm of the chair a little.
Cr: Squeeze it a little harder and hit the arm of the chair a couple more times.
Ce: (*Does so and smiles*) I have a lot of strength in this hand.
Cr: Strength that you'll be able to use in the game tonight?
Ce: Yeah. My strong hands are what helps me to make tackles as well as I do.

This counselee was summoning strength for an athletic event. The counselor accurately noted how he was also doing this nonverbally. Through the brief work with his hand the counselee was able to contact some of his physical strength and the confidence he has in it.

Ce: Next Friday we have the placement tests. They come around every couple of years at this time.

Cr: How do you feel about them?

Ce: They don't bother me. I really don't think that they mean that much, anyhow. I don't worry about them.

Cr: While you are saying that I'm aware that you are wringing your hands together.

Ce: (*Stops wringing*) I hadn't noticed that.

Cr: You seem a little surprised that you were doing it.

Ce: That's something I do when I'm worrying about something.

Cr: What are you worrying about now?

Ce: (*Sighs*) Those tests. If I don't do well on them, I won't get into the classes I need. I get all nervous when I take them and make all kinds of dumb mistakes which occur to me later.

This counselee's hands communicated something different from her words. Verbally she tried to discount the tests and their meaning to her. Had the counselor not noticed the discrepancy between her verbal and nonverbal behaviors, she may have continued her masquerade. This would have prohibited her from discussing her concerns and worries with the counselor and engaging in some counseling focused on her test anxieties.

Torso

The torso of the body contains organs which perform functions essential to life. Breathing, blood circulation, nerve conduction, digestion, reproduction, and excretion are but a few of these vital processes. The organs are all responsive and interrelated to the person's feelings. Breathing and heartbeats change pace with different emotional states. Stomach pains and elimination problems are often related to difficulties of a broader scope. Sexual excitement or the lack of it can be an indicator of experiences that are not totally sexual in nature. Backaches are one of the most common indications of anxiety and tension. As such, the torso can emit several kinds of nonverbal expressions.

Self-Experiment

Now attend to the feelings associated with your breathing. You are holding your breath. . . . You are taking short, panting breaths. . . . You are taking long deep breaths. . . . Your breathing is irregular. . . . You inhale quite quickly. . . . You release a breath you've been holding. . . . Your breathing is labored. . . . Your heart beats harder and faster. . . . You feel pressure in your bladder. . . . You feel sexual arousal. . . . You feel pain in your stomach. . . . You feel pressure in your intestines. . . . Your lower abdomen is jerking. . . . You feel somewhat nauseated as if you are going to throw up. . . . You feel empty in your torso. . . . You cannot feel sensations in your genitals. . . . You feel stiffness around your pelvis. . . . You feel pains in your back. . . .

Counseling Applications

Ce: I'm preparing for the exams that we have next week. I'm kind of afraid of them.

Cr: Do you feel some of that fear now?

Ce: Yes, it's been with me for a while. I get real tense as the time gets closer.

Cr: And as you talk about them you sometimes hold your breath.

Ce: I do? I wasn't aware of that. (*Exhales*)

Cr: What do you feel as you do that? Try it again and see what it is like for you.

Ce: (*Does so*) I feel a little more relaxed. I didn't know that breathing was connected to how I feel.

This counselee, by cutting off the regularity of his breathing, was increasing his anxiety about the exams. Further, he was unaware of the relationship between his breathing and his fear and anxiety. The counselor was able through working with the counselee's present behavior to help him experience how breathing affects how he feels. Additional work on this may be helpful in preparing the counselee for the exams such that his anxiety will not be damaging to his performance.

Ce: I'm trying a whole bunch of new things and I'm really enjoying them.

Cr: That's terrific. What kinds of things?

Ce: Well, for one, I've decided not to wear a bra any more. (*Has chest covered with arms*)

Cr: And look what you're doing with your arms.

Ce: What do you mean?

Cr: Just stay the way you are. See how you have your arms?

Ce: (*Laughs*) I'm covering up my breasts, aren't I?
Cr: Looks that way.
Ce: Boy, some liberated woman I am!

Here is a counselee who was trying some new things and who may not be really wanting to do some of them. Her self-consciousness was indicated by keeping her breasts from being seen. The idea may have sounded appealing and carried a symbolic importance, but her experience suggests that she might not be quite ready for this kind of freedom.

Legs and Feet

The legs and feet serve more than one function for a person. One of their main purposes is mobility. The lower part of the body can be viewed as a carriage which is responsible for getting the person around. A second important function of the legs and feet is support for the upper torso. The upper part of the body derives its contact with the ground through the legs and feet. A third function of the legs and feet is defense. Fighting is usually thought of as an endeavor of the hands. Manual arts such as karate and Kung Fu, however, demonstrate that the legs and feet can be lethal weapons.

The legs and feet are also significant in nonverbal expression. One of the reasons for this is that they are often less likely to be the subject of control. A person may carefully monitor facial expressions, hand movements, and other body gestures. The legs and feet, however, are usually subject to less scrutinizing and awareness and thereby often emit more spontaneous nonverbal expressions.

Self-Experiment

You tap the floor rapidly with your feet. . . . You keep your feet motionless. . . . You flex and reach with your toes. . . . You stamp your foot on the floor. . . . You tap your feet against each other. . . . You shuffle your feet around busily. . . . You make a kicking motion. . . . You dig your heels into the floor. . . . You keep your feet close together. . . . You sit on your feet. . . .

You cross and uncross your legs repeatedly. . . . You bang your knees together in a pattern. . . . You keep your legs in a closed position. . . . Your legs quiver and shake. . . . You tie your legs in a knot. . . . You continuously move your legs back and forth. . . . You keep your legs stiff. . . . You stretch your legs. . . .

You stand with your feet touching each other. . . . You take large, quick steps. . . . You walk very slowly. . . . You drag your heels as you walk. . . . You stand with the balance of your weight on one leg. . . .

Counseling Applications

Ce: I tried some of the things we talked about last week and they didn't work.

Cr: What did you do?

Ce: I tried adjusting my homework schedule and I still didn't get every-thing done.

Cr: Judy, look at what you are doing with your feet right now.

Ce: I've got them sort of digging into the floor.

Cr: What does it look as though you're doing?

Ce: Looks as though I'm in a tug-of-war. When I dig my heels in I can't be pulled very easily.

Cr: My guess is you are feeling as though you are in a tug-of-war.

Ce: You're right. I feel pulled a lot. I guess I do quite a bit of pulling, too.

This counselee was trying to regulate her behavior without taking into account some tug-of-war in which she is involved. Without an awareness of it she would, of course, experience difficulty in trying to change herself. By exploring the pulling forces in her life she may be able to make some discoveries that would lead to some of the creative adjustments she is seeking. The concept of the tug-of-war which grew out of her nonverbal behavior may help to begin that exploration.

Ce: There are still some unresolved problems that I have with my parents.

Cr: And you want to get into them?

Ce: Yeah. Because I think about them so much.

Cr: I'm aware of something different about you as you mention your parents.

Ce: What?

Cr: Other times when they have come up in our sessions you have started fidgeting your legs all over. You're not doing that this time.

Ce: Actually, I'm feeling a little less fidgety about them. I hadn't noticed the thing with my legs though. What does that mean?

Cr: Suggests to me that you mean what you say when you tell me you are feeling less fidgety about your parents.

Ce: I'm feeling as though I might be able to talk to them.

Some changes were taking place in this counselee's feelings about his parents. The counselor noted the nonverbal behavior that accompanied these changes. Further, the counselor was able to indicate to the counselee how the nonverbal behavior matched and validated his feelings about his parents.

Total Body

Nonverbal behaviors can vary from pupil dilation to a total body posture. Between these two poles are numerous nonverbal behaviors which involve various parts of the body individually and in combination. Counselor responses to these more encompassing segments of behavior are primarily the same as those involving specific parts of the body.

Self-Experiment

You sit with your arms and legs folded tightly. . . . You slouch in your chair. . . . You stand with your weight unevenly distributed. . . . You rock your body as though your pelvis is a hinge. . . . You sit with your legs tucked under you. . . . You sit or stand very erect as if in a military position. . . . You sit on the very edge of your chair. . . . You lean forward with your head in your hands. . . . You hold or cover part of your body with your hands. . . . You are in a constant squirming movement. . . . You shrink back. . . . You have your body bent to a side angle. . . .

Counseling Applications

Ce: Lately when I try to study I have a lot of difficulty.
Cr: What kind of difficulty?
Ce: I get all distracted and not involved in it.
Cr: Jim, are you aware of how you are sitting as you mention this?
Ce: Sort of.
Cr: Describe how you have yourself.
Ce: I'm leaning back in my chair with my legs out in front of me. I've got my head on my right hand with my right elbow on the arm of the chair. My left arm is hanging over the side of the chair.
Cr: What do you feel as you sit this way?
Ce: Sort of just plopped down here as though I don't expect to do much or have much happen. Actually, I feel a little bored.
Cr: Is this posture familiar to you?
Ce: (*Smiles*) Yes. This is often how I sit when I study.

This counselee is resisting doing something that he doesn't find interesting and doesn't want to do. His body posture is telegraphing this lack of involvement which he had been experiencing as a "difficulty."

As the postural message comes through the counselee gains some awareness of his boredom.

Ce: I don't seem to get along well with other people. I try but nothing seems to work.

Cr: That can be frustrating for you.

Ce: What is there about me?

Cr: I have a hunch about one thing that you do. Watch me. (*Counselor assumes a stiff, erect posture with very little motion*). . . . How do I look to you?

Ce: You look like a ramrod or a statue or something.

Cr: (*Stays in position*) And how do you feel about me when I'm this way?

Ce: I like it better when you're the other way. You look very unnatural this way.

Cr: O.K. Now you take a look at how you are sitting there.

Ce: I'm a lot like you were just a few moments ago. Is that the way that I look to other people?

Cr: Just be aware of your body and see for yourself.

Ce: No wonder people think I'm standoffish!

This counselee was not aware of the nonverbal messages sent by his stiffness and rigidity. The counselor used his own body to nonverbally convey the image that the counselee presents. This type of feedback can be much more effective than describing nonverbal behaviors, especially when the behavior involves so much of the body that the message might get lost in the words. It might be profitable now for the counselee to explore his stiffness and perhaps experiment with some new body behaviors.

Autonomic Responses

Autonomic responses are body functions which are involuntary. They include blood presure, pupil dilation, skin temperature, and sweating. These responses stand in contrast to reaching, talking, and other behaviors which are primarily intentional. Recently, researchers have discovered that some autonomic responses such as heartbeat, brain waves, and skin temperature can be controlled by persons who are trained in disciplines such as yoga or who have learned about their bodies through bio-feedback apparatus. For the most part, however, there are few individuals who feel in control or who are able to control autonomic body reactions. Consequently, they can serve as valuable nonverbal expressions to be explored in counseling.

Self-Experiment

You shiver and feel cold. . . . You have a tic. . . . You have goose pimples. . . . Your body jerks in a startle reflex. . . . Your hands are sweaty. . . . You feel warm. . . . You are getting pale. . . . You are blushing. . . . You are getting sleepy. . . . You feel rushes of energy in your body. . . . You feel dizzy. . . . Parts of your body are shaking.

Counseling Applications

Ce: Hi, I've come in to check which period I will have science next semester.

Cr: You've asked about that before. Unfortunately, the rosters are not set up yet.

Ce: Oh.

Cr: The science course must be pretty important to you. If I recall correctly you enter projects in the science fair, don't you?

Ce: Yeah.

Cr: How was your project rated this year?

Ce: (Blushes)

Cr: I see that you're turning all red and I'm not sure what that means.

Ce: I won the prize in my division. (More blushing)

Cr: Good for you! And now you're blushing even more.

Ce: I get embarrassed when I tell people about it.

Cr: How so?

This counselee has a difficult time sharing her accomplishments with the counselor and probably with others. The counselor's cue for this was the blushing, which indicated that the counselee was experiencing something which was not being expressed directly. With this in the open the counselee will be able to explore the feelings she has about letting other people know what she is doing.

Nonverbal Awareness
in Group Counseling

Since as much as two thirds or more of interpersonal communication is related through nonverbal behavior, the group setting can be quite valuable in learning about this aspect of interpersonal living. Not only does the group member have the opportunity to become aware of relating on the nonverbal level, there also are many occasions for increasing sensitivity to the nonverbal signals of others.

*Individual Differences
among Counselees*

Nonverbal behavior has been the subject of considerable public attention in the past several years. Articles in weekly magazines and Sunday supplements of newspapers have popularized the notion that nonverbal behaviors have expressive purposes. While these publications have been valuable in increasing the attention paid to nonverbal behavior in understanding others, they have complicated the issue by attaching specific meanings to specific behaviors. As a result, there are now numerous individuals on the cocktail circuit who are ready and willing to do a complete analysis of another through observing the person's nonverbal behavior. This oversimplification is not an idea to be promulgated in a group. Rather, it is preferable that counselees learn to appreciate that the meaning of a nonverbal behavior can vary from person to person. There are several methods that the counselor can use to enhance learning in this area.

One method consists of suggesting to the group members that each of them demonstrate the nonverbal behavior that they feel is most closely associated with a specific feeling. For example, the feeling may be disappointment. Behaviors may consist of clenching fists and striking downward, letting head hang loosely forward, frowning, slouching low in the chair, and others. Through this exercise the group members are able to see a sample of the range of nonverbal behaviors that can be used to express disappointment.

This short exercise can be reversed such that each person will show a nonverbal behavior and the other members of the group state what they believe the behavior means. The nonverbal behaviors can be anything the counselee wants to enact. One suggestion might be "What I am feeling right now." The nonverbal responses of the remaining counselees will reveal how different meanings can be imputed to the same behavior by different persons.

In addition to the appreciation of individual differences in modes of nonverbal expression and their interpretations, these exercises can serve yet another purpose. That is, they will demonstrate that there are enough commonalities in the nature and meaning of nonverbal expressions that patterns of "best guesses" do emerge. If this were not so, then the power of nonverbal communication would not be so potent and any attempts at sharpening skills in observing nonverbal behavior would be meaningless and futile. Patterns may be observed both in the nonverbal behaviors used to express a feeling and interpretations of the second set of behaviors. However, the counselor needs to be cautious that the responses of the counselees are to the tasks rather than to the previous counselee's behavior or interpretation.

Some counselees are more able to accurately assess another's feeling through observing the person's nonverbal behavior. These counselees may share how they come to their understanding. This can be a valuable learning experience for the other group members and help them to build their observational skills.

Discrepancies

One of the principal aims of Gestalt approaches is to assist individuals in becoming aware of the degree to which their behavior is integrated. One aspect of this is the matches or mismatches between verbal and nonverbal behavior. In the former instance the person will be relating the same message through both verbal and nonverbal expressions. For example, a person may say, "I feel hurt" and convey this in a low, depressed voice, slouching in a chair and avoiding eye contact. In the latter case the verbal message may also be "I feel hurt," and at the same time the person is void of nonverbal expressions suggestive of hurt.

The members of the group will probably be aware of discrepancies and mismatches in their daily interpersonal relationships. Chances are, however, that they will not have been in a situation in which this type of behavior was the subject of focus. Increasing awareness in this area can be helpful to counselees in understanding the extent to which they and others communicate mixed messages.

The group can be used to enhance this understanding through experiencing both proceses. Counselees, for example, can be asked to verbally report on something and at the same time express the opposite nonverbally. Also, the counselees can make a verbal statement that is congruent with nonverbal expressions. Discussions of the nature of the matches and discrepancies can follow and amplify the meaning of the personal experience and observations of each counselee.

Feedback

One of the principal advantages to a group is the opportunity to receive feedback on behaviors which are outside of or on the fringes of awareness. This feedback can be especially meaningful when it comes from peers. After some of the work on nonverbal behavior discussed above, counselees with the assistance of the counselor in beginning phases will be able to offer feedback to each other on nonverbal expressions.

Ce₁: I just don't know what to do about this crazy situation with my brother. I'm getting fed up with it. *(Slight smile)*

Cr: Can anyone in the group show Renée how she appeared when she told us how fed up she's getting?

Ce₂: I noticed that you . . .

Cr: Rather than tell her, try to show her how she appeared. Repeat what she said and include the nonverbal behavior too.

Ce₂: "I'm getting fed up with this crazy situation with my brother." *(Slight smile)*

Cr: Renée, what do you notice about Judy's feedback?

Ce₁: The smile. I wasn't aware that I had done it. There's nothing for me to smile about.

Cr: There's no enjoyment or satisfaction in this for you?

Ce₁: Well, I am pretty good at getting him riled up. But he does it to me all the time, too!

This counselee had presented a mixed message about her feelings of being "fed up" in her relationship with her brother. The counselor had noticed it. However, since the group had done some previous work with nonverbal behavior, the counselor chose not to respond to Renée's discrepancy but rather decided to have one of the other counselees do it. The counselee mirrored the behavior rather than tell Renée about it. This follows from an assumption that the best kind of feedback on nonverbal behavior is nonverbal behavior. Renée was able to see how she had expressed herself rather than hear a report on it. This made the feedback clearer and more vital.

This approach has a double advantage. First, the feedback is received from another member of the group who is a peer, which means that it may have more impact than if it came from the counselor. In the same vein, the counselor is demonstrating that there are others in the group who can give feedback on nonverbal behavior. In fact, the group may develop to the point where members can offer each other feedback without prompting from the counselor. Finally, through actively engaging in giving such feedback the members of the group will have the opportunity to expand their observational and communicative skills in this area of interpersonal relationships.

Summary

The importance of nonverbal expression rests on several theoretical principles basic to Gestalt therapy. First, every behavior emitted is an expression of the person at the moment. Second, in most cases a person is likely to be less aware of his nonverbal behavior than of his verbal behavior. Third, nonverbal behaviors are generally more spontaneous than verbal behaviors and are thereby likely to be more valid indications of present experience than what is being said. Fourth, the person who is functioning in an integrated fashion will have verbal and nonverbal expressions which match. Finally, exploring nonverbal behavior can be a valuable means to enhance the counselee's overall awareness.

There are four basic ways that a counselor can respond to the non-verbal behavior of a counselee. One way is to indicate how the coun-selee's nonverbal behavior is congruent with and validating what is being said. The counselor may also respond to discrepancies between the coun-selee's verbal and nonverbal behavior. Third, there are times when the counselor will respond to nonverbal behaviors which are exhibited when the counselee is not speaking. Finally, the counselor may suggest the extension of or experimentation with nonverbal behaviors to clarify their message.

In working with nonverbal expressions the counselor should be aware of several considerations. One of these is the differences across persons and situations in the meaning of nonverbal behaviors. Second, changes in nonverbal behavior patterns can be used to indicate changes in the counselee. Also, the counselor should be aware that responding to a counselee's nonverbal behavior can be somewhat disturbing, especially if the rationale behind the responses is not understood. Fourth, respond-ing to the irrelevant nonverbal expressions can disrupt the counselee's experiential flow.

Gestures, movements, voice tone, and other nonverbal behaviors comprise the vocabulary of body language. The high degree of relation-ship between body language and emotions is thoroughly consistent with the tenets of Gestalt therapy, which assume that a person is a unified system of thoughts, emotions, and body. Numerous Gestalt approaches to body language can be used in counseling.

The group is a natural setting for counselees to increase awareness of how they relate nonverbally and to increase sensitivity to the non-verbal behavior of others. Appreciating individual differences in non-verbal behavior, exploring discrepancies between verbal and nonverbal behaviors, and giving and receiving feedback on nonverbal behaviors are examples of how a group can work in this area.

REFERENCES

Perls, F. S., *The Gestalt Approach & Eyewitness to Therapy*. Menlo Park, Calif.: Science and Behavior Books, 1973.
Schutz, W., *Joy: Expanding Human Awareness*. New York: Grove Press, 1967.

7

Fantasy Approaches

Fantasy is often viewed with high degrees of misunderstanding and suspicion. In a world which places a premium on computers and their ability to codify, analyze, and report on "reality," there is little tolerance for fantasy. In part this is due to the association of fantasy with delusions, hallucinations, and being "crazy." The case often goes like this: "Crazy people live in a world of fantasy. In fact, they are crazy because of all these fantasies. So as long as I keep my nose squarely in touch with reality, then there is little chance that I will go crazy."

There is a population, however, which is allowed to indulge itself in fantasy, and that is children. In fact, fantasy is encouraged among children. They are told fairy tales and encouraged to play and pretend that they are animals, parents, pirates, and other figments of their imaginations. Adults delight in the spontaneity of children engaged in fantasy. They also sometimes envy children for the freedom of which they were deprived when they started receiving messages such as, "You're getting to be a big girl now. You'd better cut out that nonsense and start getting ready for your place in the world." Slowly and surely, pretending and fantasy are pushed into the background in favor of the alphabet, cognitively oriented schooling, preparing for a career, marriage, parenthood, and numerous responsibilities in which fantasy is considered more of a distractor than a contributor.

These restrictions are unfortunate because fantasy can be one of the richest experiences available to a human being. There are several ways that fantasy can constructively serve a person. One of these has to do with a temporary reprieve from reality. There are in life many experiences which are boring, wearisome, or frightening. Play, enjoyment, and positive fantasies can be helpful antidotes to such experiences. This is not to say that fantasy is to be relied upon as an escape valve for all that is unpleasant. It does indicate that fantasy can be a salve which when used judiciously can offer momentary relief so that resources can be contacted to deal with the experiences which precipitated the fantasy.

Events which are not readily available to a person can be vicariously experienced through fantasy. To scale a majestic peak, to live in a ghetto, to be of the opposite sex, to be an athletic hero, or to discover a vein of gold in the Wild West are experiences not available to all persons. However, through fantasy it is possible vicariously to contact some of these experiences, and the result can be an expanded understanding of the events and the people involved in them.

Fantasy can also be useful in adapting to the world. Through fantasy it is possible to examine past events so that learning can be derived from them. Planning and anticipating can result in a state of preparedness and confidence. Carried further, it is possible to rehearse for future activities to maximize the chances that they will occur as desired.

A person can also learn a great deal about himself through fantasy. Reveries, daydreams, and dreams have messages which sometimes reveal concerns that are not being dealt with or which are unfinished. Other times they reveal a person's avoidances and denials. In other instances fantasy offers suggestions about what a person would prefer or like to be doing in life. These messages are available through the spontaneity of fantasy.

Fantasy is highly related to creativity. Fantasies following the question "What would happen if . . ." have resulted in some of the most startling and profound inventions and discoveries in history. Conceptualizing situations outside the realm of customary thinking can offer fresh perspectives which can be very valuable for problem solving.

Finally, experiencing the process of fantasy is in its own right enjoyable and enlightening. Limits which have been experienced as real can be subjected to a new evaluation. Events which have been kept as remote possibilities can be converted into probabilities with contingencies and implications. Also, since conscious fantasy is an experience unique to man, experiencing it is a way to contact one of the essences of humanity.

How these constructive usages of fantasy can be employed in counseling is most clearly evident in the difference between "aboutism" and "enactment." When a counselee is talking about an experience, facts are being chronicled or reported. Such narrations are often devoid of the fullness of the experience because the counselee is in one sense somewhat removed from it. These reports usually do not include the constructive usages of fantasy. In contrast, enactment is the process of bringing life into an event by experiencing it in fantasy. In the security of the counseling relationship the counselee can invest in fantasies and by enacting them bring life and spontaneity into the focus of the counseling at that moment. The greater involvement that comes through enacting as opposed to talking about will enhance the person's sense of awareness and allow discoveries. Gestalt approaches involving fantasy have this process as their goal.

Identification and Projection

When identifying with something a person is associating closely with it and claiming many of its characteristics. A clear example of this occurs among adolescents who identify with each other to the point of similar dress, language, values, and other behaviors. Someone who is committed to a cause such as equality for women will identify with that cause.

A good deal can be learned about a person by exploring that with which he identifies. The old adage "You can tell a person by the company he keeps" attests to this. Imagine, for example, a person you have never met. You are told that this person identifies with Abraham Lincoln. What can you now assume about the person? Then you learn that the person is young, black, female, and identifies strongly with all of these dimensions of herself. What meaning do these identifications have in your image of her?

The Gestalt approach of working with identification combines with it the use of projection. The psychological process of projection occurs when a person is actively attributing characteristics to make something that which it is not. For example, three dots placed fairly close together are seen as a triangle even though the three connecting lines are absent. The person fills the gaps and "creates" the triangle. Projection can also be used as a defense mechanism such that a person will impute to others characteristics of himself which he deems unacceptable.

Projection can also creatively be used as a means of exploration and discovery about a person by enhancing identifications. In this approach the person is asked to project himself into or to "be" whatever or whoever it is that he is concerned with at the time. By "becoming" and experiencing himself as the object of the identification the person can clarify which aspects of it he assumes as his own. This can be an important means of self-exploration and discovery. In the same vein, the person can, by "becoming" something that he dislikes, make some discoveries about parts of himself that he is less willing to recognize and accept.

There are no limits on the object of the identification. It could be a color, an animal, a plant, something to eat or drink, a piece of clothing, another person, a concept, a situation, a part of the person's body, or a part of the person's psychological make-up. In any case, through "becoming" whatever it is, the person comes closer in contact with it and through that process enhances self-awareness.

An Object

Self-Experiment

Select an object that is in the room. Study it carefully for several minutes. . . . Notice its size, shape, and other characteristics. Be aware of its function. . . . Keep in mind that your task in this experiment is to "be" the object.

Now set the object aside and assume its identity. . . . Describe yourself. . . . Tell about what you are like. . . . State what your purpose is as this object. . . . What do you like and dislike about yourself? . . . What other feelings do you have as the object? . . . What did you observe about yourself as you did this? . . .

Counseling Applications

Cr: Let's try a fantasy experiment about who you are. Pick an object that you would like to work with.
Ce: I'll take this ashtray.
Cr: O.K. Now study it closely for a few minutes and then we'll pretend you are the ashtray.
Ce: (*Counselee examines ashtray closely*)
Cr: Now, ashtray, tell me about yourself.
Ce: Well, I'm made out of glass. I'm round and sort of greenish with some black smudges on me. My sides are smooth and I have a small chip on my side.
Cr: What kinds of things do you do?
Ce: Mostly I just sit here and hold ashes, cigarette butts, and burned-out matches.
Cr: What do you like about yourself?
Ce: I'm useful. If it weren't for me this desk would be messy. I also like that I'm a prettier color than most of the things around me.
Cr: What do you dislike?

Ce: Being dirty a lot of the time and not being able to do anything about it. I have to wait for someone else to clean me.

Cr: What else do you feel about you?

Ce: I would like to be bigger. And it would be fun if some other ashtrays were around.

This example typifies what often happens with these experiments. The person begins by describing the physical characteristics of the object. However, as he moves further into the identification he begins to attribute characteristics of himself to the object. This person's ashtray felt useful and attractive, disliked being dirty and not being able to clean itself, and wished for some companionship. Another person's ashtray might feel the opposite of all of these. The differences, of course, are within the persons creating them; the actual ashtray remains the same.

Another Person

Identification can be a very helpful process in working with interpersonal relationships. It can be used in fostering understanding of people who are different. Role reversals between whites and blacks involved in racial encounters have served to help each side see the viewpoint of the other. The same principle also holds for other types of interpersonal conflicts. Discovered similarities between persons can contribute to mutual understanding, especially when the relationship has been based on imagined or assumed differences. Sometimes the opposite is true, as in cases where "becoming" the other reveals differences which need to be taken into account where only similarities were apparent.

Self-Experiment

Think of a person with whom you have a conflict. Go over the situation of the conflict from your perspective. . . . Now think about the other person and his understanding of the conflict. . . . Now imagine yourself as the other person. Try to experience yourself being the other person as fully as you can. As this person, what do you feel about the conflict? . . . What is your perspective on the other person? What are your arguments and ideas about how the conflict can be resolved? . . .

Now, as yourself, compare and contrast your experience of thinking about the other person and being the other person. . . . What differences in perspective do you notice between the two methods? . . .

Counseling Applications

Ce: My brother Bob and I are still in constant hassles as to who gets to use the car on weekends. He is being so bullheaded!

Cr: George, suppose you imagine yourself being Bob and let's hear what he has to say about using the car. As Bob, how does your side go?

Ce: George is always trying to gyp me out of my turn for the car. Every time I get something planned he steps in and wrecks the whole thing.

Cr: How does he do this?

Ce: I don't know. He always gets his way though. Just because he goes out with girls!

Cr: And what do you do?

Ce: Well, I'm not going out with girls yet but the things I do are just as important to me.

Cr: How does this sound to you, George?

Ce: (*Smiles*) I can remember how I used to look forward to going out with the guys when I first started driving.

Cr: Yeah?

Ce: But Bob was only 14 then and there was no competition for the car. I guess I've been spoiled these last couple of years by getting it whenever I wanted it.

George had lost touch with previous developmental experience and its importance to him at the time. From his current perspective going out with the guys is child's play compared with dating girls. Apparently he had also done a job of convincing his parents. The experiment helped George to appreciate Bob's situation and perhaps opened the door for a little more sharing.

Parts of Self

According to Gestalt theory the natural state of growth for a person is toward integration, which is a state in which all parts of the person function interrelatedly. There are no parts of the person alienated when integration is achieved. Such divisions, however, are common. Sometimes a person will no longer wish to identify with a part of himself and try to disown it. This is counter to the forces of integration. Until such time as the part is owned and accepted the division will be maintained and the person will not be fully functioning. Identifying with the part and "being" it can be a first step in this process.

Self-Experiment

What personal characteristic is there about you that you know is there but which you express infrequently? See if you can let yourself feel some of that part of you. Don't push yourself into it. Just try a little at first. . . . Try not to evaluate this part of you while you experience it. . . . Let whatever feelings and needs you have come into your awareness. . . . Experience them. . . . Now see if you can be this part by saying "I am _____" and filling in the blank with the part. In other words let yourself become this part of you. . . . Now express yourself as this part of you. Put life into it. . . . You might find it helpful to exaggerate yourself a little in order to enhance the identity and the expression. . . . What do you discover about this part of you as you do this?

Counseling Applications

Ce: I have to be careful all the time that I don't lose my temper because when I do all hell breaks loose.

Cr: And so what do you do with this part of you?

Ce: I keep it well in tow.

Cr: Let's try something with this. Could you try being your temper?

Ce: How would I do that?

Cr: Just imagine yourself as your temper and describe yourself.

Ce: I'm a lot of anger. I can be very explosive. If I'm touched off and come out I can do all kinds of things.

Cr: Such as?

Ce: I can yell at people and go storming around. Sometimes I throw things. People have to watch out for me.

Cr: And so you have to be kept hidden all the time.

Ce: Yes.

Cr: And how does this feel?

Ce: Not good. Sometimes I feel as though I'm bursting at the seams.

Cr: And if one of your seams did burst, what would you do?

Ce: I'd come out at my girl friend who's been giving me all kinds of crap lately.

Cr: And what would this do for you, Bob?

Ce: I'm not sure, but I'd probably feel better about myself instead of taking everything from her.

This counselee has been closing off his temper. In so doing he has made unattainable a considerable amount of strength and energy. As he got into being his temper, what emerged was that he has cut off the expression of appropriate anger at some cost to his self-esteem. He could profit from working on this unfinished business with his girl friend and learning how to differentiate the expression of appropriate anger from outbursts of temper. He may find that these occasional expressions will result in less building up and storage of anger.

Nonverbal Behaviors

In the last chapter the point was made that nonverbal behavior is often quite valuable in assisting a person to become more self-aware. The methods mentioned in that chapter can be extended through identification with parts of the body, gestures, or other personal mannerisms. Through identifying with nonverbal behavior such as a sly smile, nodding head, or erect body, a person can give it a voice and feelings, thus extending awareness of it and enhancing self-understanding.

Self-Experiment

Choose a part of your body that you are aware of using to communicate nonverbally. For example, you could select your hands. . . . Now make some nonverbal gestures with your hands that indicate your feeling state at the moment. . . . Now become your hands. Give them a voice and allow them to speak aloud. . . . Listen carefully to what they say. . . .

Counseling Applications

Cr: Sue, I'm noticing that you are shuffling your feet around a great deal today.

Ce: I guess I have been. I don't know what to make of that.

Cr: Try imagining yourself as your feet and let's hear what's going on. They might be saying something like, "Here I am shuffling around and . . ."

Ce: Here I am moving all around. First I'm here then I'm there. I don't know where I'm supposed to go next so I just keep trying all kinds of new places.

Cr: How do you feel, not knowing where to go next?

Ce: Sort of unsure. A little bit lost.

Cr: Where are you wanting to go?

Ce: That's just it. I don't know.

As Sue identified with her shuffling feet she began to become aware that there is a more general kind of shuffling going on in her life. She has uncertainties about her current sense of direction and so is "moving all around." Further counseling might assist her in recognizing how she can establish direction.

Ce: There's just not enough time in the day for me. Everything gets so crowded. It seems as though time goes so fast. (*Talking very rapidly*)

Cr: Larry, do you hear your voice?

Ce: What about it?

Cr: Let's try an experiment to help you. Suppose you try being your voice, and describe yourself.

Ce: I'm my voice?

Cr: Yeah. Now talk about yourself as Larry's voice.

Ce: I don't know what to say. I suppose I could just talk about anything. All kinds of things come to mind. I'd like to talk about all of them. (*Speaks in rapid staccato*)

Cr: So I do what?

Ce: I talk fast.

Cr: Try feeling just how fast. Exaggerate the speed. "I'm a fast voice."

Ce: I'm a very fast voice. I have to go fast to get everything said. I don't want anything to get away.

This counselee's use of rapid speech is indicative of his not wanting "anything to get away." As such he fills his schedule with more than he can do and then lives like the rabbit in Alice in Wonderland who dashes around stating "I'm late. I'm late. For a very important date. No time to say 'hello.' Goodby, I'm late. I'm late, I'm late." A continuation of this work might help the counselee to realize how he rushes.

Fantasy Situations

In Chapter 2 the point was made that a person cannot be understood outside of his environment. The environment is the context which imparts meaning to the person's behavior. Life is a series of person-in-environment situations. The projections employed in the last section can be expanded to include situations. Several variations can be used in working with them. They can be real or imagined. The person can be himself in the situation or he can project himself into a past of the situation. In both cases the possibilities for interactions are expanded with the addition of stimuli, and there are increased opportunities for new awareness.

Introductory Scene

For persons who have not done this type of fantasy work before, starting with a pleasant and familiar situation to imagine and experience is recommended. There is less fear involved. Feeling safe, the person is more likely to get into the experience and feel the worth of the method. He can be more relaxed and spontaneous when he is not feeling anxiety or threat. Starting this way also sets a base for subsequent work. In becoming more familiar with this type of "work" the person will be able to use it as a tool for further self-exploration and discovery in other situations which are not as pleasant or safe.

Self-Experiment

Think of a situation that is familiar and nonthreatening to you. . . . Now put yourself in the situation. . . . Visualize your surroundings. . . . What do you hear there? . . . Can you contact the situation with other senses? For example, if the place is a restaurant, can you smell and taste? . . . What do you feel in the situation? . . . What thoughts come to you while you are there? . . .

Counseling Applications

Ce: . . . and so I find it difficult seeing what is going on with me.
Cr: I'd like to suggest a way for us to help you become more aware of what you do so that you can understand yourself better. It involves the use of make believe, sort of like acting.
Ce: I don't get it.
Cr: Well, it goes like this. Instead of telling me about what you are doing, we set up a scene for you to act it out, as if it were happening right now. That way we both see you in action. It's as though you were writing a script for a part in a play and then acting it out.
Ce: What good does it do?
Cr: If you are actually doing the part and if you are involved in it, then we can check in to see what you are feeling at various times during the action.
Ce: Why do that instead of just talking about what I've done and what I feel?
Cr: Well, one of the advantages is that while you are doing the experiment you might forget about the usual way that you think about what you do. You might find yourself saying and feeling some things which sound strange to you. Very often the things which come out spontaneously can lead to some new learning about yourself.

Ce: I think I'd feel funny doing that.

Cr: You probably will at first because it's something new for you. We can practice a little bit and see how it goes, O.K.?

Ce: What could we start with?

Cr: Suppose you imagine yourself doing something that you like or enjoy doing. Try to experience yourself doing it now and just sort of say out loud what you are doing.

Ce: One of the things I like best is going to baseball games.

Cr: O.K. Let's start with that. Imagine yourself at a baseball game right now and tell me what you are seeing, hearing, and smelling. What is it like for you being there?

Ce: I would say that I go to games and there are these guys who hit the ball a mile. It's great watching them.

Cr: Try relating it as if you were actually there. Let me give you an example. One of my favorite things is going to the beach. So my script is something like this: "Here I am at the beach and I love it here. I can hear the waves crashing and smell the salt water. The sun is bright and I feel the warm sand under my feet." Got the idea?

Ce: Yeah. I'm here at the ballpark. My friend is with me. I can hear organ music playing because the game hasn't started yet. There's this jeep I'm watching pull some chains to smooth out the infield.

Cr: What are you feeling during this?

Ce: I'm excited. I can hardly wait for the game to start.

The counselor did several important things during this interchange. First, she explained the difference between "talking about" and "doing" so that the counselee had some understanding of the method. Second, she offered support when the counselee said he would feel "funny." Third, she let the counselee choose the situation. Fourth, she did some modeling by sharing a situation of her own and relating it in the present through "I am." As a result the counselee was able to contact the scene and feel some of the anticipatory excitement he experiences in the situation. For now this is sufficient. Being able to enter into his experience in fantasy situations may be valuable in later phases of counseling.

Stump, Cabin, Stream

One advantage of fantasy situations is that there are several parts in them into which the person can project. This allows for several dimensions of the person to emerge, reflecting a broad range of needs, self-perceptions, and feelings. Dialogues among various components of the situation can make the experience even more rich in possibilities for discovery. The self-experiment example which follows was written by John O. Stevens and is contained along with others in his book *Awareness: Exploring, Experimenting and Experiencing* (1971).

Self-Experiment

Now I'd like you to imagine that you are a tree stump in the mountains. Become this tree stump. Visualize yourself and your surroundings. . . . Take some time to get the feel of being a tree stump. . . . It might help to describe yourself. What kind of a stump are you? . . . What's your shape? . . . What kind of bark and roots do you have? . . . Try to get into the experience of being this tree stump. . . . What is your existence as a tree stump? . . . What kinds of things happen to you as this stump? . . .

Fairly near this stump, there is a cabin. I'd like you now to become this cabin. . . . And again, I'd like you to get the flavor of the experience of being this cabin. . . . What are you like? . . . What are your characteristics? . . . Explore your existence as a cabin. . . . What do you have inside you, and what happens to you? . . . Take some time to get in touch with being this cabin. . . .

Near the cabin, there is a stream. I'd like you how to become this stream. As a stream, what kind of existence do you have? . . . What kind of stream are you? . . . How do you feel as a stream? . . . What kinds of experiences do you have as a stream? . . . What are your surroundings like? . . .

As this stream, I would like you to talk to the cabin. What do you say to the cabin? . . . Talk to the cabin and imagine that the cabin answers back, so that you have a dialogue, a conversation. . . . As this stream, what do you say to this cabin and what does the cabin answer back? . . . Now become the cabin again and continue the conversation. What do you have to say to the stream? . . . Continue this dialogue for awhile. . . . (You can also have dialogues between the stump and cabin, or between the stump and the stream.)

Now say goodbye to the mountains. Say goodbye to the cabin, the stream, the stump, and come back here to this room and your existence here. . . . Open your eyes when you feel like it. . . . (p. 139)

Counseling Applications

Ce: I don't like being the stump. A lot of me has been cut off. Anyhow, all of the rest of the trees are tall and pretty.

Cr: You are comparing yourself with them.

Ce: Yes. I would rather be a full tree rather than a stump.

Cr: How about the cabin?

Ce: As the cabin I enjoy myself. I'm warm inside and there's room in me for people to come and enjoy themselves. I have walls which keep the wind out and even though the wind is strong it can't get into me.

Cr: You are a durable cabin with nice things going on inside.

Ce: Uh huh. Sometimes, though, there are no people in me and I feel a little empty. I like it better when there is activity in me.

Cr: As the stream what do you experience?

Ce: I like being able to move around and make noise and carry things along. Sometimes I'm big and sometimes I'm small. I provide water for the people in the cabin.

Cr: Can you say that to the cabin?

Ce: I have water and when people are staying in you they can use some of me to drink and wash.

Cr: Any response from the cabin?

Ce: I'm glad you're there, stream. Besides your water, I like to listen to you babbling along.

Cr: Is there any dialogue with the stump?

Ce: He's a little hard to talk to sometimes because he broods a lot because he isn't tall like he used to be.

A number of different figures emerge from this fantasy. A part of the counselee is judging himself, comparing himself with others, and finding himself "short." He sees himself as durable and prefers an active inner life which seems to be related to other people. He likes freedom of movement and sharing himself as the stream. The dialogues reveal that while there is some inner harmony, the judging part of his personality is somewhat alienated. Further exploration of these identifications and projections can result in increased levels of self-awareness.

The Positive Withdrawal

Life consists of a rhythmic flow of contact and withdrawal. Staying in contact with a task, an individual, or a situation for too long can take away some of its interest and excitement, especially if the person is forcing the contact. There are times when withdrawal into fantasy is needed, although it is not always noted until the person realizes that he has been daydreaming for several minutes. He will have withdrawn without being aware of having done so.

Purposeful and positive withdrawals can be refreshing and revitalizing. In the positive withdrawal the person "goes" to a "place" where all wants and needs are satisfied. He knows what he wants and needs and creates a place where he can satisfy himself. By withdrawing, the person recharges personal strengths and allows some respite from environmental situations which are unpleasant or threatening.

A positive withdrawal is similar to and different from the process of avoidance. Both have the immediate result of shifting awareness and contact away from what is occurring at the moment. The similarities end there. Avoidance is getting away "from" with no indication of "where to." A positive withdrawal, in contrast, is both getting away from and a place to go to. It is not the same as merely escaping regardless of the alternative. Avoidance may not result in going to a place which is energizing and comforting. It does not account for returning to the present situation to be able to deal with it more effectively. The positive withdrawal does. The purpose of the positive withdrawal is to make contact with feelings of security, strength, and competence. By establishing contact with these feelings the person is more able to act effectively on the situation precipitating the withdrawal.

Self-Experiment

Make yourself comfortable and relax. Take a few deep breaths. Close your eyes. Now imagine a place where you feel safe and happy and where you have everything that you want. . . . Take yourself there. If you wish, take somebody with you. . . . Try to experience the place as fully as you can. Use all of your senses. Move around in the place. . . . If there are any things which you want to change, adjust them to your liking.

Now come back to the room and make contact with it. Look around, touch a few things, do whatever gets you back here. . . . Do you notice anything different in your present surroundings? . . . Now go back to your place. . . . This time notice whether you go back to the same place. . . . Can you find the way easily? . . . Do you notice anything different? Stay there for a while and then come back. . . . Shuttle back and forth between your present surroundings and your place so that you can learn how to get there easily. . . .

Counseling Applications

Cr: Let me introduce you to something you might use to relax some. It involves the use of fantasy. Want to give it a try?

Ce: O.K.

Cr: Close your eyes and think of a place which is very special and nice for you. Everything is just the way you like it. You have everything you want or need there. If you don't already have such a place, then make one up for yourself. Now imagine yourself in this place.

Ce: You mean as if I were actually there?

Cr: Yes. Now while you are there go around and touch things. Listen to the sounds and look at everything. What do you smell and taste?

Ce: (*Quiet and with a slight smile*)
Cr: Now stay there for a little and come back when you want. I'll know when you want. I'll know when you open your eyes.
Ce: (*Opens eyes*) That was nice.
Cr: Want to share where you went?
Ce: To my grandparents' farm. I always feel so good there. So many fun things to do. Great food. My grandparents love me. There are these big fields and I love to go in them with my friends. There's nothing there for me to worry about.
Cr: Sounds like a nice place for you, especially if you don't worry there. Now let's see if you can get back there.

In previous sessions this counselee had been working on his worrying. It was the counselor's hunch that teaching him how to withdraw from it for brief intervals would be helpful to him. In this way he could have more of the resources needed for exploring how he makes himself worry so much. The positive withdrawal revealed that the counselee is capable of letting go and not worrying. After the session the counselor suggested that the counselee "go to the farm" for a little while each day and perhaps to try it at such time as he was aware of worrying. In this way the counselee can begin to work on new behaviors at the same time that he is dealing with his established patterns.

There are, of course, numerous other day-to-day situations into which the counselee can withdraw. Some of these will involve situations in the past and others will be anticipated in the future. Sections of Chapter 8 will focus on how the counselor can approach past and future situations.

Dialogues

Fantasy dialogues have become a trademark of Gestalt therapy. They are by no means the only method that the therapist uses to enhance awareness. However, dialogues are one of the most readily identifiable methods that differentiate Gestalt therapy from other approaches.

Dialogue work extends the use of identification and projection as discussed thus far. The person is asked to identify with and to project himself into a part of himself, another person, or something in the environment and to "become" it. A dialogue is then held between the person and whatever it is that he is acting out. Since the dialogues rely heavily on fantasy, limitations on the parts of the dialogue are subject only to the imagination and willingness of the person. The examples which follow in this and the next chapter are but a limited cross section of how dialogues can be used.

Since using dialogues will probably be a unique experience for the counselee there are two orienting points to be considered. First, the object of the dialogue is to have the person enact both parts so that the interaction between them becomes real in the present. It may be, however, that an intermediate step could profitably precede enactment. The counselee might find it easier at first to "write a script" for the dialogue. The counselor's introduction might go as follows: "Now suppose these two were speaking to each other. What would they be saying? Suppose you write a script about how the dialogue would go. Have one side say something and then have the other side answer, and so on." This approach is one step short of enactment and may be more appropriate for a first experience with dialogue work.

A second point is that dialogues are usually carried out with two chairs. In moving back and forth between the two sides the person physically changes places as he enacts one side and speaks to the other. Changing places helps to clarify and differentiate the sides of the dialogue. Nonverbal cues noted on each side can add significantly to the interaction and awareness. It is possible, however, that some counselees will find moving between two chairs somewhat uncomfortable, especially the first time. This can be resolved by having the counselee enact both sides of the dialogue without changing chairs. As familiarity with the approach accrues the counselee can begin using two chairs.

Within Self

Dialogues can be especially productive for working with divisions within a person. Such divisions represent internal conflicts. For example, the person may have a decision to make. One part of the person may be pitted against another or one part of a bipolarity within the person may be being used to cover the other. The purpose of dialogues focused on divisions within a person is to enhance the awareness of each side and the interaction between them so that adjustments can be made and conflicts resolved. (Chapter 9 includes additional work with bipolarities.)

Making decisions comprises a large proportion of problems experienced by counselees: "I want to and I don't want to." Often the counselee, feeling stuck at a stalemate, will have gone over the pros and cons and will have developed a short circuit in which he reaches the point of balance between the pros and cons. Being stuck at this point of psychological neutrality renders the person inactive. If the decision is not made, confusion ensues and frustration is not far behind. Having a person engage in a dialogue between that part which is "pro" and that part which is "con" may shed some light on the balance through making explicit the arguments that implicitly have been waged time and time again.

Self-Experiment

Select a decision that you have to make, preferably one that you have been pondering. Your task is to have a dialogue between the part of you that is "pro" and the part of you that is "con." If you wish, set up two chairs opposite each other so that you can move back and forth as you enact each side. Now select one side and become it. You may begin with either side. Express yourself as this side, being aware of your feelings and nonverbal behaviors. Direct what you have to say to the other side. . . . Now switch over to the other side. Respond in terms of a rebuttal or expressing the point of view of that side. . . . Continue the dialogue. . . . What difference do you notice between yourself as each side? Are there any feelings or body reactions which suggest a favoring of one side over the other? . . . On which side do you feel more convincing and committed? . . . Do you sound different on each side?

Counseling Applications

Ce: So the problem boils down to my not being able to make up my mind whether or not I want the job.

Cr: You've been putting off the decision?

Ce: Yes. I get it all figured out in my mind that I will and then zap! I turn right around and convince myself that I don't want it. It's the same old jazz.

Cr: The song being "First you say you will and then you won't."

Ce: Yeah.

Cr: Let's try a dialogue. There are two parts to you on this. One says "Take the job"; the other says "Don't take the job." Perhaps if we let the two sides argue openly we may get a fresh perspective on the argument. Want to try it?

Ce: O.K.

Cr: Which side do you want to be first, pro or con?

Ce: Pro.

Cr: Then feel yourself as the side who is for taking the job. State your position to the other side, the one which doesn't want to take the job.

Pro: The job will be great for me. You are wrong about it. It will give me the chance to earn some money. The hours are O.K. I think I'll like the work. Some nice people are working there.

Cr: Now switch over to the other side. What does the con person have to
        say? Try to relate your point of view.
Con: That job is not right for me. It will tie me down. So what if I'm earning
        money. I won't be doing the traveling I want. Anyhow, they didn't
        say how long it will last. You know I wouldn't be happy.
Cr: Now continue the dialogue between the two parts.

As the counselee becomes engaged in the dialogue she may clarify
where her feelings lie on the pro–con continuum. This may come out in
a new perspective offered by one side or the other. Also, the counselor
may direct the counselee's awareness of differences in her behavior while
being the parts of the dialogue. For example, one side may speak louder,
more emphatically, or with more animation, suggesting a more convincing argument. In addition, the counselee may become aware of a difference in her feelings between the two sides. She may feel more afraid,
sure, anxious, or confident as she alternates. Further, the counselee may
become aware of how she carefully balances the arguments with both
reasons and affect, thus perpetuating her felt balance and guaranteeing
that she will not decide! Refusing to decide can then become the focus
of counseling.

Self–Other

Dialogues involving another person can also be usefully employed
in counseling. This type of work rests on the assumption that a large
proportion of a person's interaction with another person takes place in
fantasy. Also, responses to the other person are often based on perceptions which are tainted by projections. Fantasy dialogues with the other
can offer a fresh perspective on the relationship. They can also serve as
a situation for practicing interacting with the other or completing some
unfinished business.

The possibilities of who the other person can be are virtually
unlimited. The person can be someone from the past, the present, or the
future, and can be alive or deceased. In fact, the person can be wholly
imaginary. One of the most common self–other dialogues in counseling
is with one or both parents.

Self-Experiment

Picture one of your parents sitting before you. . . . What do you
feel as you look at your parent? . . . Now slowly begin to speak to your
parent. Say whatever comes to mind. . . . Does your parent appear to be

hearing you? . . . If not, what do you have to do to be heard? . . . Try
that and see if you can get through. . . . What do you feel about your
parent as you do this? . . . Can you relate this? . . .

Now switch over and be your parent. What do you feel about your
child? . . . What do you have to say about the remarks addressed to
you? . . . State these to your child. . . .

Now return to being yourself and continue the dialogue. . . . What
sorts of themes come up in the dialogue? . . . Are there any differences
in your perceptions of your parents? . . . Are there any differences in
your feelings about your parents? . . .

Counseling Applications

Ce: It has been a long time since I've talked with my parents about how I
      feel about things.
Cr: You sound as though you would like to do that.
Ce: I suppose that I would, but I doubt if it'll happen because they don't
      understand me anymore.
Cr: Try saying that to them. Imagine they are sitting here and tell them
      how you would like to talk with them.
Ce: I'd like to tell you how I feel about some things, but I don't think
      you'd be able to understand.
Cr: Now be your parents and respond.
P: It's been such a long time since we have been able to understand you.
      You don't tell us much about yourself anymore.
Cr: Go ahead with this dialogue.
Ce: You never ask me anything about me.
P: What good will it do? We used to ask you and you would tell us to
      leave you alone.
Ce: Yes, I did that. I feel differently now though.
Cr: Are you willing to take a chance and see if they can understand you?
Ce: I'm not sure that they want me to.
Cr: Ask them.
Ce: Do you?
P: Yes. But you'll have to try to be patient with us if we don't understand
      it all at first.

This counselee, along with scores of others, felt estranged from her
parents, who in turn felt a great deal of distance between themselves and
her. Through the fantasy dialogue with her parents she became aware
of some of her responsibility for the estrangement. She also came to the
point where she felt that her parents would like to know her better and
that she would take a risk in this direction. The dialogue could con-

tinue by having her share herself with her parents. She may then be ready to approach her parents in actuality in the same way as in the fantasy dialogue.

Self–Object

Sometimes the "other" in a dialogue will be something other than a part of oneself or another person. It could be a source of frustration, a favorite pair of shoes, a building, a piece of clothing, an accomplishment, or anything else of relevance to the person. The dynamics are the same. The dialogue is between the person and whatever the "object" happens to be.

Self-Experiment

Choose something which is of significance to you. . . . Relate to it and what meaning it has to you. . . . Now try to become whatever it is and respond. . . . Carry this dialogue on for a while. . . . Listen very carefully to what you say as you are being the other. Are you hearing anything new? anything familiar? . . . As you do this are there any differences in your attitudes toward the other part of the dialogue? . . .

Counseling Applications

Ce: Last night I spent the whole evening trying to write my English composition and just couldn't do it.

Cr: How were you stopping yourself?

Ce: I'm not sure. I do know, though, that I didn't get anything done.

Cr: Let's try an experiment with this. Imagine that it's last night and you're working on the paper. What would you say to the paper?

Ce: I don't know what to put in you. I know that you have to be good and I'm not sure that whatever I put down will be good enough.

Cr: Now what does the paper say to you?

Paper: You are the one who says I have to be good. How do you know how I'll be until you get started on me?

Cr: Continue this exchange. How do you respond to the paper?

Ce: I just don't know where to start.

Paper: Well, if you start me and don't like me you can always start me again.

Cr: As the paper you sound as though you have some suggestions for Joe.

Paper: I think I do.

Cr: Go ahead and make them and let's see what happens.

Paper: Look, right now I'm blank paper. You write in pencil and you know how to erase. Try putting down whatever comes to mind. Then if you

don't like me you can change me. I won't mind. By trying something
you might get some other ideas.

Cr: And how does this sound to Joe?

Ce: Worth giving a try, that's for sure.

This counselee had momentarily lost sight of the fact that the first
words written do not necessarily have to be those in the finished product.
As he took the role of the paper the part of him which was aware of how
he could change his work came through. This awareness may be quite
useful to him when he again attempts the paper.

Object–Object Dialogues

Sometimes dialogue work can take the form of two objects speaking
to each other. Usually the two objects will be related to each other in
some functional way. Examples might be a car and a road, canvas and
paints, rain and an umbrella. In this way the person can project two personal aspects which tend toward opposites and heighten awareness of
both sides. One such dialogue is between a puppet and a puppeteer. (A
puppeteer is not actually an object. An imaginary person can serve
equally as a screen for projections.)

Self-Experiment

Imagine yourself as a puppet. Describe yourself with strings and
all. . . . Feel yourself as a puppet by itself. . . . What can you do? What
feelings do you have? . . . Now imagine a puppeteer approaching. What
do you feel toward the puppeteer? . . . Speak to the puppeteer about your
relationship. . . .

Now switch over and be the puppeteer. . . . What do you have to
say in response to the puppet? . . . What are your feelings about the
puppet? . . .

Continue this dialogue. . . . What differences do you feel in the two
roles? . . . Which feels more familiar to you? . . . Which do you prefer?
. . . What do you discover about yourself as you compare and contrast
your experience on each side of the dialogue?

Counseling Applications

Ce: I'm not sure what makes me go. Things get done, but I'm puzzled
       about what causes them.

Cr: You sound sort of mechanical.

Ce: I feel that way sometimes. Like "who's running the show around here."

Cr: George, would you be willing to try an experiment in this area?

Ce: What is it?

Cr: In the experiment I would like you to imagine yourself as a puppet and then as a puppeteer and have a dialogue between the two parts.

Ce: O.K.

Cr: Where do you want to start? As the puppet or the puppeteer?

Ce: The puppet.

Cr: All right. Sit here and imagine yourself as a puppet. Start out by describing yourself—"I'm a puppet . . ."

Ce: I'm a puppet. I have a body with arms, legs, and a head. I am brightly painted. My hair is red. There's a smile on my lips. Strings are connected to parts of me.

Cr: Can you move around?

Ce: No. I can't move unless the puppeteer pulls my strings.

Cr: Say this to the imaginery puppeteer sitting across from you.

Ce: You have to pull my strings before I move. Otherwise, I'll just sit here not able to do anything.

Cr: Now imagine yourself as the puppeteer talking to the puppet. What does he have to say?

Ce: You can't do anything without me. You're only a puppet. Until I pull your strings you are lifeless. In fact, I can make you do anything I want.

Cr: Make him do something now.

Ce: I'm making you wave your arms all around. You can't do it for yourself, but I can make you do it.

Cr: Now try being the puppet again. What do you feel about being manipulated and controlled like this?

After the counselee has continued the dialogue for awhile he may be able to experience both sides of the bipolarity a little more clearly. This will enhance his awareness of himself as both the "moved" and the "mover" and may assist some growth in responsibility. The counselor can then interject some questions about how the counselee identifies and feels as he assumes the two roles. One counselee (as puppeteer) may come to a realization of the power he has in his affairs. Another counselee (as puppet) may have some complaints to register with the puppeteer. Perhaps another counselee may come to appreciate the part of himself which can sit still without having to "do" anything.

Fantasy Approaches
in Group Counseling

Fantasy approaches in a group can be valuable for self-awareness. In a group setting they offer the advantage of learning and exploration through activities which have an element of spontaneity and playfulness. Under these conditions there can be less threat in revealing oneself. Also, the use of fantasy approaches can dispel some of the "heaviness" that counselees often assume has to be the case in counseling.

Identification and Projection

The object-identification approach can be valuable in the beginning phases of a group for helping the counselees to get to know one another. There are a couple of ways that this exercise can be done. One way is to give each counselee the same object and have them "be" that object. After some introduction about the nature of the exercise the responses might go as follows:

Cr: I'm going to give each of you a pencil. Study it for a few minutes and then imagine that you are the pencil and tell us about yourself. (*Counselor gives an identical unsharpened pencil to each counselee. A few moments are allowed for studying it.*) O.K. Who wants to begin?

Ce_1:   I'm a pencil. I can be useful but not yet. I have to be sharpened first.

Ce_2:   I'm yellow and I have six sides. As I look around I see that there are lots of other pencils around just like me.

Ce_3 I have a soft inner part and a layer of wood around that to protect me.

Ce_4:   I have a part of me that makes marks. There is another part of me, though, that can correct mistakes made in the marks.

Ce_5:   There's not much I can do by myself. Someone has to pick me up before I can do my thing.

Ce_6:   I can go along writing for awhile and then I get dull and have to be sharpened before I can go any further.

All of these counselees were responding to the same object. Each, however, imputed some aspect of himself to the pencil. The counselees are put in touch with some important aspects of themselves and these are shared with others. At the same time, the counselees can gain some appreciation for the differences among themselves in how they responded as the pencil and how these responses are expressions of self.

There is another variation on this exercise. Instead of the counselor giving each person an identical object, the group members are to select and distribute objects in the room such that each person receives an object given him by someone else. Each counselee studies this object, "becomes" the object, and relates his "story" as the object. This variation offers some interesting follow-up discussions. For example, the counselee who gave the object may share what he would have done with it. Also, counselees may respond to each other in terms of what they expected each other would do with the object. This variation is somewhat more complex than the identical-object approach and can be used as a sequel which adds these latter interaction opportunities.

Extending identification approaches from objects to persons can also be used in the group. This type of work can go in several directions. For example, a group may be having difficulty with parents. The counselor might ask them to be their parents and have a discussion about what it is like to be a parent, how they are trying to raise their children, and other areas of difficulty. This same approach could be done with teachers, siblings, and other significant persons.

Another aspect of this approach might be to do role reversals within the group. For example, a heterosexually mixed group might be concerned with relationships with members of the other sex. Having members of the group assume the identity of the opposite sex and relate to each other from that perspective can raise significant issues for the group's consideration. A similar approach might also be done with other subdivisions within the group if they become a focal topic, such as race and religion.

Fantasy Situations

Fantasy situations can be set up so that group members can imagine themselves in circumstances which are of common concern to them. For example, there may be a group of counselees who are disruptive in the classroom. To help find out how they experience their classroom settings the counselor might introduce the following situation:

Cr: Imagine that you're in the classroom. The other students are there along with the teacher. Now what are you experiencing in the classroom?

Ce_1:   As usual, I'm bored. The stuff that we do is strictly from Dullsville. I'm getting restless.

Ce_2:   I'm watching the teacher. As soon as her back is turned I'm going to get back at Susie for that wisecrack she made at me before class.

Ce_3:   Any minute now Mrs. Smith is going to turn around and say something to me about my not doing the work or something.

Ce_4:   I'm failing this course anyhow, so what's the use of busting my ass in here.

Ce_5:   My folks were fighting all night last night. I wish I could sleep, but I'll get in trouble if I do.

Each counselee has his story which takes place in a situation. Since these students have difficulty with the classroom situation they will be able to identify with and understand each other. Setting the scene can enliven reports of their experiences to a greater degree than talking about them. It is quite likely that one or more of the counselees will be willing to expand his story through this fantasy approach.

The counselees may also enjoy creating a group fantasy. They can, for example, make up a situation with one or more characters and then take turns adding to the fantasy. This can be an enjoyable way for counselees to interact in a common purpose. Once the group has decided the general scene of the fantasy and the main character, each counselee can take turns being the character and relating what he is doing in the situation. The situation can be a purely enjoyable fantasy or it may be one which is of concern to the counselees.

The group could also be used as a social situation. For example, there may be a few counselees who have difficulty in social situations outside the group. The group may assume the identity of the situation, perhaps a party or some other social gathering, and the counselee can enter the situation and behave in his normal fashion. This allows here-and-now exploration of the person's behavior. The situation also allows for feedback from other members of the group.

Sharing positive withdrawals is also an enjoyable activity for the group. In many cases fantasies which have often been secrets are shared. They have not been secrets in the sense of something fearful or shameful, but rather secrets in the sense of something just not normally shared. Hearing about each other's "places" can bring about a feeling of relatedness and intimacy that most group members will appreciate.

Dialogues

Fantasy dialogues are primarily an intraindividual approach whose purpose is to facilitate awareness of the "how" and "what" of the counselee's behavior. They can be used for this in the group or in individual counseling. Using such dialogues in the group can be to the advantage of both the counselee doing the dialogue and the others.

The counselee doing the dialogue benefits from the group's presence. He is receiving attention in a special way as he explores himself. The presence of the group provides him with persons with whom he shares himself. He can receive feedback, support, and understanding from the other group members. Relationships between counselees can take on a new dimension when each has witnessed the other work on a concern of significance to both.

The counselees witnessing the dialogue are not passive viewers. Much can be learned about oneself through vicariously experiencing another person's dialogue. This can be especially so when the topics of the dialogues are germane to the purposes of the group. For example, some counseling groups are set up to help counselees with their decision making. Being able to view other counselees doing decision-making dialogues can serve as valuable input to a counselee who is accustomed to making decisions through one formula.

Summary

There are numerous ways that a person can constructively use fantasy. First, fantasy can provide a means to withdraw temporarily from certain situations for relief and replenishment. Second, through fantasy a person can vicariously experience events and situations unavailable in reality. Third, fantasy can also be useful in helping persons adapt to reality by reviewing past events and preparing for the future. Fourth, fantasies, dreams, and reveries can be suggestive of a person's current concerns and needs. Fifth, active fantasy is a primary determinant in creative behavior. Finally, fantasy can be enjoyable in its own right. All of these uses of fantasy have their place in counseling and allow counselees to enact certain circumstances in contrast with talking about them.

There are two fantasy processes which are frequently used as Gestalt approaches. Identification is the process through which a person takes on the characteristics of a person or object. Projection is the process through which a person attributes characteristics of himself to a person or object. New areas of awareness can be attained when a person, through identification and projection, "becomes" an object, another person, a part of himself, or a nonverbal behavior.

The power of projections and identifications in enhancing awareness can also be extended in situations. In this work the person can be himself or a part of the situation. It is also possible to have parts of the situation interact with each other. Situations can be imagined or based on the person's reality. In either case fantasy is used to allow the person to enter into the situation as if it were reality.

Dialogues are an additional approach which employ fantasy. In working with dialogues the person is asked to identify with and project himself into whatever is of personal concern at the moment and to carry out an imaginary dialogue with it. Dialogues can be held with a part of oneself, with another person, with an object or with two objects, neither of which is the person.

Fantasy approaches in group counseling offer a wide diversification of activities which promote personal awareness. Identifying with and becoming an object or another person can help counselees get to know each other and gain more understanding of persons with whom they may be in conflict. Fantasy situations can be used to explore means of coping with common environmental concerns and can add to the relationships among counselees. Intrapersonal dialogues in a group setting offer unique opportunities for direct and vicarious sharing and for receiving feedback, support, and understanding.

REFERENCES

Stevens, J. O., *Awareness: Exploring, Experimenting and Experiencing.* Moab, Utah: Real People Press, 1971.

8

The Past and the Future

In Chapter 5 the point was repeatedly made that Gestalt therapy focuses primarily on the present, the actuality of experience in the here and now. There was no denial, however, of the existence of the past and the future or the impact of these time dimensions on the present. Perls (1947) has written:

> Although I have tried to deprecate futuristic and historical thinking, I do not wish to give a wrong impression. We must not entirely neglect the future (e.g. planning) or the past (unfinished business), but we must realize the past has gone, leaving us with a number of unfinished situations and that *planning must be a guide to and not a sublimation of or a substitute for action.* (p. 97)

The focus of this chapter is Gestalt approaches to dealing with the past and the future.

The Past

The most famous name associated with the significance of the past is Freud. At the outset Freud conceived of psychotherapy as a process through which a person's past was searched as a means of gaining understanding of his current life. Once the person achieved insight into the significant determining events of his life and their causative effects on him, the theory held that he would then be relieved of his symptoms or maladjustments. While this sketch is oversimplified, it does represent the general thrust of Freud's work for several years in which the past was the focal point of the psychoanalytical school.

It was not until Freud became aware of transference that he realized there were therapeutic fruits also available in the present. He noted that some patients would begin to react toward him in ways that were typical of their behavior with significant others. However, in most instances the person who was the object of the transference was someone in the past. Thus, the dynamics of the present were then often still used as a springboard to the past. Freud used the present to explore the past in another way. He would instruct his patients to free associate in the present. Here again, though, subtle reinforcements through selective questions, comments, and interpretations encouraged free associations which were not really "free" but geared to the past.

While psychoanalysis has splintered into several schools, the place of the past remains prominent. The impact of psychoanalysis on psychotherapy and counseling has been so great that today a large proportion of practitioners spend time working with past events.

From the viewpoint of Gestalt therapy there are several problems inherent in focusing on the past. Principal among these is the complexity of causations. Too often it is assumed that "an" outcome is the result of "a" cause. There is, however, little evidence for this assumption. For example, specific toilet-training methods have not been found to have the significant impact on child development that was once attributed to them. Taken in context of a pattern or set of parental attitudes, however, toilet-training practices emerge as "a" factor in subsequent development. Thus, the hunt for the needle in the haystack is usually just that—a hunt.

Relatedly, there are times when it appears that "the" significant past event is identified. One counselee would not write essays and consequently failed or received low grades in all courses which required writing. In her first session she related how when she was young her mother used to stand over her with a yardstick and hit her hands to force her to write. When she did write something her mother would read it and tell the girl how awful it was and how stupid she was. The mother would then write papers and force the girl to copy them, sign them, and turn them in as her own. The A's received on the papers were rewarding to the mother! The girl's clear recall of this repeated event had been evident for many years and did not produce a relief to the writing block.

Focusing on the past often leads to a view of the person which is represented by the cliché "As the twig is bent, so groweth the tree."

This type of thinking is particularly significant when there is a long history of events which have been deleterious to the development of the person. The therapist or counselor who focuses on the person's past may feel that the person's abilities to change are damaged and blocked by the sheer weight of past evidence to the contrary. "If he could have changed, why hasn't he by now?" Further, the more that the past is plumbed, the more likely it is that this feeling on the part of the searcher will increase. This dynamic is often reflected in the counselor's feelings of futility by expressing statements such as, "What in the world can I do in the face of all of that?"

At the same time a similar process may be at play within the person. The counselee may become aware of all the problems and negative events in the past and use this knowledge in disadvantageous ways. One way this can be done is to use the past as a scapegoat. "I am the way I am because of all that has happened to me. There is nothing I can do about it. Therefore, no one should expect that I can be different." In this way the person puts the responsibility for his current behavior onto the past. The past is used as a shield against suggestions that he could behave in different ways if he chose. Sometimes this person will be only too happy to spend time focusing on the past because he can continue to uncover events to use in his defense and as justification for who he is.

Behavior such as just described fits into another pattern that emerges when the past is the central focus: avoidance of living and being responsible in the present. Insofar as time is spent dwelling or sifting through the past, the person is not then capable of doing much otherwise. There is little energy or time left for contacting the present in ways that creative adjustments and changes can take place. In short, focusing on past "if's" or "why's" is antithetical to a "what now?" in the present.

Finally, the past was lived once and cannot be re-experienced other than in fantasy. Usually, however, when the past is considered it is done so in the past tense. This common habit detracts significantly from discovering the meaning of the past event in terms of the person's current situation. Talking about the past in the past tense usually results in leaving the past in the past.

The counselor is fully aware that the counselee is the sum total of his experiences up to that moment of contact. The counselor is also aware that some past experiences may be having a disruptive effect on the counselee's current living and development and that a good deal of counseling will be focused on these past events. The problem the counselor will face, then, will be how to work with the counselee on the past events while avoiding the difficulties just discussed. The Gestalt approach offers several perspectives to this problem.

Presentizing the Past

The counselee's past is ending as each moment develops into the present, thus making the past impossible to relive. He can never actually relive his past. Changes in himself, situations, and other persons make this impossible. Does this mean then that Gestalt approaches, which are geared toward the immediate and the present, have no validity in counseling focused on the counselee's past? The answer to this question is "no."

"Presentizing," the process of working with the past, is definable as using fantasy to bring the past into the present. Through presentizing the counselee is asked to relate past events as if they were occurring at the moment. Instead of saying "I was" the counselee says "I am." Relevant nonverbal behaviors related to the incident are also utilized. The more ways the counselee can contact the past even through fantasizing it in the present, the more life he brings into the past event. As life is breathed into the event there arise possibilities for re-examination, discovery, expresson, changes in attitude, and the completion of unfinished business. The counselee may gain a fresh perspective on the event as it actually occurred, which may be different from the distorted memory. Such discrepancies can be quite illuminating and show the advantages of presentizing over discussing memories.

Self-Experiment

Thy the following presentizing experiment. Recall a past event of some significance to you. Go over your memories of the event. Try to recall it as clearly and as completely as possible. . . . Now imagine yourself being in the context of the event and actually experiencing it. Try to feel the physical sensations and emotions that occurred then. See if you can approximate your behavior and total experience at the moment. . . . As new elements associated with the event emerge into the present integrate them into your presentizing experiment. . . . Now compare and contrast your recalling memories of the past event with the presentizing work. . . . What difference or similarities did you notice in vividness, emotionality, completeness, and spontaneity? . . .

Counseling Applications

Ce: I guess you heard about what happened to me last week.
Cr: No, I haven't, Judy. I'd like to know.
Ce: I got beat up by three girls. I was on my way to school and they just

tore all my books away from me and started hitting me. (*Reporting story in matter-of-fact style*)

Cr: Judy, could you tell me the whole thing as if it were happening now. Like, "Here I am walking to school . . ."

Ce: I'm on my way to school, walking the way that I always do. Suddenly I see these three girls standing on the corner looking at me. I know they are tough girls.

Cr: And what do you feel as you see them?

Ce: I got a little nervous.

Cr: "I am a little nervous."

Ce: I'm nervous because they're looking at me funny. I start walking faster to get past them and then one of them says "Hey, Judy." (*Voice gets a little shaky*)

Cr: Go on.

Ce: I'm getting scared and I'm about to run and they grab me. They're hitting me and . . . (*Begins to cry*)

This counselee began relating a recent historical event of deep personal significance. By talking about the event her feelings were not connected with it. When the counselor asked her to bring the event into the present, its emotional impact became more vivid. Feelings experienced during the event were allowed into the present where they could be expressed and shared in full.

Reclaiming

Splits within a person take place at all phases of development. The result of this can be that the person leaves behind some part which was of value then, but abandoned nonetheless. Anger, playfulness, appropriate dependency, spontaneity, and creativity are but a few dimensions of a person which might get lost in the shuffle of growing up. As long as the person no longer experiences the lost part, the person will not be capable of reclaiming it. Identifying with this split part and experiencing it in the present is a first step in reclaiming.

Self-Experiment

This experiment is similar to the one in which your task was to identify with and "be" an alienated part of you. The difference is that now your task is to select a part of you which you once experienced but no longer seem to have available even though you would like to. . . . Try to recall the last time you experienced this aspect of you. . . . Bring that experience into the present. Do the behaviors and allow yourself the feelings that come along with them. . . . What is your overall experience as you do this? . . . What have you learned about the availability of this part to you? . . .

Counseling Applications

Ce: When I was younger I used to be able to play and have fun more than I do now. I envy young children for being able to be so free.
Cr: Sounds as though you've put the childlike part of you under wraps.
Ce: Quite a while ago, actually.
Cr: At about what age?
Ce: Around the time I turned 13. I was always told that teenagers were supposed to be grownups and all that.
Cr: O.K. What I would like you to do is imagine yourself as you were when you were 12.
Ce: At 12 I'm shorter and pretty chubby. I'm going into the seventh grade.
Cr: What kinds of playful things do you like to do?
Ce: I go around making up ridiculous rhymes that make no sense at all. I just babble them out and sometimes I put them into sort of songs and dance to them.
Cr: Try doing one of them now.
Ce: Wow, I don't know if I still can.
Cr: Go ahead and try one.
Ce: One of the last times I remember doing it was out on the lawn of my parents' house. I was making up songs about my sister.
Cr: Fine. Go ahead and do that one.
Ce: Now I know what you are, you are a fishcup dee dum dum dum. Catch you out and bake you up, always got you on my mind.
Cr: What do you feel as you do this?
Ce: (*Smiles*) Sort of like I did then. I like it.

The childlike part of this counselee has not been lost. Covered and relinquished to the background in the name of maturity, it has managed to survive a long hibernation. Perhaps realizing this, the counselee will permit himself to feel and experience and enjoy this part of him more than he has been. The part needed some revitalizing which presentizing can do. Now that he has made this discovery the counselee and counselor can go on to explore how the counselee currently prohibits himself from experiencing and expressing this part of him.

Differentiating the Past
and the Present

Sometimes a person will live in accordance with an experience from the past. He may have acquired certain behaviors which were important at the time, have outlived the need for them, and yet still be living as if they were necessary. Allport termed these "functionally autonomous" behaviors. An example of this is the person who after many years of frugality and poverty wins a lottery ticket and still continues to live "as if" there were no money. The behaviors have become rewarding for their own sake and are not easily abandoned or replaced. By holding onto them the person remains stuck in the past. An albatross is being carried which is deleterious to development. Counseling which differentiates the past and the present can help to remove some of these behaviors and allow development to proceed.

Self-Experiment

See if you can identify something that you do which was important and necessary to you at one time and of which you have not questioned your current need. . . . Now imagine yourself at the time the behavior was important to you. Try some "Here and now it is important that I . . ." statements. . . . Can you contact the importance of the behavior at that time? . . .

Now bring yourself into the present. Try the same "here and now" statements about the behavior in your current life. . . . Do you discover anything about the significance of the behavior now? . . . Alternate between some "there and then" and "here and now" statements to feel the differences. . . .

Now experiment with some "Here and now I don't have to . . ." statements. . . . Do you feel there's room for some changes here? . . . Are you willing to give this up? . . .

Counseling Applications

Ce: I'm having a difficult time getting along with the other kids here. They're so different from the ones I grew up with.

Cr: How so, John?

Ce: Those kids were tough. Every time I turned around I had to fight someone or avoid a fight. I was afraid a lot of the time. These kids never fight and there's no gangs here but I still feel afraid.

Cr: You haven't been able to switch gears.

Ce: That's it. I don't know how.

Cr: Let's try something. Imagine yourself in your old school. Feel yourself there and describe what's going on in you. You might start with "here I am at Oxford and . . ."

Ce: Here I am at Oxford. I have to be careful today because I've heard the Diamonds are thinking about making a move. Christ, I hope it isn't me. I'll have to watch out for them.

Cr: You had to live in anticipation there.

Ce: If you wanted to survive you did.

Cr: And here at Barson.

Ce: I don't have to be afraid here. That's why my parents moved. So I could go to school without being afraid.

Cr: Repeat what you said about "I don't have to be afraid here."

Ce: I don't have to be afraid here. I can come and go as I please.

Cr: "No one is out to hurt me."

Ce: Yeah. No one is out to get me. I'm safe here. There's no hassles in the halls and the bathrooms. I don't have to sneak home.

Cr: Do you feel this as you say it?

Ce: Some. Not as much as I would like. I guess it'll take a little while.

Cr: You've lived with those fears a long time. We can't expect them to dissolve overnight. The important thing now is to try to let this safe feeling grow.

This counselee's change in environments occurred quicker than he could psychologically absorb it. He has been living with the fears, anticipations, and preparations that were necessary in his previous environs. The counselor recognized how the counselee brought these behaviors with him and respected them. The counselor's approach was to help the counselee expand his awareness of the safety about him so that he could begin to give up his fears.

Unfinished Business

Unfinished situations continue to clamor for attention until closure is attained. In one study a group of students were given a series of progressively more difficult arithmetic problems. A few days after the tests they were asked which problems they remembered. The findings revealed that the unresolved problems were recalled more frequently and more clearly than the completed ones.

This dynamic reveals itself in the total spectrum of life situations. Most people have numerous unfinished or unresolved situations in their lives. These situations compete for attention which they cannot all receive at the same time. Thus, the unfinished situation which is most pressing will be the first to claim present attention, only to be replaced by the next most pressing, and so on.

A counselee who has amassed a vast array of unfinished situations will not have full attending power available. The counselee will be like the person who in the midst of relating a story forgets the name of one of the principles and pauses until he can remember it. However, this may be magnified several times over depending on the number of unfinished situations. A certain amount of tolerance for unfinished situations is necessary in everyday living. However, they can sometimes result in a sapping of energy, resembling a bucket pin-pricked with holes. Conversely, a counselee can become preoccupied with finishing a situation. In either case the counselee's energy is kept from being fully utilized in the present.

Self-Experiment

Try these experiments to feel the power of the unfinished situation. Sing the first four words of the national anthem and then stop abruptly. . . . Bang your finger on a table to "Shave and a hair cut, two bits," only leave off the "two bits." . . . Were you able to do these without completing them? . . .

Recall the feeling you had the last time you were engrossed in some activity and were interrupted. . . . See if you can get in touch with the feeling you have when you finally complete a task that has been hanging over your head for awhile. . . .

Now select an unfinished situation that involves another person. The event may be from the immediate or the distant past. The person may or may not be attainable in reality. . . . Imagine that the person is before you and say what you have to say to him. . . . Express yourself fully to the person. Do you feel an impulse to hug the person, to strike him, or to make some kind of physical contact? If so, you might use a pillow. . . . Feel yourself now and see if you have completed your situation. . . . If not, continue. . . . Now compare how you experience the situation with how it felt to you before doing this experiment. . . . Are there any differences in your feelings?

Counseling Applications

Ce: The other night I was at a movie and there was this guy who kept bugging me all during the show. Do this, do that! I felt like telling him to bug off.

Cr: And you didn't.

Ce: No, I didn't. I wish I had. Boy, I've thought about it so many times. If I ever see that guy . . .

Cr: Suppose he were here right now. What would you say to him?

Ce: I'd tell him a thing or two.

Cr: O.K. Just imagine that he's sitting right here and say it to him.

Ce: You've got no right ordering me around here. I've got just as much right as you do!

Cr: Is there more?

Ce: Yeah, I'm sick of your pushiness. If you don't like being around here, then take your ass and haul it someplace else!

In this situation the counselee had some unfinished business with the "guy at the movie." The lack of closure kept it alive. By working on the situation in the present she was able to bring some excitement into it. Her expression of feeling in fantasy permitted her to finish out the scene. Chances are she will not be plaguing herself with it any longer. Talking about what happened and what she would have liked to have done, and so on, would not have permitted her to put enough energy into the situation to attain the closure.

Unfinished business often is in the form of a resentment from the immediate or the distant past. There is a full range of other types of unfinished business.

Ce: All of us kids feel terrible about Mrs. Martin's leaving the school. She did so much for us and we never did let her know. Now it's not possible.

Cr: I gather that there are some things which you wish you would have said to her.

Ce: Yes. And I regret now that I never did it.

Cr: George, let's just imagine that she's sitting here with the two of us. You say what you want to say to her. Suppose she were sitting in this chair. Want to give it a try?

Ce: Yeah. I would tell her that . . .

Cr: Say what you want to say rather than saying what you would say.

Ce: Mrs. Martin, thank you for being such a marvelous English teacher. I've never said this to you, but you have been so encouraging to me that I'm thinking about being an English teacher myself.

Cr: Is there more?

Ce: Yes. You taught me how to believe in the things I think and feel and have been so great in teaching me how to express and communicate them. Somehow you've been much more than a regular teacher to me.

This counselee's unfinished business was one of gratitude and appreciation. The value and meaning of expressing them to the person involved is quite important, as is evidenced in "thank-you's" often present in eulogies and final farewells at funerals. Unexpressed appreciations can weigh as heavily on a person as unexpressed resentment.

Learning from the Past

An often quoted statement claims that those who ignore the past are condemned to repeat it. While this statement usually comes up in the context of nations, populations, and generations, its meaning is not lost on the individual. Reviewing an event which was not carried out satisfactorily can provide a basis for changes in behavior. Often the person was unaware of mistakes and feels puzzled later. "What did I do wrong?" The frustration from this not knowing can prohibit a review of the situation to discover what was done erroneously. The frustration is experienced in the present. Going back to the event as if it were occurring now momentarily leaves the current frustration and allows a clearer perspective for reviewing the event.

Self-Experiment

Identify something you did recently which did not turn out the way that you planned. . . . Put yourself in that situation as if it were occurring at this moment. Now replay the scene bit by bit. "Now I'm . . . and now I'm . . . "and so forth. . . . Focus your attention on each part of the process as you enact it. . . . Can you discover what you did that caused the difficulty? . . .

Counseling Applications

Ce: Ed is not speaking to me.
Cr: What happened, Sue?
Ce: I don't know. We were talking the other day and all of a sudden he pulled out this package for me. I opened it and all hell broke loose. He's been avoiding me ever since. I can't figure it out.
Cr: You don't know what you did that got him upset?
Ce: I didn't do anything.
Cr: Let's explore this a little. Suppose you re-create the scene just before the trouble started.
Ce: O.K. We're standing there talking about this TV show we both saw and now he's reaching in his pocket and hands me this little package.
Cr: How do you react?
Ce: What's this?

Cr: Now speak his part in the dialogue.

Ed: Just a little something I picked up for you. Go ahead and open it.

Ce: I am. There I've got it opened. Pierced earrings? What am I supposed to do with these? Then he turned around and walked away. I tried to stop him but it was no use.

Cr: Can you say the part about the earrings again. Just like you did a moment ago.

Ce: Pierced earrings? What am I supposed to do with these?

Cr: Once more and listen to yourself carefully.

Ce: Pierced earrings? What am I supposed to do with these?

Cr: What do you feel as you say this?

Ce: My ears aren't pierced. It's silly for me to have these.

Cr: Imagine Ed was here and try saying to him, "You're silly for buying these for me."

Ce: You're silly for buying these for me. . . . God, I might as well have said that. No wonder he was ticked off. He has been hinting that I would look nice with pierced ears.

This counselee was apparently not aware of the impact of her comments upon receiving the earrings and couldn't understand her boyfriend's reaction. By re-enacting the situation some cues emerged which helped her to realize her impact on him.

The Future

At the opposite pole of the time continuum lies the future. This is life yet unlived which can clamor for a great deal of attention nonetheless. Insurance policies, pension programs, and detailed planning of innumerable events are very common occurrences in our society. Particularly notable is the high premium on delayed gratification. Certain religions counsel their adherents to bear with this life in order to reap the harvest of the next one. Hedonism, the opposite dynamic, is scorned and looked upon as a sign of weakness.

The future is the world of goals, expectations, wishes, predictions, and purposes. Several psychologists such as McDougall, Tolman, and Holt devoted their work to examining these futuristic behaviors and their significance in a person's life. In general, they posited that a person was something more than a collection of causations and reflexes. Rather, they believed that a person's concepts of what he willed were related to what the person would do and become.

Alfred Adler's Individual Psychology is one of the most currently active futuristic schools of psychotherapy and counseling. Adlerians believe that the person relies on his past and current life situation and then works out logical predictions of what will come. Interacting with these predictions are expectations or prophecies which it is believed the person attempts to realize and confirm. One of the main functions of the Adlerian therapist is to assess the person's "life style" and the meaning of current behavior so that this data can then be used to rework expectations into more appropriate, constructive, and encouraging directions.

Just as there are notable problems in heavily focusing on the past, so is a focus on the future encumbered with obstacles. One of the main problems here is that the future is often predicted from past data, which can lead into a closed circuit that does not take into account changes in the person. If the prophecy is based on how the person is, then subsequent behaviors will consistantly reflect that state.

When this point is recognized there are often programs or plans set up so that the person can change to fit himself into the scheme of his futurizations. One of the most common examples of the difficulties encountered here is the New Year's resolution lists dutifully prepared in December and often dissipated by mid-January. In sum, attempts by the person to mold himself into what he feels he "should," "ought," or "would like" to be are not often successful. The ensuing frustration and disappointments then discourage attempts at further changes.

Sometimes the future will be so prominent that the person will live in a world of intentions. Perls (1947) has aptly described the course this behavior may take:

> A man, on going to bed, worries about how he will sleep; in the morning he is full of resolutions as to the work he is going to do in his office. On his arrival there he will not carry out his resolutions, but will prepare all the material he intends conveying to the analyst, although he will not bring forward this material in the analyses. When the time comes for him to use the facts he has prepared, his mind occupies itself instead with his expectation of having supper with his girlfriend, but during the meal he will tell the girl all about the work he has to attend to before going to bed, and so on and on. This example is not an exaggeration, for there are quite a number of people always a few steps or miles ahead of the present. They never collect the fruits of their efforts, as their plans never make contact with the present—with reality. (p. 95).

Thus, living with eyes focused into the future can result in not seeing what is at hand. This often occurs in daydreams, which can be employed as a means to flee from the present into "better" times. Sometimes, however, these future states are not better and the person anxiously spends considerable time worrying, catastrophizing, scheming, and rehearsing.

While the future is still fantasy, the impact that it has on the present is real. Planning, anticipating, worrying, and preparing are all present experiences that have the future as their referent point. It is undeniable that these experiences are paramount in the lives of counselees who have so much of their life ahead of them and who are engaged in making decisions with possible long-range consequences. The counselor, then, is well advised to be able to assist counselees to deal with their current concerns about the future. Gestalt approaches can be valuable in avoiding the difficulties often encountered in future-oriented counseling. These approaches also employ presentizing.

Presentizing the future has the same objective as presentizing the past. Each is an attempt to bring that which is not occurring in the present into the now through an "as if" experience. In contrast with presentizing the past, presentizing the future is focused on that which is anticipated rather than having been experienced. These anticipations can be subdivided into happenings which "will" occur and those which "might" occur.

Presentizing "When"

When a person is concerned with an event which will occur, he is fairly certain about the likelihood of its occurrence, or else he would not be concerned about it. The question then becomes, "What will I do when?" This question is one source of uncertainty about future actions that contributes to the felt need for planning and preparedness. The assumption underlying presentizing the future is that by projecting into the anticipated event as if it were occurring at the moment the person will enhance his awareness of himself in the situation. This awareness will allow more spontaneity, which will free and make available a broader range of resources which can be brought to bear on the situation.

Self-Experiment

Select an event in your life which you are fairly certain will occur, preferably one which you are not so sure about what you will do when it does occur. Now reflect on this event and your anticipated reactions in your usual fashion. . . . What do you feel as you do this? . . .

Now change the scene. Fantasize yourself in the situation as if it were occurring right at this moment. . . . You might try an "I am . . ." rather than "I will . . ." approach. . . . Feel yourself in the situation. What emotions do you experience? What thoughts do you have about alternatives you can choose? . . .

Now compare your experiences of reflection and presentizing. What similarities are there? . . . In what ways were the experiences different for you? . . . Did any new awareness come to light in presentizing that were not available in reflecting? . . .

Counseling Applications

Ce: Next year I'll be going to Jones High School. It's going to be scary.

Cr: "I'm going to be scared."

Ce: I am. It's a big school and there probably won't be many kids there that I'll know.

Cr: Let's try something. Imagine yourself at Jones. It's the first day and you're walking in. Start out by saying, "Here I am at Jones" and carry on from there.

Ce: Here I am on my first day at Jones. What a huge school. Look at all the people. I wish I would see somebody that I know. Maybe I will some time today.

Cr: Now what are you imagining all of those other kids are feeling?

Ce: I'm not sure.

Cr: Imagine yourself being one of them and let's hear what he has to say.

Ce: I've never seen so many people in one school. I wish there was someone I could talk to.

Cr: So you imagine he feels the same way you do.

Ce: Probably.

Cr: Now what can you do to meet some people?

Ce: I can just start talking to someone. Maybe ask them a few questions about the school or something.

Cr: O.K. What else can you do?

Ce: I can wait until I get to my classes. Then there will be some kids sitting by me and we'll probably say some things to each other.

Cr: And what else can you do?

Ce: I can keep looking around for some kids who live around my new neighborhood. I don't know if they're going here or not.

This counselee was scaring herself about a situation which was several months away. She had been spending more time with her fear than with some things she might do to make the situation more manageable. By bringing the event into the present, she began to realize that she would probably not be the only person feeling that way and that there were some ways to go about meeting people. Further counseling might include some practicing of the alternatives.

Presentizing "If—Then"

While some of the future is predictable within reasonable limits of probability, a great deal of it is not. Not knowing whether an event will or will not materialize has serious implications. There is the uncertainty to deal with. The unknown is necessarily ambiguous and thus can stimulate worrying, anticipating, and anxiety. Related to this uncertainty are the "if-then" propositions. If an event occurs, then this suggests one set of consequences, and if the event does not occur, then another set of consequences is suggested. Each of these sets unfolds a chain of additional "if-then" conditions that carry their own levels of uncertainty and consequences.

Often the futurizing centers around the probability of the "if." The person worries and ponders "if it's going to happen." What often occurs is the person will spend so much time with the "if" that no allowances are made for considering the "then" of the consequences. With vague consequences and alternatives another source of the unknown is introduced, contributing even more stress and discomfort. The purpose of presentizing the "if" is to bring the situation into the now so that the consequences of the event can be explored.

Self-Experiment

Find an event in your life which "if" it did occur would be a source of difficulty for you. . . . Now be aware of how you think about this event and the feelings you have when you consider it. . . . Now imagine that the event has just occurred. You have just gotten the news. What do you feel? . . . Now what are you going to do? . . . What alternatives do you have open to you now? . . . Stay with this exploration for a while. . . .

Now go back and consider that this exercise has not changed the reality that the event "might" occur. Have you experienced any change in your feelings about how you will be or what you do "if" it does? . . .

Counseling Applications

Ce: If I don't get that job as camp counselor this summer, I don't know what I'm going to do.

Cr: It sounds important to you.

Ce: It is. Jodi and Bob have applied there, too, and we could have a ball.

Cr: And if you don't get the job?

Ce: I've got to! There's nothing else for me. I wait every day to hear from them.

Cr: Just for the sake of exploration, let's imagine that you just got the

word that you haven't been hired. The letter has just come. What are
you feeling and thinking?

Ce: I'm very disappointed. The summer is going to be awful now. I've been
hoping for that job. I don't know what to do now.

Cr: You have no other alternatives?

Ce: No. I didn't apply any place else because I wanted this job so much.

Cr: Then, here you are. You applied for one job and didn't get it and
you're empty handed.

Ce: I guess maybe I should have applied to some other places.

This counselee had placed all of his eggs in one "if." Small wonder
that the likelihood of its occurrence was loaded with such importance to
him! He had done little exploration beyond the "if." By presentizing that
the job did not come through he became aware that he had spent little
time considering the "then" consequences of that event. He may now
rechannel some of the energy spent on worrying about the "if" to generating some alternatives in case the job in fact does not come through.

Predictions Based on the Past

A person will usually make predictions about what he "will" do
in a given situation by drawing upon what he "has" done in similar or
related situations. This type of predicting on the basis of experience is,
of course, a double-edged blade. The person who predicts negatively on
the basis of negative past experiences can get into a restrictive downward
cycle. Conversely, the person who predicts positively on the basis of
positive past experiences can get into an upward cycle. Each kind of
experience can germinate the expectancy of more of its own kind. The
main difficulty with this dynamic is with the person on the downward
cycle.

Unless the validity of the predictions is challenged, it can become a
principle for living. A Gestalt approach for dealing with such concerns
is to assist the person in becoming aware of how he stacks the deck
against himself.

Self-Experiment

Locate in your life something which you believe you cannot do well
because of negative experiences doing it. . . . Now select a specific example from the past and put yourself there as if it were happening now. Go
over the event carefully. What are you thinking? . . . What are you feeling? . . . What else are you aware of? . . .

Now imagine yourself in a similar situation in the future. . . . Predict how you will react, what you will do, how you will feel. . . . Now notice the correlation between your behavior in this event and that from the past. . . . At what point do you begin laying out the same sequence for yourself? . . . What do you feel as you begin it? . . . Do you have any alternatives for other predictions? . . . If so, what are they? . . .

Counseling Applications

Ce: I have a social studies test coming up and I'm certain not to do well. I always go in feeling like I know the material and then, "bang," I get so rattled that I forget things and make stupid mistakes.

Cr: Suppose you were taking the test now. Let's see what your reactions would be. Imagine yourself sitting in the room just before the test is given. What are you doing?

Ce: I'm looking around and it seems as though everyone is calm and confident. They don't get riled up the way I do.

Cr: Try to feel how you are getting yourself so riled up. Do it now.

Ce: Here I go again. Every damn time. I'm going to blow it again, I just know I am. There go my chances for a decent grade in this course. How the hell will I ever get into college? Then what will I do? If only I could do well on these exams.

Cr: Sounds like familiar turf for you. Are you aware of how you start this chain reaction?

Ce: I suppose by predicting how lousy I'll do.

This counselee raises his test-taking anxiety by catastrophizing about how poorly he will do and predicting the dire consequences which may follow. Through presentizing he was able to describe what he does to himself in the test situation. The counselee can then focus on how he does this. Working on test-taking methods, some simple slow breathing, and a new, positive prediction may help him alleviate some of the deleterious effects of this performance variable so that he can demonstrate his learning.

Differentiating the Future
and the Present

Anticipation of stressful events which are imminent can be the cause of stress in the present. For example, if a person is anticipating that he is going to lose something, the chances are that he will begin to live as though the loss were taking place currently. This results in two kinds of discomfort. First, there is the dread of the loss. Second, while living in the anticipation the person may not permit himself to enjoy and appreciate the present.

In this dynamic, what is "going to be" crowds what "is" out of awareness. The future is clouding contact with the present. A Gestalt approach which may be used in such situations would focus on staying with what "is." This is not meant to discount the advantages in pre-paredness. It does suggest that when preparing supersedes or replaces the present, the preparedness has been carried too far.

Self-Experiment

Think of some anticipated event which will result in some important changes in your life. Imagine that the event is taking place and the changes have occurred. . . . Feel yourself in this new place. . . . What are you faced with? . . . How do you feel about yourself and the adjustments you must now make? . . . What else are you aware of about this event? . . .

Now bring yourself into the present and realize that the event has not and is not occurring at this moment. . . . Try some shuttling between "Then, I will . . ." and "Now I. . . ." Can you differentiate the "then" from your "now"? . . . Does this, in any way, make your "now" different? . . .

Counseling Applications

Ce: My father got transferred in his job and we're going to have to move to a new town. I feel awful about it.

Cr: I see your tears and your lips quivering.

Ce: (*Begins to cry*) I'm going to have to leave everything behind me. All my friends. School. Everything.

Cr: And you don't want to have to do any of those.

Ce: I don't! It's hard starting all over again in a new school and a new town. I won't know anyone there. (*Crying subsides*)

Cr: When will you be moving?

Ce: Not till next year.

Cr: Then you'll be here about eight more months.

Ce: Yeah, but what an awful thing to have to be looking forward to.

Cr: When you look ahead eight months you get sad.

Ce: Yes. I'm going to lose a lot.

Cr: How about if you look around you now? What are you losing?

Ce: Nothing actually. Susie is waiting for me outside. We're on our way to practice gymnastics.

Cr: You mean you don't have to go out and say goodbye to her right now?

Ce: No. (*Smiles*) We've got a lot of time to spend together.
Cr: Hopefully you'll let yourself enjoy that time.

This counselee was experiencing her forthcoming move as if it were occurring immediately. She could conceivably live that way for the next eight months and miss out on a lot of what is going on around her. The counselor helped her to differentiate this future event and the present by asking her about what she was losing at that moment. She was able to realize that she was not losing anything at that time. She will be sad when the move occurs, but at the same time she doesn't have to let her anticipation of it distort her present enjoyment.

The Past and the Future in Group Counseling

Counseling with individuals cannot be devoid of attention to the counselee's past and future. This is no less true for group counseling.

The Past

Presentizing the past can help a counselee to contact the total experience of a past event. Presentizing enlivens through enactment, and the counselee becomes much more involved with the experience than if it were reported as history. With this greater involvement comes a higher likelihood of increased awareness and discovery.

Presentizing also has an enlivening effect on the other members of the group. They respond to the increased liveliness of presentizing. They will attend more closely and become more involved in responding to the counselee and offering feedback.

The group can also serve as a meaningful backdrop against which the past can be differentiated.

Ce: I've always found it very difficult to talk when there was more than one person around.
Cr: In the past you have found this difficult.
Ce: Yes, I would stammer around and not know what to say.
Cr: Are you aware of what you are doing right now?

Ce: Yes, I'm talking about the difficulties I've had trying to speak up when there was more than one person around.
Cr: You seem to be able to talk right now.
Ce: Yeah. So?
Cr: So, how many people are here right now?
Ce: (*Laughs*) Seven.

This counselee had been living a long while with the self-image of a person who found it difficult to speak when more than one individual was present. She was, however, relating this in the presence of six other people. Her immediate experience, then, was quite different from her past conceptions. The group will offer her further experience in speaking in social situations.

Unfinished business plays a significant role in the life of the individual and can also have considerable impact on the development of a group. Unfinished business can develop between group members and evolve into hidden agendas that thwart or render ineffective other kinds of group activities. This means that the social interactions within the group can provide a natural setting for learning to recognize and deal with unfinished business.

Handling unfinished business in the group can be facilitated if the counselor introduces the group to it early in its development. One of the ways this can be done is by allowing some time toward the end of each session to allow the counselees the opportunity to say some things they may not have been able to get in. As this becomes a part of the group's format, dealing with unfinished business will be able to be worked into the meetings at other times. For example, the counselor may be aware of some unfinished business in the group and inquire about it during the session. It may also be that unfinished business which was brought up at the end of the previous meeting and not completed could be the opening topic for a meeting. This would be particularly important when the unfinished business from the previous meeting was broached at the end of the session and tabled until there was more time to devote to it.

The Future

Presentizing the future has the same enlivening benefit in a group counseling situation as presentizing the past. That is, it then allows the counselee to experience events and situations not yet lived on an "as if now" basis. There are several ways that presentizing the future can be used in a counseling group. The counselor, for example, can suggest that counselees in a vocationally oriented group imagine themselves as a person in their chosen career.

Ce: I am planning to be a carpenter.

Cr: Roy, imagine that you are a carpenter now and tell us about you and your work.

Ce: I'm a builder. I can go somewhere where there are no buildings and help put them up.

Cr: What do you feel doing this?

Ce: I feel good. This is what I do best. I enjoy working with my hands. There's a lot of satisfaction for me when I stand back, point to something, and say, "I built that."

Cr: What else do you like about your work?

Ce: I start early every morning, which is good for me because I'm a morning person. And I'm not cooped up in an office all day. I'm tan because I'm in the sun a lot. Also, there's no one always looking over my shoulder.

Cr: Who do you work with?

Ce: There are some other guys that I usually work with. They're not always the same though. But carpenters are interesting people and I like meeting different ones.

Cr: What else?

Ce: I work on different things. It's not like I'm doing the same thing year after year.

This counselee revealed a number of significant points. He demonstrated how carpentry was consistent with his interests and aptitudes. Also, he seemed to have a good idea about the life style of being a carpenter and found it agreeable. Apparently, he had done some exploration about carpentry and was thereby able to project himself into what it would be like for him. Counselees who are unable to do this probably will not have explored themselves or their chosen vocation sufficiently, and thus the experiment can point out gaps in the information they are using in decision making. As members of the group observe each other doing this type of presentizing they may gain new perspectives of what things are important to them about their future careers.

Presentizing the future can also be used for other situations. Some of them may be short ranged, such as impending examinations, going away to school, choosing courses, and handling interpersonal problems in and out of school. They may also be longer-range situations such as marriage, growing older, where to live, and parenthood. The situations for which presentizing can be used in this fashion are also limitless.

Summary

Much of counseling is concerned with the past. Problems in dealing with the past include the multiplicity of causation, the insufficiency of insight from the past as a primary determinant of change, the belief that change is unlikely in light of a long history of difficulty, the use of the past as a scapegoat, the avoidance of the present by focusing on the past, and the leaving of the past in history by speaking of it in the past tense.

Gestalt approaches for dealing with the past employ presentizing, which is defined as using fantasy to bring the past into the present by enacting past events as if they were occurring now. Variations of presentizing can facilitate a counselee to express feelings from the past, to contact and reclaim parts pushed aside in the past, to differentiate between the past and the present, and to explore and learn from the past.

The future also figures prominently in the lives of counselees and therefore in counseling. Some difficulties in focusing on the future include the unreliability of predicting, the tendency of persons to mold themselves into futurizations, the ease of living in a state of intending, and the anxiety and catastrophizing which can be projected onto the future.

Gestalt approaches to problems related to the future are also based on presentizing. Presentizing the future entails enacting events that the counselee forecasts will occur or events and consequences which might occur. Another approach to future-related problems consists of helping the counselee to experience how he makes predictions about his behavior. Differentiating what is being lived now from that which is anticipated is yet another approach.

Dealing with the past and the future is necessary in group counseling. Presentizing the past has an enlivening effect on the group members and enhances interaction. Unfinished business which accrues among group members is important material from the group's past that can block interaction and group development if not worked through. Presentizing the future can be a valuable group experience for exploring situations yet to come.

REFERENCES

Perls, F. S., *Ego, Hunger and Aggression.* New York: Vintage Books, 1947.

9

Approaches to Feelings

From the Gestalt perspective emotion begins in the infant as undifferentiated energy. Emotion is the basic source which drives the organism and allows it to begin to be aware of its environment. At first the energy is spent on helping the organism to survive. The organism becomes aware that some elements in the environment promote survival and development and that others may be harmful or of no value to him. The infant becomes more selective in differentiating components in the environment which do or do not meet personal needs.

As this selectivity becomes more refined, an evaluation process becomes established. The energy which was once pure and undifferentiated now is selectively used in acquiring those things which are needed and in avoiding those which are harmful or not useful in meeting needs. The former are experienced by the organism as "good" and the latter as "bad," depending on the need pressing at that time. These specific and evaluative uses of energy are referred to as emotions. Positive emotions occur when energy is used to orient the person toward some element in the environment which meets current needs or to manipulate the environment for the same purpose. Negative emotions occur when energy is utilized to avoid elements in the environment which are harmful or not helpful in meeting current needs. These emotions are given names such as love, fear, pleasure, threat, and joy.

The emotions, then, serve two basic purposes. First, they provide energy to mobilize the person. Second, they provide an orientation or evaluative function by selectively directing the person's behavior in acquiring and manipulating the environment to meet his needs.

The term "feeling" is often used synonymously with emotion. When a therapist or a counselor asks a person "What are you feeling?" the question usually is directed at the emotions. A common response to this question is to report on the experiencing of an emotion such as, "I feel sad." Hence, the word "feeling" encompasses not only the emotion but refers to the experiencing of it. From this perspective the question, "What are you feeling?" means, "What emotion are you experiencing?"

This perspective on emotions and feelings has important implications for counseling. One of the most important is that a counselee is always feeling something. There is also some emotion at work, else all current needs would be met, which is a highly unlikely, if not impossible, event. Perls, Hefferline, and Goodman (1951) have stated the following on this topic:

> It is all important that you become aware of the *continuity* of your emotional experience. Once emotion is understood to be not a threat to rational control of your life but a guide which furnishes the only basis on which human existence can be ordered rationally, then the way is open to the cultivation of continuous awareness of its wise promptings. (p. 100)

This continuity of emotion extends to the continuity of feelings as discussed herein. Some feeling is always being experienced. Too often when a person says, "I'm not feeling anything right now" what is meant is that he is not experiencing a volcanic upheaval or very strong feeling. To some persons feelings are not present unless they are clear, strong, and dramatically expressed. The person who is sitting quietly is often considered to be not feeling. Then, as feelings of love, sadness, or anger are acted out, the person is suddenly "in touch with his feelings." This orientation to the nature of feelings suggests that there is an off-on switch for them. Now the person is feeling, now he isn't. The feelings of the person between upheavals are ignored.

Awareness of feelings cannot be confined to such a cyclical approach. It must include all feelings, even the more subtle ones which are not normally considered feelings. Restlessness, relaxation, boredom, confusion, and "not knowing" are just as "real" as feelings of frustration, grief, pride, and satisfaction. Being able to enhance the awareness of less familiar or recognizable feelings is important, because if they are not attuned to, their message may be lost.

Self-Experiment

Focus your awareness on the feelings you are having now. You might try some "Now I'm . . ." statements and fill them in with your current feeling. . . . When or if you run out of feelings to complete the sentence stems, stay with that feeling ("Now I'm unsure about what to say next") and carry on from there. . . . Try to be aware of feelings you are having which you haven't considered as feelings before. . . . Does this do anything to your attitude about those experiences? . . . Compare and contrast these feelings with others which are more dramatic and intense. . . . What do you discover as you do this? . . .

Counseling Applications

Ce: I just found out my grades for this semester.
Cr: And?
Ce: And they're pretty low.
Cr: What do you feel about that?
Ce: I don't know what to feel about it.
Cr: I don't understand what you mean by that.
Ce: I could get real disappointed. Maybe I could be relieved that it's finally happened.
Cr: You could feel those and you don't?
Ce: Yeah.
Cr: Then what do you feel?
Ce: Not much of anything big.
Cr: How about something small?
Ce: I sort of feel a little as though I really don't give a damn. But then, I'm not supposed to feel that way about grades.
Cr: Try it on for size—"I really don't care about my grades."
Ce: I don't care about my grades. They're not important to me.
Cr: Now is that true for you? Is that what you feel?
Ce: Yes. I'm thinking about getting training as a mechanic and they don't care about grades in history and that kind of stuff.

This counselee did have feelings about his low grades which were different from more socially acceptable reactions. Because his feeling was not intense ("Not much of anything big") and wasn't one of the things he imagined he could feel, he was almost apologetic about what he actually did feel. The counselor attempted to help him enhance the awareness of his feelings of "not giving a damn" so that he could explore it further.

Responsibility

Persons are often familiar with the experience of their feelings and may know when they are mad, bored, happy, pleased, frustrated, and so on. The imputed source of these feelings, however, varies by person and by situation. Commonly heard are statements such as, "She makes me feel worthwhile," "They make me so mad," and "That place depressed me." In such cases the speaker is asserting that external forces are at play in determining feelings. Something or somebody out there is making him feel the way he does. Another variation of this is the "came over me" dynamic represented by statements such as "I don't know what came over me. All of a sudden I was so pleased," or "I feel my temper rising." In these cases the feeling is "coming" from within, but from a place that is alien enough that it might as well be "out there."

The common element between these two scenarios is not assuming responsibility for the current feeling. The person is not aware of his responsibility for feeling the way he does; he is not able to be aware of what he does to make himself feel. All he knows is that the feeling is there, like it or not. If it is a pleasant feeling, the person feels rewarded and gratified. Conversely, he feels victimized and plagued by feelings that are unpleasant and that he would like to get rid of immediately.

Not being aware of who is creating the feelings leaves the person deprived in several ways. First, he is "at the mercy" of his feelings rather than being the creator or the master of them. As such, an unpleasant degree of powerlessness and, in some cases, hopelessness is experienced. Second, the person will be unable to dismiss or substitute an alternate feeling for one which is inappropriate or destructive for him. These both involve choices which the person is not aware of having. Third, the person will not know how he brought about his pleasant feelings and thereby does not have ready access to them.

There are several Gestalt approaches whose purposes are to assist persons to realize the responsibility they have for their feelings.

I Give You the Power

When a person believes others are making him feel the way he does or that his feelings "just come over him," responsibility is not being accepted for those feelings. The person is investing power to make him feel in other persons or in that mysterious place within himself that "puts" feelings on him. Usually the person is not aware of giving away this power and is therefore unable to recall it. Helping to experience how he gives away this kind of power to what he believes is the source of his feelings is necessary before the power can be reclaimed and converted into his own sense of responsibility.

Self-Exercise

Think of some persons who make you have certain feelings. Select one of them and in a fantasy dialogue say some of these things to him: "I give you the power to make me feel . . . ," "I let you make me feel . . . ," "It is because of you that I feel. . . ." . . . Now do this with a few other persons. . . . Now repeat some of the statements, only this time address them to that part of you which makes you feel certain ways. . . . Can you get in touch with how you give away this power? . . . What is your feeling about doing this?

Counseling Applications

Ce: One of the things that I like most about Mr. Smith is that he makes me feel good. Lots of other people make me feel bad.

Cr: Other people have a lot to do with what you feel.

Ce: Yes, I guess so.

Cr: Are you aware of how you let them do this?

Ce: No.

Cr: Let's try something. Suppose Mr. Smith is sitting right here. Now try saying to him, "I let you make me feel good."

Ce: I let you make me feel good. I like when you do it.

Cr: There were others that you mentioned who make you feel bad. Could you tell them how they affect you?

Ce: There's my brother. You make me feel dumb.

Cr: I give you the power to make me feel this way.

Ce: I give you the power to make me feel this way.

Cr: And what do you feel as you say this?

Ce: I don't like it.

Cr: I believe you. When you let people make you feel things you're going to get all kinds of results. Let's try the experiment with a few other people.

This counselee developed a slight awareness of his tendency to let other people mold his feelings and started feeling a little uncomfortable with that awareness. Chances are that he feels resentment toward his brother. The counselor could have chosen to respond to that but rather chose to recognize that the counselee would have to become much more aware of how he gives power to others to make him feel before he would be ready to assume responsibility for his feelings. As this awareness increases, the counselee's desires to change these relationships will increase, and he will become more ready to assume responsibility for his feelings.

Now I Feel ...

To many counselees the notion that they are responsible for their feeling is unique and strange. This is especially true for those counselees who fit the two situations mentioned above. It is not expected that all counselees will embrace the notion they are capable of assuming the responsibility for their feelings. Once they become aware that they can be responsible, counselees are confronted squarely with their own avoidance of it, which leads to the powerlessness already described. On the other hand, movement toward the acceptance of responsibility can result in a feeling of power. A hurtful feeling if perceived as self-inflicted is more tolerable because it is less tainted by mystery. Acceptance of the responsibility opens the door to curtailing such inflictions.

Self-Experiment

Concentrate for a few moments on the flow of your feelings. Be aware of them as they bid for attention. . . . Your task in the experiment is to fill in the blank in the statement, "Now I feel . . . and I'm responsible for that." Do this continuously, allowing whatever feeling you are experiencing to be noted in the blank. . . . Do you accept this responsibility? If not, spend some time with your objections. . . . Do you accept responsibility for the objections? . . .

Counseling Applications

Ce: Sometimes I get these strange feelings and I don't know where they come from.

Cr: You have no idea where they are coming from?

Ce: No. It just seems as though they are there all of a sudden.

Cr: What I believe is that they come from inside you.

Ce: What do you mean?

Cr: I mean that you are the source of your feelings and you are responsible for them.

Ce: You mean I should blame myself for them?

Cr: I don't think in terms of blaming. Just responsibility—that it is you who makes you feel the way you do.

Ce: That sounds a little strange to me.

Cr: It does to a lot of people. Want to try a little experiment with the idea?
Ce: What's the experiment?
Cr: Take the sentence, "Now I feel, and I'm responsible for that" and state whatever you are feeling. For example, if you were feeling happy you would say, "Now I feel happy and I'm responsible for that." Try it.
Ce: Now I feel kind of confused, and I'm responsible for that.
Cr: O.K. Do some more. Just put in whatever you're feeling at the moment.
Ce: Now I feel this is funny, and I'm responsible for that. Now I'm not sure what to say and I'm responsible for that.
Cr: Good. You're getting the idea.
Ce: Now I'm feeling pleased and I'm responsible for that.

This counselee's response to this approach was fairly typical. She was unclear about what being responsible for feelings meant. When she did get a glimpse of the notion she converted responsibility into blame. The counselor briefly differentiated blame and responsibility and then suggested the experiment. She was supportive of her first efforts, especially since this work was taking the counselee into a new area of awareness. The counselor was well aware that the counselee's parroting of the experiment did not result in her fully experiencing responsibility for her feelings. It did, however, give the counselee a chance to taste the idea and did serve as an orientation to it.

Creating Feelings

Once the idea of being responsible for feelings is accepted, the person can then begin to work on actually creating them. The main thrust of this kind of work is to set up some experiments allowing the person to experience how he creates feelings. Until these processes of creation are contacted the person will not be able to feel the responsibility for his affective state.

One way to start enhancing awareness in the creation of feelings rests on the assumption that teaching provides an occasion for the teacher to learn a great deal. Operationally, this translates into an approach in which the counselee is asked to tell the counselor what to do to make himself feel the way the counselee does.

Self-Experiment

Select a feeling that you find yourself experiencing frequently. Now imagine that you have someone there with you. Tell this person about your feeling as if you were experiencing it now. (Don't be surprised if you do start experiencing the feeling.) Suppose that this person is unfamiliar with your feeling and is interested in experiencing it. Your task is to provide instructions on how the person can go about doing this. Tell him specifically what he has to do, think, or say to experience what you feel. . . . Listen to yourself very carefully as you do this. . . . Do you come across any new process or awareness as you do this?

Counseling Applications

Ce: Sometimes I get this very good feeling about myself and I feel how well I can do things.

Cr: How do you make yourself feel this way?

Ce: I'm not sure. It just sort of happens. I like it, that's for sure.

Cr: Tell me what I would have to do to feel this way about myself. How can I feel the same way?

Ce: Well, you would have to set up some things that you want to do and that you believe that you can do. Then you figure out what you have to do to get the things done.

Cr: O.K. I've got you so far. Now what else should I do?

Ce: You have to realize that the things you want to do may not be easy and that it's O.K. if you sometimes get frustrated as you do them.

Cr: What do I do when I get frustrated?

Ce: You cool it for a while and then come back to what you're doing.

Cr: What else is important in this?

Ce: You give yourself the time to do what you want because the things are important to you. You just keep at them until you do them. After a while you can begin to tell yourself that you can do most things that you set out to do. That's the good part.

This counselee was able to share her feelings of competence and her belief in herself. Her instructions indicated that her feelings about herself were grounded in her experience. The lucidity of her instructions indicated that her awareness in this area was not as dim as her initially communicated "It just sort of happens." Nonetheless, giving the instructions, or "writing the script," which was Perls's terminology for this approach, can make that which is fairly clear even more so.

Giving instructions or writing a script can serve to enhance awareness of how certain feelings are produced. It does not, however, engage the counselee with the part which has the power to produce the feeling. Before responsibility for producing feelings can be accepted it must be experienced. This experience can be attained through enactment of the producer.

Self-Experiment

Again select a feeling that you experience with some regularity. Now imagine that you have the power to make others feel that way too. Enter into a fantasy dialogue with someone and produce the feeling in the person. You might try some sentences like, "I'm making you feel ..." "Now you are feeling ... and I'm doing it to you." You can make up some of your own. . . . Tell the person in detail how you are making them feel this way. Be sure to address the person in the present tense. Feel yourself doing it right now. . . . What do you observe about yourself as you do this?

Now change the dialogue. Instead of addressing someone else, do the experiment on yourself. Do to yourself what you were doing to the "other" in the dialogue. . . . What differences and similarities do you notice in the two dialogues?

Counseling Applications

Ce: Sometimes I get confused and am not sure what I think about something.

Cr: How do you bring about this confusion?

Ce: That is a good question. I wish I knew.

Cr: Let's try something that might help you to see how you do it. Let's assume that you have the power to make me feel confused the way that you do. Now go ahead and make me confused.

Ce: I'm not sure how to start.

Cr: Perhaps by telling me, "I'm confusing you" and then going on from there.

Ce: I'm confusing you. You don't know what you think or feel.

Cr: And how are you doing this to me?

Ce: I'm making you have an idea about something. You no sooner think that's right when I slip in another one. Then you doubt the first one and decide on the second one. . . .

Cr: And?

Ce: And now I'm bringing in still another alternative. Now you're not sure about that one and you're thinking that maybe the first one was right. (*Smiles*) You are now confused.

Cr: And I'm making you this way?

Ce: Yes. And I'm making you confused. I guess I'm pretty good at it, aren't I?

Cr: Tell me how good.

Ce: (*Laughs*) I can keep your head spinning this way.

Cr: Does this feel familiar to you?

Ce: You wouldn't believe how familiar.

Cr: O.K. Now let's try the same thing, only this time instead of confusing me, try confusing yourself.

This counselee was to do unto someone else what he does unto himself. In so doing he experienced some of the power in the "confuser" part of him. He, like many other counselees, was lightly amused at discovering himself in his own game. Further work on this will help him to realize that it is he who keeps his head spinning.

Bipolarities

A person is composed of a myriad of aspects which are organized into his present level of integration. Each aspect of the person is one part of a duality, even though only one side of the duality may be observable. As Polster and Polster (1973) have stated:

> There is nothing new about looking at polarities in man. What is new is the gestalt perspective that each individual is himself a never-ending sequence of polarities. Whenever an individual recognizes one aspect of himself, the presence of its antithesis, or solar quality, is implicit. There it rests as background, giving dimension to present experience and yet powerful enough to emerge as figure in its own right if it gathers enough force. When this force is supported, integration can develop between whatever polarities emerge in opposition to each other, frozen into a posture of mutual alienation.

There are numerous examples of bipolarities. There is a defensive lineman on a professional football team who is a paragon of physical force and fierceness. Yet he spends considerable time with crippled children, handling them with gentleness and tenderness which stand in stark contrast to his Sunday afternoon behavior. It is not uncommon to read that neighbors of a person who has just committed a mass murder describe the criminal as a "nice person who wouldn't harm a soul." Changes which come about when a person is inebriated often reflect normally undisclosed tendencies. Contrasting aspects of a person will often emerge during stresses or crises. Strengths which haven't been used will emerge. Controls which have been rigidly adhered to may be dissolved.

There is a tendency for one side of a polarity to be in the foreground with its counterpart residing in the background. The relationship between the two ends of the polarity are often like a seesaw, such that when one end is up the other must be down. The end that is up is more in awareness, while the down side is less in awareness.

Polster and Polster (1973) have stated the objectives of working with polarities:

The task in resolving the polarity is to aid each part to live its fullest while at the same time making contact with its polar counterpart. This reduces the chance that one part will stay mired in its own impotence, hanging on to the status quo. Instead, it is emergized into making a vital statement of its own needs and wishes, asserting itself as a force which must be considered in a new union of forces. (p. 62)

Restated, as one side of the polarity emerges and makes contact with its counterpart a reorganization will be taking place within the person. Take, for example, the person who lives the role of the "toughy." As he begins to get in touch with the "softy" in him, there will be a change in the "toughy." This is not to say that the end goal is to blend the two components into a gray composition that is neither tough nor soft. Rather, the idea is to let each emerge, depending on the situation at hand. The person will be able to be tough when the situation calls for it and appropriately soft in other situations. He will not have to be tough in places where that is inappropriate but where he normally would be tough because of the inaccessibility of his softness.

Topdog–Underdog

One of the most famous bipolarities identified by Perls (1969) is that of the topdog and the underdog. He describes them as follows:

The topdog usually is righteous and authoritarian; he knows best. He is sometimes right, but always righteous. The topdog is a bully, and works with "You should" and "You should not." The topdog manipulates with demands and threats of catastrophe, such as "If you don't then— you won't be loved, you won't get to heaven, you will die," and so on.

The underdog manipulates with being defensive, apologetic, whee- dling, playing the cry-baby, and such. The underdog has no power. The underdog is the Mickey Mouse. The topdog is the Supermouse. And the underdog works like this: "Mañana." "I try my best." "Look, I try again and again, I can't help it if I fail." "I can't help if I forget your birth- day." "I have such good intentions." So you see the underdog is cunning, and usually gets the better of the topdog because the underdog is not as primitive as the topdog. (p. 18)

Neither the dominance nor the absence of the topdog or underdog is a satisfactory formula for living. Dominance by the topdog can result in an insatiable search for perfectionism. Dominance by the underdog can result in a state similar to inertness or constant resistance. In con- trast, there is strength and power in the topdog which would be notable in its absence. Likewise, the absence of the underdog would leave the person without a necessary check on the topdog. Each has its place in the integrated personality.

Self-Experiment

Start out by feeling your topdog. Now imagine yourself in a dialogue with your underdog. Make some "should" statements and levy some criticisms. . . . Listen to the kinds of things you say. . . . Continue expressing your displeasure. . . . What feelings do you have as you do this? What do you experience in your body? . . .

Now switch over and be the underdog. Answer the criticisms. Listen to your reasons, excuses, and explanations. . . . What do you feel toward the topdog? . . .

Continue the dialogue for a while. . . . What differences do you experience as you switch from side to side? . . . Which side feels more familiar to you? . . . Do you notice any difference in your feelings about either side? . . .

Counseling Applications

Ce: I've given up my diet for the third time. I just don't seem to be able to hold to it. I get so mad. Other people I know can lose weight. I should be able to do it.

Cr: There's a part of you that says you should be able to diet and yet you don't do it.

Ce: That seems to be my life's story.

Cr: Let's try a dialogue between the two parts. Start out with being the "should" part and tell Sharon what she should do.

Ce: You are so fat. Just look at you. Who likes a fat girl? You could lose that weight if you wanted to. Why don't you? What's the matter with you, anyhow?

Cr: Now switch over and be the other side.

Ce: You're always hitting me with that. It's not fair. You know that I've tried time and time again. What am I supposed to do?

Cr: Continue the dialogue. Let's see how this battle goes.

TD: You know what you should do. You should pick out a diet and stick to it. Do you want to be fat all your life?

UD: No. And I wish you would leave me alone about it for a while. It's hard for me.

TD: Leave you alone. Ha! If I did you would get even fatter. You know that as well as I do.

UD: I'm not so sure about that. I've gotten to the point where I'm reluctant to even start another diet because if I don't lose fast, you jump on me. If I don't hold it to the letter, I catch it from you. You think you're helping, but what you're really doing is making it almost impossible for me.

TD: You don't think I'm helping?

UD: I think you're trying to. The way you're going about it, though, is lousy.

This counselee's conflict reflects an often-heard topdog–underdog dispute—the self-torture of dieting. In this case, however, there is some movement toward a reorganization of the two sides. The topdog's hint that it had seen that efforts to "help" were having an adverse, almost bludgeoning effect suggested that the underdog's message appears to have been getting through. An extension of movement in this direction might result in a realignment of these forces within Sharon such that the diet could be attained.

In addition to topdog–underdog disputes which can focus on any number of issues such as school performance and interpersonal behaviors, there are numerous other polarities which exist within the person. These may include the frustration–frustrated, victimizer–victim, domineering–submissive, frightener–frightened, active–passive, and strong–weak.

Ambivalences

Just as personal characteristics and behaviors exist in polarities, so do feelings. It is not possible to know happiness without having been sad, to feel powerful without having experienced helplessness, or to hate if love has never been felt. These polarities are reflected in ambivalent feelings which occur when both ends of the duality are experienced in close temporal relationship.

Such ambivalences can be a source of stress and confusion. A child may find that he alternately loves and hates his parents. An aggrieved person at a funeral where everyone is lauding the deceased may experience some ill feelings about the deceased or feel pleasure in the person's death. A person who has been wishing and wanting something may quite suddenly become fearful that the wish may be granted. The person cannot explain and may be frightened by these feelings which seem very much out of phase with what "should" be felt in the situation.

The relationship between feeling polarities can be clarified by considering appreciations and resentments. Where either is present, the other is there, albeit hidden and subtle. A person can be very resentful of another person or situation. However, if he remains in the relationship or stays in the situation, there must be some appreciations at work or the person would sever himself from that which he resents. Likewise, a person can feel very appreciative of a person or a situation and also experience resentments toward them.

Self-Experiment

Consider a person or situation about which you feel resentful. . . . Now imagine yourself in a dialogue and relate your resentments. Listen to them carefully and attend to how you feel toward the person or situation. . . . Continue doing this and see if you discover any new resentments.

Now relate what it is you appreciate about the person or situation. . . . This may feel strange at first. Ask yourself, "What is this person or situation providing which is of benefit to me?" . . . Relate the answers to this question as appreciations. . . . What do you feel toward the recipient of your appreciations? . . . How does this compare with the feelings you had when you were relating resentments? . . . Are you able to differentiate the resentments and appreciations? . . . Can you accept that both are present about the same person or situation?

Counseling Applications

Ce: Now that I'm wanting to go out evenings by myself, my parents are getting stricter and stricter with me.

Cr: You resent that they are getting stricter.

Ce: You can say that again!

Cr: Better if you say it. Only let's imagine that they're here, so you say it to them. Suppose they are sitting here. Now tell them how you resent their strictness.

Ce: You're treating me like a baby and I resent it.

Cr: Tell them specifically what you resent.

Ce: I resent that I have to ask you if I can go places. I resent you're asking me who's going to be there and what's going to go on. . . .

Cr: I imagine there's more.

Ce: Yes. I resent that I have to be home by 11:30 and that you are sometimes waiting up for me.

Cr: Is there anything about this that you can appreciate?

Ce: What do you mean?

Cr: Is there anything in your parents' rules that is good for you?

Ce: Well, they do let me go out alone.

Cr: Tell them what you appreciate about this.

Ce: I appreciate that you do let me go out alone. You used to say I wouldn't be able to until I was sixteen. Some of my friends' parents won't let them go places at all.

Cr: Any other appreciations?
Ce: Well, I guess you care about me and don't want me to get in any trouble or anything.
Cr: "And I appreciate that."
Ce: I do, but I resent all the rules sometimes, too.

This counselee came in feeling his resentments quite strongly. When the counselor suggested there may be some appreciations also associated with his parents' strictness, he was able to identify a couple of them. His last statement showed, however, that his resentments were not to be easily submerged under a flood of appreciation. A growing awareness of the latter might take some of the sting out of the resentments. Where there are appreciations, resentments may also exist, as evidenced by the following counselee.

Ce: There is something about my relationship with one of my best friends that is puzzling to me.
Cr: What's that?
Ce: I don't think there is anybody that I like more or am closer to than Judy, and yet sometimes I have these bad feelings about her.
Cr: Suppose you try telling her what you appreciate about her. Let's just have her sit here.
Ce: I'm glad that you're my friend. You like me and I appreciate that. I can trust you. You're smart and we like a lot of the same things.
Cr: Now I want to play a hunch. Can you tell her some of the things you resent about her?
Ce: What do you mean? She's my best friend.
Cr: I believe you on that. I also believe that there may be some things you resent about her.
Ce: I'm not so sure about that. There might be, though.
Cr: You can test that out if you wish.
Ce: How?
Cr: Try a few "I resent" statements and see if anything comes up.
Ce: I resent that . . . that you don't want to go to the same college as I do. You sometimes act as if State is not good enough for you.

This counselee found the idea that she would have some resentments about her best friend to be a little strange. She had hinted, though, that she sometimes did have some "bad" feelings about this person whom she appreciates so much. The counselee had a little trouble in voicing her resentment. She may have felt that she shouldn't resent things about a "best" friend. She may learn that she can have her appreciations and her resentments and her friend. Dealing with the resentments may even enhance the relationship and the appreciations.

Opposites

Counselees will often get locked into certain identities, behaviors, or feelings. The adherence to "one side of the coin" necessitates the lack of awareness of the other. Often what is on the other side of the coin can be of value to the counselee. Asking a counselee to experiment with opposites can often unlock new dimensions of awareness such as discovering an unmet need, a dormant talent, or an unexpressed feeling.

Self-Experiment

Let's see if you can make some discoveries about yourself by working with some opposites. Take a particular characteristic of yourself with which you are familiar. Now try getting in touch with the opposite of the characteristic. . . . Can you allow yourself to experience some of this? Now try this with a behavior. Take something that you enjoy doing and see what happens when you allow yourself to feel that you don't enjoy it. . . . Do you come up with any new awareness?

Counseling Applications

Ce: Whenever I'm around people I feel funny.
Cr: How do you experience this funniness?
Ce: Well, it seems as though they are all looking at me and watching what I do.
Cr: What are your objections to that?
Ce: I don't like being looked at.
Cr: Would you be willing to try an experiment on this?
Ce: Well, that depends on what it is.
Cr: Could you try telling me the opposite of what you've been saying? Sort of elaborate on how much you enjoy being seen by others.
Ce: I'll try it, but it feels funny.
Cr: Give it a whirl. Perhaps you could start with, "Here I am and I like being seen."
Ce: Here I am liking to be seen. People are looking at me and I am grooving on it.
Cr: What pleasure do you find in being seen?
Ce: Then I know that people are noticing me. They know that I'm around and I don't feel like some invisible person.

This counselee "feels funny" around people because she is not accepting something that she needs—to be seen and noticed by others. When she is hiding a need from herself or not accepting it, there is little chance that she can mobilize to meet it. Further counseling may help her to come up with some alternatives for further expression and development in this area.

Ce: I have always been the sweet little girl of the family, the block, the school, the world.

Cr: And?

Ce: And I sometimes get sick of it.

Cr: If you were the opposite of a sweet little girl, how would you be?

Ce: I'd be mean and spiteful. I wouldn't always smile when I don't feel like it. I'd say "no" when people ask me to do something I don't want to do. I wouldn't always put other people ahead of me. I'd say a few things to some people, believe me.

Cr: These sound pretty real.

Ce: They are! I can feel them.

Cr: My hunch is that these are some things this sweet little girl would like to do.

Ce: Maybe I can try a few.

Sweetness is nice. Too much sweetness isn't, especially when it is associated with holding check on behaviors that allow the experience and expression of strength. There are lots of "sweet little girls" and "nice little boys" who have themselves so type cast that they consider any behavior inappropriate that is not "sweet" or "nice." In practically all cases there are opposite behaviors waiting for their chance in the awareness limelight.

Avoidance

The awareness of a particular feeling falls somewhere on a continuum which ranges from full vividness to no awareness. There is little doubt about the reality of feelings which are experienced at the moment. In fact, experience validates the existence of those feelings. The reverse of this proposition, however, does not hold. It cannot be said, for example, that a feeling which is not currently experienced does not exist.

The process through which feelings are present in a person yet not in the person's awareness is avoidance. A person can have feelings of fear, happiness, loneliness, or competence and through actively avoiding them deny their existence. From the Gestalt perspective, avoidance is an active rather than a passive process. The person purposefully insures not experiencing certain feelings, or if so, to a dim degree.

A misconception is that the avoidance of feelings is quite different from the expression of feelings. In one sense, the difference is true, since avoidance insures that feelings stay within and are not acted upon directly, although there may be leakages, displacements, or other dynamics through which the feelings are partially and indirectly expressed. An example is the child who is angry with his parents and berates his younger sibling without provocation. Conversely, the expression of feelings occurs when they are experienced and acted upon directly. The joyful person beams, hugs, and prances. Anger comes out as loudness, physical exertion, and perhaps retaliation.

The problem in comparing expression and avoidance is that the former is seen as a necessary adjustment behavior while the latter is viewed as a barrier to adjustment. Expression is something the person has to do, while avoidance keeps the person from doing what must be done. In short, expression is viewed as doing, while avoidance is viewed as not doing. Nothing, however, could be further from the truth than to say that avoidance is not an active process. A person who is avoiding a feeling is operationalizing an adjustment that he believes is necessary. The avoidance behavior is just as personally meaningful and purposeful as any overt expressions of feelings. The avoidance is, in essence, the manifestation of an expression of self at that moment. The person feels threatened or endangered by a feeling and is not allowing it into his awareness at the moment. This adjustment and self-regulation process rests squarely on the assumption that at any moment a person is doing what he truly believes to be best for him. If this were not so, he would be doing something else.

This outlook on the process of avoidance yields implications for counseling. The first is that avoidance deserves respect as an ongoing self-regulatory process. It is not merely resistance to be cracked like the "shell" of a nut in order to get at the "meat" of the problem. Avoidance should be regarded as what the person *is* doing rather than the result of what is not being done. Counseling focused on how or what a counselee avoids is as legitimate a topic as any.

Second, there is considerable energy and strength involved in avoidance. Avoidance is not a sign of weakness. A powerful feeling will clamor for attention in the person's awareness. The force necessary for restraining or avoiding the feeling must be at least equal or the feeling would emerge. To experience this dynamic you need only to put your palms together in front of your chest and push equally with each.

A third implication for counseling lies in the knowledge that a vast majority of counselees will engage in avoidance some time during counseling and that a significant proportion of them will not be aware of how they do it. Helping a counselee to explore how he avoids certain feelings can lead to his questioning whether he has to continue doing so. This, in turn, can result in experimentation with experiencing and owning the feeling, which is a necessary process in reintegrating the avoided feeling within the counselee's personality.

Avoidance Questions

Any feeling that a person has can be subjected to avoidance processes. Some persons will avoid feeling their hurt, frustration, sadness, and anger. Others may choose to avoid feelings of peace, pleasure, fulfillment, and happiness. The mechanisms of avoidance keep the feeling in a sufficiently low state of awareness so that the person is not able to come to grips with reorganizations that could be advantageous. Because the feelings are kept on the perimeters of awareness the person is perhaps only dimly aware of having them. A question by the counselor as to whether a feeling is being avoided or, in cases where avoidance seems apparent, as to what is being avoided can help to facilitate the emergence of the feeling into awareness.

Self-Experiment

Start with the "Now I am aware" experiment and tune into your feelings at the moment. . . . As you find yourself on a particular topic ask yourself, "Is there a feeling about this that I am avoiding?" . . . Stay with this for awhile and see what comes to you. . . .

Now consider a situation about which you suspect you are avoiding a feeling but are uncertain as to what the feeling is. You may experience the feeling as vague but there nonetheless. Try to stay with the vagueness and the presence of the feeling. . . . Now ask yourself, "What is it that I'm avoiding here?" . . . Don't force an answer. Do you experience any difference in the vagueness of the feeling?

Counseling Applications

Ce: My parents keep telling me that I can't buy my stereo. I've saved up for it and everything.
Cr: What do you feel about this?
Ce: Oh, nothing much. They always pull these kinds of things on me.
Cr: And you don't mind?
Ce: As I said, I'm used to it.

Cr: Is there something about this you are avoiding?
Ce: What do you mean?
Cr: Is there some feeling you have about this that you're not stating?
Ce: I get a little angry sometimes, but I keep myself pretty well in control.

This counselee was not nearly as accepting of her parents' control as she made herself out to be. The counselor suspected that there would be some feelings of anger or resentment underlying the resignation in the "Oh, nothing much" exchange and posed his question on that hunch. As long as this counselee is living as though this type of treatment of her is satisfactory, there will be no efforts made to change it. Mobilization from the energy involved in the anger and the avoidance of it may result in efforts to seek some changes. Awareness of the feeling, however, must precede this type of movement.

Ce: I didn't take my English exam again. The same for math.
Cr: That seems to be becoming a pattern with you.
Ce: Well, I don't care. I just don't want to do them.
Cr: What are you avoiding, George?
Ce: Taking the tests.
Cr: Try just repeating "I don't want to take those tests."
Ce: I don't want to take the tests. I don't want to. I don't want to have to.
Cr: What else about the tests are you avoiding?
Ce: The low grades that I get.
Cr: And the feeling that . . .
Ce: That I'm some kind of dummy. They've got me in classes with all those smart kids. Who wants to get the lowest grade every time! I don't.

The counselee was clearly manifesting avoidance behavior in not wanting to take exams and had reasons for not wanting to. The counselor could not be certain about what the counselee was avoiding and inquired. Underlying the avoidance was frustration and fear of failure, which could then become the topic for further counseling.

Avoidance Rules

One reason a person will avoid a feeling may be due to teachings that it "shouldn't" be felt. The teaching may have been overtly enforced by punishment or more subtly established by parental behaviors such as "good boys don't feel that." In either case the teachings are established into a code or a set of rules about what may be felt and what may not be. Often the person will take over the writing of the rule book and add new rules by extrapolating from the older rules. In effect, the person becomes his own teacher and rule writer. Clarifying the rules and experiencing responsibility for writing them can lead to a fresh perspective on a code which has gone unchallenged.

Self-Experiment

Observe yourself and see if you catch glimpses of feelings that you avoid letting yourself experience. Now write some rules about those feelings. You might try some rule stems such as "I'm not supposed to feel this because. . . ." "I don't want to feel. . . ." Now carefully examine your rules. . . . Can you experience yourself as the producer of these rules? How much of the responsibility do you accept for these rules as you live them?

Counseling Applications

Ce: I sometimes feel jealous of some of my friends. And then I get upset with myself because I know I'm not supposed to feel that.

Cr: Who says you're not supposed to feel jealousy?

Ce: Everybody. It's not a nice feeling.

Cr: Who says you shouldn't feel it?

Ce: My parents used to always tell me that.

Cr: Who says it to you now?

Ce: I guess I do.

Cr: You have a rule "I'm not supposed to feel jealous."

Ce: Yes.

Cr: What other rules do you have about what you should and shouldn't feel?

Ce: (*Laughs*) There are so many.

Cr: I believe you. Now let's see if you can see how you create them. Suppose you were writing a book called "Rules for Sam to Live By." What would you put down as the first rule?

This counselee lives by a set of rules. The problem is that many of them may be implicitly accepted to the point of reflex. He may also experience them as being chipped in stone and therefore inviolate. Further, he may have little sense of the degree to which he formulates the rules and on what basis he does so. Working on his "rule book" may offer some new perspectives for awareness in these areas.

Censoring

Some feelings are experienced and expressed. Others are kept alive and inactive. This means that somewhere in the person a gate-keeping function is being carried out. A part of the person is permitting some feelings to come into the light of awareness and relegating others to dimmer shadows of awareness. This part of the person may be referred to as the censor.

The censor carries a significant amount of responsibility for controlling and regulating the awareness of feelings. This responsibility is rarely experienced clearly. By assuming the role of the censor the responsibility and functions it carries out can be made more explicit. With this comes the awareness of "It is me who is deciding which feelings I will or will not let myself be aware of, and this is how I do it."

Self-Experiment

Your task in this experiment is to carry out a dialogue between your censor and your feelings. First take the role of the censor and talk to your feelings. You might begin with some statements such as "I'm here to decide which of you gets out," or something to that effect. . . . Elaborate on your functions and how you carry them out. . . . As the censor, tell the feelings how you perceive them. . . . How do you experience yourself in this role? . . .

Now switch over and be your feelings. What is it like for you, being monitored and controlled? Say this to the censor. . . . Tell the censor what you feel about it. . . . Continue this dialogue and see where you go with it. . . . Do you find there are certain specific feelings which speak up more intensely than others? . . .

Counseling Applications

Ce: I have been very blah lately. Not many ups or downs, just blah.
Cr: And how about now?
Ce: The same. Just sort of here and not feeling much. It's as if I haven't been having feelings.
Cr: How do you keep yourself cut off from your feelings?
Ce: I don't know. That's how I feel, though.
Cr: Let's try something with this. Let's assume that you have feelings and that there is a part of you that is censoring them. Now imagine that you're the censor and tell the feelings how you handle them.
Cen: I've got you all cooped up somewhere so that I can keep you under control.
Cr: Tell them some more about how you control them.

Cen: It's like I've got you in a container. Sometimes you want to get out but I won't let you.

Cr: I have to keep you closed off.

Cen: Yes. I have to keep you closed off. I have to keep you where you can't get out.

Cr: Now switch over and be the feelings.

Feel: You know that we are here. You might try to ignore us but you can't make us just go away. We don't know why you keep us in here the way you do.

Cr: How does the censor answer?

Cen: Because you are trouble, that's why. You know what happened when I told Julie how much I liked her. Pow! I don't want that to happen again.

Ce: You're talking to some hurtful feelings you don't want to feel.

Cen: And I'm not going to. I've had enough of that. You are staying right where you are.

This counselee was able to connect with his censor and experience himself as the controller of his feelings. This puts him a step beyond feeling "blah" and not being aware of how he got there. Even though he may not yet be ready to allow himself to experience his feelings, he is aware that they are there. He can now explore the strength and determination in himself as censor and may find that these qualities in himself may be helpful in allowing him to experience some of the cloistered feelings. At the very least he will have realized that he has feelings, that he is responsible for the extent to which he avoids them and some of how he handles the avoidance.

Acceptance

There are few feelings which are universally accepted or avoided by all persons. One person may accept the experience of fear, while another person may not. In the same vein, one person may feel affection toward others while another person will avoid that feeling. It can be said, then, that most persons have some feelings that they accept and others that they avoid. The avoided feelings are not always "negative," while the accepted feelings are not always "positive."

Feelings which are avoided can be a source of difficulty. Take, for example, the person who steels himself against feeling fear. One day he is walking along and a rabid dog charges up to bite him. Not allowing himself to be afraid increases his chances of being bitten, as he takes no precaution to remove himself from the situation. If he did feel fear he might quickly scan his horizon and see a tree, a fence, or a car which he could climb to avoid the dog. This rather oversimplified example illustrates that avoided feelings can have messages and purposes which are to the advantage of the person.

A second ramification of avoiding selected feelings bears on the overall awareness of feelings. There are times when a person's awareness of his feelings is quite low. To avoid experiencing these negative feelings, the person may have restricted awareness of all feelings, including those which are positive. As the person begins to accept some feelings, it may be that a negative feeling may be one of the first to emerge. This can be a critical moment, as that feeling may be the one which precipitated the avoidance in the first place, and there may be temptation to avoid it again. This would leave him right where he was.

If he could accept the feeling and be aware of it, then other things can happen. The person might find that the feeling is not as threatening as it was at the time he began avoiding it. Learning that he can experience this part of himself and survive can build a sense of confidence and strength. Also, he may find that current conditions in his life are such that he is better able to do some things which the feeling suggests would be constructive for him. Further, by staying with this emergent feeling even though it may be a negative one, the person may be open to experiencing some positive feelings which have also been held in abeyance. A further outcome may be a sense of excitement and energy that comes with readmitting into awareness some feelings which have been avoided. As such splits within the person are rectified the sense of integration is enhanced. The object of working with counselees to help them accept their feelings is to allow the opportunity for some of those dynamics to unfold.

Sometimes when a feeling has been avoided or rejected the idea of accepting it as part of oneself seems inconceivable. So much energy has been put into keeping the feeling at bay that to suggest owning or accepting it can seem very strange to the person, especially if one of the reasons for coming for counseling was to learn how better to avoid the feeling.

Self-Experiment

What is a feeling you sometimes have which you attempt to avoid? . . . See if you can let the feeling into your awareness now. . . . Can you stay with the feeling and allow yourself to experience it? . . . Can you accept that you feel this and let it be a part of you? . . . What would happen if you allowed this? . . .

Counseling Applications

Ce: Usually I feel strong and able to do the kinds of things I have to do. (*Voice trails off*)
Cr: How strong do you feel now?
Ce: Not as strong as I really am. I don't know what the heck's wrong with me. You'd think I was some kind of pushover or something. (*Voice is low*)
Cr: Do you hear yourself as you say this?
Ce: Yeah. A little.
Cr: How do you sound?
Ce: Kind of quiet and soft.
Cr: And what do you feel?
Ce: Kind of afraid. I get to feeling weak sometimes. I fight it and try to ignore it but then it comes back.
Cr: You are afraid to feel weakness.
Ce: Yes, because I'm a strong person. And I feel as though there's something wrong with me when I feel weak.
Cr: Can you allow yourself to feel some of your weakness now?
Ce: I don't want to and yet I do feel that way.
Cr: Just stay with what you feel. What is feeling weak like for you?
Ce: I feel kind of run down. I don't know what to do. I'm not very sure of myself.
Cr: Just let yourself feel this.
Ce: (*Sits quietly*)
Cr: How do you experience this now?
Ce: I feel a little less afraid.
Cr: No harm has come to you.
Ce: Yeah.
Cr: Can you accept this feeling of weakness as part of you?
Ce: I guess it's not as awful as I thought. I didn't dissolve, did I?
Cr: Try this: "It's O.K. for me to feel weak."
Ce: It's O.K. for me to feel weak.
Cr: Again.
Ce: It's O.K. for me to feel weak.
Cr: True?
Ce: Well I guess I'm not positive. More so than before, though.

This counselee had been avoiding feeling his weakness. The purpose of this work was to see if he could allow himself to experience a little of it in the present. By attempting this he found that he "didn't dissolve" and didn't have to be as threatened by his weakness as he had been imagining. This is an important step in his moving toward accepting his feeling of weakness. This acceptance, once further developed, will permit him to not have to feel strong all the time. Also, he may more genuinely experience his strength once the weakness is assimilated. This counselee also made it clear that it was not totally O.K. for him to feel weak. He has been doing the opposite for too long to expect an immediate turnaround.

Approaches to Feelings
in Group Counseling

The work with feelings as presented in this chapter can be used for working with counselees in a group to expand their awareness of how they deal with feelings.

Responsibility

Building a sense of responsibility for one's feelings is an indicator of maturity and could be an important goal in a group whose purpose is personal growth. One of the main ways that counselees can use the group setting for experiencing responsibility for their feelings is imagining that they have the ability to "create" feelings in others. This approach was introduced earlier in this chapter where the counselee worked with "creating" feelings in the counselor. The group offers the advantage of offering the counselees a wider range of persons to work with in this way.

This approach can be very significant for the other counselees besides the person doing the "creating." They can experience that the person who is working on "making" them feel something actually cannot and does not. In this way each counselee can experience that only he is responsible for his feelings and is immune, if he chooses, to being "made" to feel on someone else's demand. The "creator" meanwhile is expanding his awareness of his responsibility for his feelings and how he implements it. Through doing to others what he does to himself he becomes more aware of what he does to himself.

It is important in this experiment and similar ones that all counselees realize when a person takes on and acts out the role of the "feeling creator" the purpose is for that person to become more aware of that part of him through expressing it openly. If, for example, a suppressed counselee is practicing being angry at the group members, he is usually not actually angry at the other counselees but rather contacting that part of himself which is angry and bringing it up front to be experienced. This type of work with the group is an extension of the fantasy dialogues. Contact with other persons does make the experience more real. However, it is important not to lose sight of the fact that most of what is being said is a projection and not a reflection on the person being spoken to.

Bipolarities

Working with bipolarities can be a very significant process for the group. A few examples of extending the approaches covered in the first part of this chapter will serve to illustrate how.

Since the topdog–bottomdog split is at the center of so many internal civil wars, it is important that the counselees have some sense of this process in themselves. Working with the topdog–bottomdog polarity can be done in the group. To begin, the counselor orients the counselees to internal divisions and arguments, perhaps by giving a personal example. The counselees are then given instructions similar to those in the topdog–bottomdog self-exercise (p. 194). This will allow each counselee to gain awareness of his own topdog-bottomdog struggle.

Follow-up on the individual exercise can take one of several directions in the group. The counselor could ask the counselees to finish the statement, "As topdog I say . . ." or "As bottomdog I say. . . ." Another variation could be to ask each counselee to share some of the dialogue between their topdog and their bottomdog. These approaches will encourage identification with each of the parts. Further discussions can focus on similarities and differences among counselees, which side of the polarity feels more familiar, the positive and negative aspects of the topdog and the bottomdog, and how these kinds of arguments can take place over a vast array of issues significant to the person.

Another type of bipolarity in feelings occurs in ambivalences in which a person feels some of both ends of a continuum such as good–bad or love–hate. The group provides a significant social situation for helping counselees to become aware of such ambivalences. An example of ambivalent feelings which can be worked within the group is appreciations and resentments.

Some preliminary work with the group can be valuable for subsequent interactions involving appreciations and resentments. For example, each counselee might speak of something that he resents and then explore what it is that he appreciates about the same thing. The opposite experiment can also be done with the total group. This would entail each counselee relating appreciations about something and then adding resentments. This brief exercise can help the counselees to grasp the notion that their feelings can and usually are mixed rather than rigidly dichotomized.

Sharing ambivalences and resentments can be used in situations where interpersonal conflicts arise between members of the group. For example, if two counselees engage in a confrontation of saying what they dislike about each other, the counselor could also involve them in sharing appreciations for one another. In this way each counselee experiences the full range of feelings for the other. Each counselee, on hearing what is appreciated about him, may be more open to consider the validity of resentments expressed about him.

The group can also be a significant place for a counselee to experience an aspect of himself that is the opposite of his usual behavior. This can be done with an individual or with all of the counselees. For example, the soft-spoken counselee can be given an assignment to speak loudly. The counselee who always feels put down can be given the opportunity to put down the other members of the group to help him become aware of a part of him that projects onto others. The somber, serious counselee could take on the role of a sport. The group provides an opportunity for counselees to experience and express some of their opposites in an *in vivo* situation.

Avoidance

During the course of the group counselees will demonstrate that they have certain feelings they wish to avoid experiencing or expressing. One way for the group members to enhance their awareness of these feelings and to share them with each other is to write a collective "rule book" on feelings to avoid. The counselor can ask each group member to contribute a rule or two.

Ce_1: You shouldn't be angry at someone because they will just get mad back at you.

Ce_2: My rule is that I'm not supposed to expect good things to happen and that way I won't get disappointed.

Ce_3: I don't like to let people know how foolish I sometimes feel because then they won't like me.

Ce_4: If I trust people with my secrets then they can hurt my feelings.

Ce_5: Another rule could be to be careful how much you let yourself like people because then you can feel rejected.

These are but a few of the kinds of rules that might emerge from the group. Through their compilation each counselee has suggested what is probably his most important rule. This kind of sharing can result in

"I thought I was the only one who did that" feelings among the coun-selees. Due to the personal nature of these disclosures the level of trust in the group can be elevated through the process of sharing them. Sub-sequent interactions can focus on the meaning and importance of the rules among the group members and the responsibility they have in creating them.

Censoring is an important aspect of avoidance and the group can provide an opportunity for the counselees to experience their "censor" and how it functions. One way that this can be approached is for coun-selees to practice censoring each other. As the counselees imagine them-selves able to censor the feelings of others they will become more aware of how they censor themselves.

Cr: From what you're saying, Bob, you experience your feelings as being cut off and you don't know how this happens. Here is an experiment you can try to help you become more aware of how you censor your feelings. I'd like you to censor a feeling for each member of the group. Tell them what the feeling is and then how you are blocking it out.

Ce: O.K. I'll give it a whirl. I'll start with Sam. Sam, you look as though you're feeling happy today and I can censor that happiness.

Cr: Rather than "can," do it now. "I am censoring. . . ."

Ce: I'm taking your happiness away. I'm not going to let you feel it.

Cr: And how do you do this?

Ce: I'm making you feel that you really don't have any right to be happy. And even if a little bit does slip by it won't last very long.

Cr: Now try something like this with someone else, Bob.

As this counselee "makes the rounds," he is becoming more explicit about how he operates as a censor. The counselor, realizing that the counselee has probably not done an experiment like this before, stays with him to help make it an active, here-and-now process. Doing this experiment with several counselees and different feelings will help the counselee to gain a clearer awareness of the "how" and "what" of his censor. The other counselees will be able to clarify their own censoring functions as Bob is doing the experiment and during an ensuing follow-up discussion.

Acceptance

Being able to acknowledge and to accept oneself in the present is an essential ingredient in allowing processes of change and self-regulation to take place. The group offers counselees an opportunity to enhance and enliven their sense of self-acceptance through disclosure and sharing with others. This statement is based on a double-edged assumption. First, the person will have to have at least a minimal level of acceptance to permit sharing. Second, the process of sharing can increase the level of acceptance. This process can be used as an experiment within the group.

Ce: So I guess I am really a little more self-centered than I had realized.
Cr: Do you accept this part of you?
Ce: Somewhat. Feels strange to me.
Cr: Sara, pick out a few people here and tell them "This is the way I am."
Ce: Sue, this is the way I am. I'm self-centered. I'm more important to me than you are.
Cr: What do you feel as you say this to her?
Ce: Still feels sort of foreign.
Cr: Try it with someone else even though it might feel a little phony.
Ce: Abe, if there's something I want, I'll take care of myself before I'll pay any attention to what you want.
Cr: True or false?
Ce: (*Smiles*) True.
Cr: O.K. Do this with another person or two.

As this counselee continues the experiment her self-centeredness begins to feel less foreign. This indicates that she is allowing herself to have more of this feeling, which is, in turn, a sign that she is becoming more accepting of it.

In addition to individuals learning to accept themselves, the group can also provide an opportunity for group members to learn to accept persons different from themselves. This can be approached by asking the group members what each can accept about the other. Objections to accepting which arise can be explored on the part of the person who is having difficulty accepting. In this way the counselees can experience how accepting is more the responsibility of the acceptor than of the person who is or is not being accepted. This can often lead to some discussion of how accepting another person relates to expectations which are held of him.

Summary

At each moment a person is having an emotional experience which is recognized as a feeling. These feelings serve to mobilize the person and provide an orientation or evaluation function to selectively direct the person's behavior in acquiring and manipulating the environment to meet the needs underlying the feelings. Thus, it is important to recognize the continuous flow of feelings regardless of their content or intensity.

The responsibility for a feeling is often imputed onto environmental forces or other persons. However, from the Gestalt perspective it is assumed that persons are responsible for what they feel. There are several Gestalt approaches whose purposes are to enhance responsibility for feelings. One of these approaches engages the counselee in how power is given to others to "make" him feel. Another consists of having the counselee report what is felt at the moment, followed by the statement, "And I am responsible for that." A third approach is to have the counselee instruct or direct the counselor in specific behaviors that would permit the counselor to experience what the counselee feels.

There exists in every person innumerable dualities or bipolarities. The object of working with these bipolarities or splits in the personality is to bring each side into awareness so that a reorganization takes place which does not exclude either end of the continuum. One of the most common bipolarities consists of the topdog–underdog. Bipolarities also exist in feelings. Counselees can increase their awareness of the bipolarities of their feelings by expressing both appreciations and resentments toward something of significance to them and by behaving according to the opposite of what they normally feel.

Avoidance is a process by which a person purposefully and systematically organizes his emotional life to assure that specific feelings are not experienced. This avoidance prohibits integration of the feelings into the personality and thereby blocks growth. The counselor can assist counselees to explore "what" and "how" they avoid by asking questions. Awareness of these dynamics can also be increased when the counselees experience themselves as the writers of avoidance rules and the censors who administer those rules.

Being able to accept one's feelings is a crucial ingredient in growth and development. Once an avoided feeling is accepted and assimilated the energy invested in it can be used constructively. The counselor can facilitate acceptance by supporting the counselee in experiencing and accepting feelings.

The group setting broadens the prospective uses of approaches to feelings. Counselees are able to fantasize themselves as creators of feelings in others and to be on the receiving end of the exercise, both of which can augment responsibility for one's own feelings. Bipolarity exercises in the group can lead to significant sharing as well as providing a basis for handling ambivalences felt by group members toward one another. A collective group effort on writing avoidance rules can expand awareness in this area. Further, having a number of group members with whom a counselee can practice censoring can increase awareness of this function. The group also offers an opportunity for disclosing feelings which a counselee is experimenting with accepting.

REFERENCES

Perls, F. S., *Gestalt Therapy Verbatim*. Lafayette, Calif.: Real People Press, 1969.

Perls, F. S., Hefferline, R. F., and Goodman, P., *Gestalt Therapy: Excitement and Growth in the Human Personality*. New York: Dell Publishing Company, 1951.

Polster, E., and Polster, M., *Gestalt Therapy Integrated: Contours of Theory and Practice*. New York: Bruner-Mazel Publishers, 1973.

10

Gestalt Approaches
in Psychological Education

Psychological education is emerging as a potent force in the schools. The main purpose of psychological education is to use classroom situations as a means for promoting personal growth and development. Underlying the approach is an assumption that difficulties encountered by students are often the result of previous developmental concerns which could have been prevented through appropriate experiences in the classroom.

At first glance there does not appear to be much new or different in this notion or the assumptions underlying it. Education has always purported to be for the "whole" person. The point made by proponents of psychological education, however, is that while the development of the "whole" person has been stated as a goal, development of aspects of the person other than intellectual and academic ones have long been left to change. For example, two goals stated by a school might be learning arithmetic and learning to understand oneself. For the former, books are ordered, specially trained teachers are hired, specific time periods are scheduled, in-service days are held, and arithmetic is firmly established as a respectable and necessary component of the curriculum.

The goal of self-understanding, while no less nobly stated, is much less concretely operationalized. It is assumed through the social aspects of the educational experience that self-understanding will "happen." Relationships with other students, teachers, counselors, and administrators are indicated as means to this goal. Extracurricular activities are often mentioned and justified as contributing to the development of the "whole" person. However, in most instances, the goal of enhancing self-understanding has not been approached systematically and has been perceived as being implicit in the other goals of the school.

Proponents of psychological education have urged that this important thrust of education be made explicit. Learning English, humanities, arts, sciences, and athletics are planned for. If it is possible to integrate learning about oneself into education, and if this learning is valued, then should not a systematic approach to it be planned and implemented? The answer to this question is an emphatic "yes." Ralph Mosher and Norman A. Sprinthall (1971) have discussed these purposes of psychological education at this secondary level, but their remarks are no less relevant for lower grades:

> The essential effort is to produce curriculum, i.e., systematic educational experiences, to affect directly the personal development of adolescents. The work springs from a belief that education currently offers little help to adolescents or young adults *as people* who are trying to mature against unusual vicissitudes. Our objective is to make personal development a central focus of education, rather than pious rhetoric at commencement, a second-order concern of the English curriculum or the private guilt of committed teachers and counselors. (p. 3)

A significant point about Mosher and Sprinthall's statement is that it was written by two counselor educators who were envisioning that counselors would have important responsibilities in conceptualizing, planning, and implementing psychological education. More recently an entire issue of the *American Personnel and Guidance Journal* (1973) was devoted to this topic and was entitled "Psychological Education: A Prime Function of the Counselor." Making the involvement of the counselor even more explicit, the guest editors, Allen Ivey and Alfred Alschuler (1973) stated:

> For practicing counselors, psychological education provides a new conception of their roles. When we hear the word *counselor*, we tend to think of a person or a small group on problems in living that are brought to the counselor. Psychological education involves the counselor's taking initiative in deliberately teaching aspects of mental health to larger groups. Education, rather than remediation, is the goal . . .
>
> We anticipate that psychological education will become one of the most important roles of the counselor in the next five years. The counselor has too many skills, the counselor education movement too many concepts of effective human relations for us to keep these techniques

locked within rigidly defined roles and restrictive accreditation legislation. Psychological education offers all of us a new opportunity of promoting health while helping more individuals grow. (p. 589)

In the same issue, Ivey and Alschuler (1973) made two significant statements about Gestalt approaches in teaching. They wrote that "Gestalt concepts are increasingly important in psychological education" and then went on to note that "Gestalt may be even more important as a teaching tool than as a therapeutic alternative." These statements suggest the usefulness and value of Gestalt approaches in teaching. Two books published on this topic are *Human Teaching for Human Learning: An Introduction to Confluent Education* by George I. Brown (1971) and *Anger and the Rocking Chair: Gestalt Awareness with Children* by Janet Lederman (1969). Both books present actual examples of the application of Gestalt approaches in teaching.

There are several characteristics of Gestalt approaches which make them useful in psychological education. One is that the objectives of the approaches in teaching include the enhancement of self-awareness and responsibility—two essential components in growth and maturation. The objectives are important and advantageous in their own right. They also have a corollary advantage in that as self-awareness and responsibility are integrated into teaching, higher levels of attention, excitement, and personal experiences are brought to bear in learning. This permits an interaction between the students and the curriculum such that each can significantly contribute to a greater understanding of the other. For example, when studying literature, the students will understand the experience of a character more fully as they explore similar experiences of their own and will have learned something of themselves in the process.

A second advantage of Gestalt approaches lies in the diverse ways they can be related to the curriculum. A simple approach such as asking students to personalize their statements can be useful regardless of the course content. Approaches can be worked into the curriculum as a part of lesson plans. Finally, it would not be difficult to make self-awareness the topic of a module or a class in its own right.

Gestalt approaches can be employed in teaching from preschool to doctoral level classes. Much of early childhood education focuses on sensory and self-awareness. Brown (1971) has presented examples of how Gestalt can be integrated into classes from the first to the twelfth grades. In my own experience teaching at the undergraduate and graduate levels, I have found many Gestalt approaches useful for enhancing self-awareness in such classes as human development, group process, counseling, and practicum supervision.

The application of Gestalt approaches need not be limited to a particular structure or format. The approaches can be used with individuals, small groups, or an entire class. Because the approaches are basically geared toward self-awareness, the student can gain regardless of whether the awareness is shared in a small group or a class. Learning experiences involving Gestalt approaches can be carried out through participation exercises in a class discussion or through written assignments. "Homework" assignments can extend processes for heightening self-awareness beyond the classroom.

How can a counselor help teachers learn to feel comfortable and skillful enough to make use of Gestalt approaches in the classroom? One way is to provide in-service training sessions for them to experience some of the approaches and to explore their possibilities for classroom use. I recently conducted two such workshops, each of which lasted five days. In both workshops combined there were thirty-two teachers, ranging from preschool to secondary levels. They were widely distributed in terms of subject areas.

The subject matter of the workshops consisted of portions of Chapters 4 through 9 of this book. As facilitator I handled each of the topics three ways. First, I gave a mini-lecture on the theory and principles of the particular topic. Second, I conducted individual and group exercises (the self-experiments contained above) to experientially communicate the topic. Finally, I divided the teachers into teams by grade levels, and the teams worked on devising ways that they could integrate what they had experienced and learned into their classrooms. In this sense I acted in a way analogous to the consultative role a counselor might perform when working with faculty members.

The work that the teachers did in producing uses of Gestalt approaches in teaching is particularly significant in light of the fact that the vast majority of them had had no prior exposure to Gestalt. They were, however, able to produce a broad range of applications, a sample of which is presented below.

Awareness

After starting several sessions of the workshop by having individuals state their current awareness through completing the "Now I am aware . . ." stem, several teachers noted how they "arrived" in the sessions as they listened to themselves and others. While there would hardly be time to "make the rounds" in a class of thirty-five or so, they reasoned that having each person do the exercise by himself and then having a few students report might serve to bring the students into the present.

During one session the teachers were working in smaller groups. One of the groups was faltering. As I approached the group I looked at what was occurring, and when I sat down said, "What I am aware of here is that people are sitting a considerable distance from each other and that there are three conversations going on simultaneously." My sharing of my awareness was enough to kindle the group's responsibility. What evolved out of the interchange was how a relatively non-judgmental remark affected the group. This they felt would definitely be worth a try in a classroom situation.

Several teachers were already using the magic circle technique in their classes. In brief, the method consists of introducing a topic to a small group of students who reflect on their personalized answer and then share it with the others if they choose, under the rule that whatever is said is not open to attack by other members in the group. The teachers who had been using magic circle noted that their topics were rarely focused on here-and-now experiences. They enthusiastically increased their magic circle stems to include "What I notice in the room," "What I am hearing right now," and so on.

The body awareness exercises yielded implications for several kinds of classes. One of the teachers, a coach, noted how awareness of the structure and function of parts of the body could be tied quite naturally into athletics. Jumping in basketball, leverage in wrestling, and eye-hand coordination in sports involving catching a ball were discussed. This topic also had possibilities for the importance of integrating the emotional, physical, and mental aspects of the athlete to elicit the best performance. One experiment suggested was to have students try something like shooting a basketball and to purposefully change such variables as their level of concentration, excitement, and emotional involvement. This would yield self-awareness on the significance of these performance variables.

Courses in physiology, health, and biology were considered important avenues for exploring body awareness. There was also discussion of how awareness of anatomical and physiological structure could be increased through "homework" assignments such as taking one's pulse at various times of the day, noting how the sphincter works, purposively slowing down everyday movements for observation, measuring the size of limbs and relating that to their functions, and exploring one's body for new movements, muscles, and sensations.

A music teacher noted how breath control was important in singing and wind instruments and decided that he would devise and utilize some methods for helping students to be more aware of their vital capacity limits and diaphragm utilization. These might include experimenting with the differences between inhaling and exhaling, experiencing the effects of different postures on breathing, timing how long a note can be extended and what is involved in doing it, and listening for qualitative differences in sounds as the flow of breath is controlled.

At first brush a chemistry teacher in the workshop was unsure about how awareness could be worked into her class. It was, after all, a laboratory on "pure" science. Further exploration of the topic revealed that certain elements could be identified by the color of the solutions. The idea also emerged that the concept of the volume of an object, namely a student's hand, could be gotten by displacement of water in a measuring beaker. She then went on to explore how she could show how in many cases that one sense is not enough to identify something. By mixing certain chemicals she could produce the exact scent of a banana. Blindfolding the students and having them sniff at the ether and some slices of banana would get across the message.

A math teacher was intrigued by the different kinds of thinking that she could do and recognized that divergent thinking was not the proper channel for proving axioms in geometry. She explored the ideas of teaching students the different ways they think so they would be better able to set themselves for solving math problems. English teachers who have the same students in a following class would perhaps be equally heartened if they could change sets before coming to that class. Convergent, axiomatic thinking does not lead to imaginative creative writing assignments. These modes of thinking could be taught by conducting the self-experiment on thinking contained in Chapter 4. There could then be short warm-up exercises prior to assignments. For example, the English teacher might ask the students to respond to the "How many things could you do with a brick?" questions before they begin a creative essay.

A typing teacher related how awareness of the body related to teaching that rather specific skill. She would have students exaggerate negative habits such as always looking at their fingers and assuming a poor posture as a means of teaching the opposite of those. She also reasoned that much of typing could be practiced outside the class and even without a typewriter. Students could learn which fingers are responsible for which keys and what kinds of movements are necessary to reach them.

Two home economics teachers found that their subject lends itself well to exploring senses which relate to eating. For example, they would select some foods which were sweet, sour, bitter, or salty and have students taste them and then taste them again while holding their noses.

They could also demonstrate how sight, scent, texture, and sounds are all related to the enjoyment of food. They also noted that they could have students be aware of chewing slowly and concentrating on eating as opposed to bolting down food while watching TV and doing homework.

Language Approaches

The personalization of language to increase self-awareness touches a resonant chord in teachers. The lower-grade teachers became aware of how much of Show and Tell is focused on describing "it" and discussed among themselves how they could help students to explore their experience in relation to "it." This might help them to clarify their likes, preferences, and interests.

One teacher in the workshop had the habit of using "we." After I asked her several times to relate what she was saying by using "I" she (and most of the others) began to understand the difference in experience between the self-references and generalizations. This resulted in a deeper understanding of individual differences among the participants in the workshop. An additional spinoff of the work with personalizing language were some second thoughts about the thousands of "I's" and other self-references which have fallen under the red pencil. There came with this a sense of responsibility that depersonalized language was not a random happening peculiar to English, but rather was a systematically taught language habit which had psychological implications tied in with self-awareness and identity.

A language teacher noted that a unit could be developed on the cross-cultural implication of the relationship between behavior and language structure. The French, noted for their independence, do not say "It is interesting." Rather, they say "Je m'intéresse," which literally translates "I interest myself." The Germans, a rather precise people, have a language in which nouns, pronouns, and articles are so precisely declined that, to paraphrase a student of the language, "You could take most German sentences, cut them up and throw the pieces on a table, and the meaning would still be clear."

Teachers at all levels were favorably disposed toward using verb changes to enhance awareness of responsibility and making choices. The book *The Little Engine That Could* was considered a natural lead in for exploring the meaning of "can't" among young children. From this they could learn how much of what appears to fall in the "can't" experience is actually within their grasp if and when they apply themselves. At the same time, the children could explore things that they literally cannot do and learn to accept the idea. In this way they could learn real limitations and distinguish those from limits that they set for themselves.

There was high agreement among the teachers that the importance of differentiating between the "can't" and "won't" experiences cut across grade levels and subject matter. It seems that all classes have students who "can't" do their assignments. The teachers felt that by doing some work, such as having students change "can't" statements to "won't" statements, there would be a greater degree of accuracy as well as a greater awareness of choice than when the students say "can't." Once this unit had been introduced the teacher would be in a better position to explore the refusals often inherent in "can't" statements. From this the students could come to appreciate the strength in "won't" and learn that there are consequences in making such choices.

English teachers noted the value of the active–passive voice difference in increasing the student's self-awareness. By having students write about their own experience in first the passive voice and then the active voice, two objectives could be attained. First, the differences between the two voices would be clarified. Second, the assignment could serve as a lead in to some class discussions on responsibility and the feelings associated with each voice.

After hearing their own questions made into statements by themselves and others, this approach became one that many of the teachers stated they would begin using in the fall. Since they are the target of endless questions, many of which are unanswerable because they are not really questions at all, the teachers were excited about this simple way to distinguish real from apparent questions. Many of them became aware of resentments about questions which had been vague to them. They realized that in many cases they were being "set up." Through their own experience they also learned that there is much more responsibility in "I'm warm" than in "Don't you think it's hot in here?"

The teachers found that the use of "what" and "how" questions instead of "why" had several uses. First, many felt that this approach ("What are you doing right now?") would be helpful in discipline situations. The teachers also noted through their interaction experiences that being asked "how" and "what" is much more helpful when dealing with a person who is bogged down in solving a problem. The questions seemed to help the problem-solver get to the specifics of where he was stuck.

Several class activities designed to help students "listen" to themselves were conceived. They could, for example, listen to themselves give each other verbal instructions for doing a task. Students could also describe an object without telling what it is and let the other students guess at it. Once an understanding of listening to self was clarified in the class the teacher could occasionally ask students if they heard themselves.

Language habits could also be examined in classes to help the students to understand how dialects and jargon relate to their identity. For example, the parent or a younger sibling of an adolescent may have different ideas about what is meant when hearing "Can you dig it?" The parent may be confused, the young child may fantasize a hole in the ground, and the adolescent knows he's being asked if he understands or accepts "it." Language habits also differentiate groups of students on characteristics such as ethnicity, drug usage, socioeconomic class, and taste in music. Students can become aware of how their language habits serve as bridges and links with their peers.

Several teachers noted how words relate to different psychological experiences. Expletives serve to release tensions and express meanings far from their concrete meaning. This is true also in the study of poetry, where words are used for their symbolic intent rather than as signs to represent something explicitly. Simple word-association exercises could be used in classes to help students learn that different things "come to mind" when certain words are heard. This can be especially true with certain "trigger" words such as "sex," "hate," and "religion." Misunderstandings in communication can be tied into different meanings and associations surrounding words which are thought to be commonly understood. For example, two students could engage in a discussion of what it's like to be an "older" person, one having been secretly told that older means around sixty, the other given the age of thirty. The differences in what is meant by "older" would rapidly emerge.

Nonverbal Approaches

One idea which occurred to several teachers was to have a class discussion on the types of nonverbal behaviors they use in teaching and class management. A number of teachers did become aware of ways that they use silence, body posture, voice tone, eyes, and other "signals" to which the classes respond. They considered going through their nonverbal repertoire and having the students relate what they believed those behaviors meant. The students might also be able to provide for the teachers some feedback on nonverbal behaviors which they had been using systematically without knowing it.

The teachers could explain that the students are able to view them in ways that they cannot view themselves, and ask the students to share with them some behaviors, such as how they use their voices, body posture, hands, and other nonverbal behaviors.

The teachers could then reverse the situation and share with the classes some of their hunches about the meaning of behaviors such as restlessness, daydreaming, and focused attention. By dealing with the class as a whole no individual student would feel "singled" out or threatened. This approach and the one above could serve as introductions to the topic of nonverbal communication in interpersonal relationships. Most students are aware of the communicative power of nonverbal behaviors, yet few of them have had the opportunity to discuss them with reference to themselves and others.

A number of teachers became aware of how little attention they had been paying to the nonverbal behavior of individual students during classes and in conferences with them. The concept of discrepancies and matches between verbal and nonverbal behaviors seemed to them to be a valuable tool for expanding their understanding of the students and the students' understanding of themselves.

The teachers of younger children came up with several ideas. One had to do with finding out how the children felt about themselves, class activities, and other life situations. The idea was that these children may not have the language to differentiate between various gradations of good–bad or like–dislike. They are, however, capable of pointing to one of six faces, ranging from a broad smile to a deep frown, and indicating which one best describes their experience. Such a device could then be useful to help them acquire the words that go along with the pictures.

Young children love to study about and observe animals. A unit on the nonverbal behaviors of animals (for example, the slap of the beaver's tail, the ostrich hiding its head, the cat arching its back) would hold their interest and turn on their imaginations. From there the unit could be developed around the theme of "What kinds of things I do that are like the beaver, the ostrich, and the cat." In this way the students would have a chance to increase their own awareness of the relationship of their feelings and nonverbal behaviors.

Charades is a popular game in classes, particularly on rainy days and other times when a little fun is in order. A number of teachers noted how this could be an important means of bringing up nonverbal behavior and communication. It seems that the game is rarely talked about and is thus a potentially rich teaching resource.

Several teachers came up with the idea of teaching a lesson during which neither themselves nor the students would speak. After the lesson the class would discuss the experience and what they felt during what would have to have been a highly unusual class situation.

The teachers mentioned several methods that could be appropriate for providing feedback for students on their own nonverbal behavior. One of these was the popular mirroring exercise in which one student acts as a mirror and reflects back the nonverbal behavior of his partner. This exercise is useful at several grade levels. Other teachers mentioned that having an actual mirror in the class could be useful for helping students to look at themselves in ways other than just whether they had their hair combed correctly. Since audio- and video-tape recorders are frequently found in schools the teachers reasoned that some class time could be valuably spent on letting the students hear and see themselves. This was noted especially by those teachers who had had their classroom behavior recorded and played back to them.

Nonverbal awareness could also be worked into several other kinds of classes. A home economics teacher decided to ask her students to pay particular attention to how they selected their clothes and to relate the selections to what they were feeling at the time. The idea here was to make explicit how clothes selection is a type of nonverbal expression. An English teacher came up with the idea that characters in novels, short stories, or plays could be studied both by what they said and their nonverbal behavior. A French teacher decided to work into her conversation class a unit on the different facial expressions, shoulder shrugs, and hand gestures that seem to go along with speaking and experiencing French. One of the teachers was involved in creative dramatics and noted that practicing pantomimes was a good way for preparing students to attend to nonverbal behavior while speaking. She also decided to experiment with the idea of having students nonverbally express a feeling such as surprise by recalling a situation in their lives when they were surprised and acting it out. An art teacher discussed developing a unit around the nonverbal messages in graphic advertising. This could be done by cutting the captions away from pictures and by watching TV commercials with the sound off. A football coach noted the significance of nonverbal behavior in athletics. Preciseness in exercises, lining up in the huddle, and getting set in positions not only serves to sharpen awareness among the players but it also communicates a "we're prepared" signal to opponents which can help get that psychological edge. All of these lessons could serve as means for enhancing awareness of the students' nonverbal behavior.

Fantasy Approaches

The use of fantasy was well received by the teachers, many of whom were already using various role-playing methods in their classes. Work with identification and projection seemed to expand their thinking to include "being" things other than persons in stories or lessons.

A science teacher devised a lesson for teaching the digestive process and anatomy. First the students would be the various parts of the total gastrointestinal tract and describe their functions. Along with this method would be another in which the students would be a piece of food and then relate what happens to it as it passes through the digestive tract. These methods could be as general or as detailed as the nature of the class demanded. In an elementary science unit they would be used simplistically. In more advanced classes the anatomical parts and the morsels of food could relate chemical reactions of the organ or the food substance.

After some experimentation with the identification process a number of other teachers came up with ideas for their classes. A music teacher would ask the students to select a musical instrument. The students would then describe what they enjoyed about being the instrument either in a group discussion or in a couple of paragraphs. The teacher would respond in reflective, noninterpretive ways ("You like making smooth, low sounds"). This process was also thought valuable by a geometry teacher who would ask students to be a geometric figure, which could range from a simple line to a complex three dimensional figure. Chemistry also provides a diversification of elements which students can choose to become. Some are heavy and noninteractive and others are light and eager to join with all kinds of substances. The students can further their understanding of the differences among elements and how they are similar and different from them. Self-awareness can be crystallized in this process.

Identification with other persons offers many opportunities for learning about self. Many of the teachers had been using role-playing to depict various historical scenes and events. What had been missing in these lessons, though, was some way to enhance self-awareness. In one parochial school a teacher devised such a lesson around the biblical scene in which Christ entered the temple, found many activities going on there which he deemed inappropriate, and became quite angry. The teacher had the students imagine themselves as Christ and they expressed their feelings. She then turned the lesson to the topic "What has happened in your life recently about which you have gotten angry." The students shared several events and then discussed them in terms of what had transpired, the appropriateness of the anger, and the actions taken as a result of the anger. In this way the students were able to reflect on a human experience of their own and see the similarities and differences between their reactions and those of Christ. To affectively oriented teachers this procedure was not new. To others it added a whole new dimension to what could be done with a lesson "about" someone.

Role reversals were often mentioned as a use for "being" another person. Sex, race, religion, and nationality were frequent topics. One teacher used role reversal in teaching sex education in a secondary school.

In small groups the girls and boys imagined themselves as members of the opposite sex. In so doing students of both sexes became aware of misconceptions and distortions they had of the opposite sex.

One role reversal that many of the teachers had heard of but had not tried was letting the students be the teacher. It seems that many students are constantly amazed that teachers exist and have lives apart from teaching, a rather distressing comment on the interpersonal approach of many teachers and the stereotypes students have of them. The teachers would ask the students to be them and answer such questions as "How do I feel when the class gets rowdy?" "What do I like to do on weekends?" and others. After the students shared their answers, the teacher would answer the questions. Through this activity the students could learn how their conceptions of the teacher do or do not match the teacher's answers. They could also see the differences among themselves as to what they imagined about the teacher. Both of these could be developed into a discussion about what can happen in interpersonal relations when actions are based on fantasies about a person. From this exercise the teachers could get powerful feedback on how they are coming across to their students and the extent to which they are letting themselves be known.

The teachers found the positive withdrawal a personally rewarding experience. Not surprisingly, they first thought of it for themselves during some of those moments when they felt "one more minute of this class and I will explode." The teachers recognized that the positive withdrawal was based on the rhythm of contact and withdrawal as a means of keeping attending powers fresh. They reasoned that an occasional withdrawal would permit the students some pause from the school day. It could also be used as a transition from gross motor activities to more quiet, sedentary activities. The positive withdrawal could also be the basis for an assignment in creative writing or dramatics in which the students would act out the situation of their "place."

One teacher learned something of utmost personal significance. At first, she had trouble finding a "place" in which she could be safe and have everything the way she wanted. She therefore was somewhat dubious about whether children could find such places because many of her students were from deprived backgrounds. At a later point she excitedly discovered that while she could not "find" her "place," she was able to "create" one. She then realized that her students also have fantasies and wishes which they could use to "create places" even though they might not have them in reality. For her students, she reasoned, becoming aware that they could create positive fantasies and use them to their advantage would be a powerful learning in its own right.

There were numerous suggestions as to how students could become more aware of and enjoy their fantasizing capabilities. One of them had to do with listening to different kinds of music and producing fantasies or daydreams to go along with each kind. They might be given the beginning of a fantasy situation and then be encouraged to finish it on their own. The sharing of these finished fantasies can be fun and productive in that they demonstrate how fantasies are a reflection of the person producing them and how persons will produce very different fantasies even though they begin with the same stem. Accepting and appreciating individual differences through fantasies can lead to significant learnings about self and others.

The Past and the Future

After working with "presentizing" various aspects of their past, the teachers came up with ideas about how this concept could be used in the classroom. The ideas centered around the themes of differentiating the past and the present, unfinished business, and learning from the past.

Differentiating the past and the present would help the students to become aware of changes that have occurred in themselves. I have used a method of helping students to trace their development in courses such as adolescent psychology. The assignment is centered around several concepts or a theory of development such as Erickson's. The students write about themselves at three ages, describing themselves on all of the dimensions of development at each age. The ages might be twelve, seventeen, and the present. (The assignment came to be known as "There and Then, There and Then, Here and Now".) The students write in the present tense at all three ages. Through this assignment the students become aware of how they have changed on some characteristics and not on others. Surprises were usually in store in both cases. This assignment was, according to feedback from the students, a personally significant experience that served to enhance self-awareness and resulted in an understanding of the theory involved in the assignment.

The teachers noted that an exercise based on these procedures could be done with students at various age levels. It could easily be made less complex by eliminating the theoretical aspects and exchanging them with some topics such as "my favorite food," "what made me unhappy," and "what I most liked to do." The ages could be changed to one in the past and the present. Students could write the assignment or talk with each other by presentizing the earlier age and then having a discussion centered around "I still . . . and I no longer. . . ."

One team of teachers devised an activity which could be done at midterm or at the end of the school year to help the students become aware of what they learned. In many cases the gradual accumulation of knowledges and competencies will not have been noticed. Having students contrast what they know and can do at the end of the time interval used with that at the beginning of the interval will enable them to experience and appreciate the changes.

The teachers were also very much aware of the power of unfinished business in the lives of their students. Students arrive in class with unresolved issues from home, other classes, lunch periods, and recesses. The teachers conceived of a few activities they could use to help the students complete some of the unfinished situations. If, for example, the situation involved a conflict between two students, the teacher might spend a little time helping them to resolve it. In other cases a student might attain partial completion of a situation by finishing it in his fantasy or by writing a paragraph or two about it. Time and situations permitting, the teacher might speak with an individual student or engage him in some activity, for example, drawing a picture or operating a puppet, to work toward closure. In other circumstances there may not be an opportunity to work with finishing. In such cases the teacher may let the student know that he or she is aware of the student's experience and will have some time later to meet with the student about it. Often, knowing that there will be time set aside for dealing with unfinished business will allow the person to put it aside sufficiently to be able to attend to the present.

One way that a number of teachers would use presentizing to learn from the past was by reviewing examinations. Instead of just going over the tests to note right or wrong answers, the teacher would ask the students to recreate and presentize the experience of taking the test. In this way they could become aware of the processes they employed in answering the questions. Becoming aware of "how" they answered the questions can be as valuable a learning experience as selecting or creating the answer. This same enactment or presentizing method could be used to review how the students prepared for the test or worked on an assignment.

School, being a place where students are always being "prepared," is a natural place to learn about preparedness. Numerous teachers mentioned how their students always seemed to be getting ready for something new when going into a school day with more than one teacher, transferring to a middle school or high school, going into the labor force, or going on for further schooling. They felt that the classroom could be well used for presentizing some of these future events to allow the students some vicarious experience in preparing for them. Since many of the teachers were in schools which had "guidance" hours, they could tailor activities around the situations soon to be confronting their students.

Some of the teachers were somewhat concerned about the emphasis on preparation in schools and felt that there might be too much delayed gratification being engrained in students. They recognized that many of their students spend a good deal of their time considering intentions. A couple of alternatives were suggested for working with the students in this area. Class discussions or assignments could be focused on topics such as "What are some things I would like to be doing now that I'm not doing?" or "If I were going to move out of town in three months, some things I would do between now and then are. . . ." After the students had generated their responses the teachers could ask the students to ask themselves, "Which of these things could you be doing today and how are you stopping yourself from doing them?" The objective of the lesson would be to help the students realize that they could now be doing much of what they put off into the future.

Approaches to Feelings

The teachers were in overall agreement that helping students to become aware of their responsibility in creating their feelings could be a valuable addition to their classes. Written assignments could be focused on such topics as programming a computer or a robot to have selected feelings. What would they have to do to feel angry, excited, or happy? Puppets, stuffed animals, and other fictitious beings could be instructed by younger children on how to experience certain feelings. These exercises could then be followed up with a class discussion of how people create feelings and self-exploration in this area.

Several teachers noted how individualization in creating feelings could also be handled at a class level. A scene from a historical event could be described, a picture shown, or a piece of music played and the students asked to attend to what they feel as they look or listen. Upon sharing some of these feelings the students will have produced among themselves enough data to note how people respond differently in terms of their feelings about things. These differences can be used to demonstrate how a scene, a picture, or music does not "make" anyone feel a particular way. If these things did have the power to make people feel, then everyone would probably feel the same upon being exposed to them. There is, then, something in the person which brings about the feeling.

A math teacher who sees much frustration in his classes devised a lesson which could enhance awareness of how students frustrate themselves. His method was simple and direct. He would give them a problem which appeared solvable but which was not (at least for them) and put a time limit on the work on the problem. After the frustration levels had grown he would debrief the students by explaining the problem and then ask the students to participate in a discussion on what they had done to get themselves frustrated.

The teachers recognized that parents, schools, and society place a high premium on achievement and that along with this comes a good deal of pressure to attain it. Upon working with their own topdog-underdog struggles, several teachers noted that some work in this area could be useful in helping students to become more aware of how they put pressure on themselves. They decided to introduce their students to this topdog-underdog concept, although they would refer to it as "a part of you which tells you what you should be doing" and "a part of you that argues against the shoulds." The teachers would then share with their students some of their own conflicts of this nature to help them understand the notion. The students would then be invited to explore their own topdog-underdog dynamics on selected topics such as doing assignments, studying for tests, taking specific courses, participating in class, or on other topics of their choice. Depending on the nature of the class students might share some of their debates or their experiences in doing them.

During the workshop the teachers had an occasion to contact feelings in themselves which they did not consider as desirable or as acceptable as others. Several of them had been somewhat fearful of facing themselves in this way. The experience of contacting these feelings, having them accepted by others, and accepting them as a part of self was very enriching for these teachers. The question that arose from this learning was, "What can I do to help students recognize and accept their feelings?"

One answer to this question was to allow students the opportunity to express feelings in class. Several elementary school teachers were quite interested in the idea of using punching bags, puppets, and other toys as means of expression. They listened intently to some of the teachers who had been experimenting with such methods. Their fears were allayed upon hearing that the students did not get out of control or get hurt when they took out their frustrations on a pillow or a punching bag. The teachers would be able to support the students and convey to them that it's "O.K." for them to feel what they do.

A class unit could be formulated around the topic "What I like about me and what I don't like about me." This work would be based on the assumption that "liking" is highly correlated with "accepting." Various methods could be used for eliciting responses. Students could speak to each other in pairs, small groups could meet with the teacher or counselor, or the class could work as a whole either orally or by having each person respond in writing. The method used is less important than product in this case, which would be that students would become aware that each person feels varying degrees of liking and disliking himself or herself.

Discussion topics in the class can be developed around this awareness. One topic could be that it is important to recognize that just because the students dislike or do not accept some aspects of themselves does not mean that they are "bad." Persons can picture themselves by what they are and what they are not. Some students have the tendency of describing themselves in terms of deficits. These types of descriptions usually reflect a regret about what the person isn't, and these regrets often crowd out acceptances and appreciations of what the person is. For example, to say "I am not very tall" is quite different from saying "I am five foot eight." Consideration of these topics could help students see that they have numerous characteristics and that a few less appreciated ones do not cancel out those they accept more. This may spark in them some acceptance of those aspects of themselves they are less willing to own.

The teachers could reinforce and propagate the feeling of acceptance by demonstrating it in their interactions with the students. The teachers recognized that their levels of nonjudgmental acceptance of feelings would be a powerful model to the class. One teacher considered the idea of doing a class on the Gestalt prayer to emphasize and communicate the "I am I and you are you" aspects of it.

Consulting with Teachers

Now the question is, How do you begin consulting with teachers about using Gestalt approaches in their classrooms? Let's assume that you are working in a busy school and have neither the time nor the expertise to conduct five-day workshops with the teachers in your school. Let's assume, further, that getting groups of teachers together for systematic in-service is difficult for whatever reasons. Given these realistic and frequently encountered obstacles, where can you begin?

I suggest that you start by working with a single teacher, preferably one with whom you have a solid working relationship. If this teacher has an interest in psychological education, then that is all the better. The choice of the teacher will be quite important, especially if this is your first venture into this area.

You will want to become familiar with the teacher's philosophy of teaching, classroom behavior, students, and subject matter. This may be done through informal conversations, brief visits to the teacher's classroom, and reviewing selected samples of the students' work.

As the teacher becomes actively interested in trying some Gestalt approaches, the two of you can meet to discuss the teacher's interests more specifically. In certain instances the teacher may want to read some of the references included in this chapter or portions of this book. At this point you can significantly assist the teacher by providing an opportunity for experiencing some of the approaches which are read or discussed. This will allow the teacher the chance to select interventions with which he or she is comfortable in terms of goals and feasibility.

You can be of assistance in several ways during this selection process. First, you can suggest that the first work be done with some less complex approaches. Second, you might be able to offer the teacher some feedback on whether certain approaches seem consistent with his or her values and teaching style. Third, you might have noted some characteristics of the students or the current curriculum which would lend themselves to certain approaches. Finally, you may help the teacher to clarify the expectancies and reasons for using an approach.

You can be available in several ways as the teacher begins to use the approach. You can talk with the teacher about orienting the students to a different kind of activity and discuss ways of introducing it. Sometimes a teacher may ask you to come into the class to demonstrate an activity while he or she observes. The teacher may invite you into the class to participate in the lesson involving the approach or to observe.

After the teacher has used the approach you can be of assistance. This may involve providing feedback on how the teacher behaved and on the students' reactions. The teacher may also wish to discuss needed modifications in the approach or the possibility of trying another.

What will hopefully come of this? For one, the teacher may find excitement and interest in promoting psychological development in the classroom and learn how to devise and adapt Gestalt approaches as they are appropriate. Another positive outcome could occur when the teacher speaks to a faculty colleague who then wishes to consult you about using Gestalt approaches in his or her class. What this could mean for you is the beginning of a new dimension in your role as a counselor.

Summary

Psychological education is becoming an important thrust in teaching. Activities and teaching approaches which promote personal development comprise psychological education. Advocates of psychological education maintain that it can serve as a powerful means of preventing developmental difficulties. They also maintain that the facilitation of personal growth is better achieved through purposeful planning rather than being left to chance.

Psychological education has been described as a prime function of the counselor. By initiating the promotion and teaching of mental health and personal development the counselor is able to expand his or her impact in the school. In this way the counselor can truly serve students in ways other than through remedial counseling.

Gestalt approaches can serve as valuable tools for psychological education. They serve to enhance self-awareness and responsibility. Gestalt approaches can enliven a curriculum and promote self-understanding. Selected Gestalt approaches can' be used in classes of varying subject matter ranging from preschool to the doctoral level.

Teachers who have no prior experience with Gestalt approaches can be taught how to use them in their classes. An important role of the counselor is to serve as a consultant to teachers in this process.

REFERENCES

Brown, G. I., *Human Teaching for Human Learning: An Introduction to Confluent Education.* New York: Viking Press, 1971.

Ivey, A. E., and Alschuler, A. S. (eds.), Psychological education: A prime function of the counselor. *Personnel and Guidance Journal,* 1973, 51 (9),586–675.

Lederman, J., *Anger and the Rocking Chair: Gestalt Awareness with Children.* New York: Viking Press, 1969.

Mosher, R. L., and Sprinthall, N. A., Psychological education: A means to promote personal development during adolescence. *The Counseling Psychologist,* 1971, 2 (4), 3–82.

Stevens, J. O., *Awareness: Exploring, Experimenting, Experiencing.* Moab, Utah: Real People Press, 1971.

INDEX

Gestalt

Approaches in

Counseling